ACKNOWLEDGMENTS

THE AUTHOR EXTENDS GRATEFUL ACKNOWLEDGment and special thanks to the many friends, and heritage-making associates, parents and youth whose experiences and encouragement have contributed to the stories and intentional parenting recommendations of this work. Special thanks goes to the following people whose contributions were so significant to the work. First and foremost to my loving and supportive wife, Judy, for her collaboration on the writing and editing of the book, which has moved the project forward from concept to completion, and I give my deepest love and gratitude. My special thanks go to Debbie Pincock, John Tefft, Danelle Curtis, and Jen Cloward for their unfailing efforts in the initial reviews and editing of the work. Special thanks go to Linda Angelastro and Marin Barney of the Heritage Makers Creative Department for their reviews and suggestions regarding the content of the cover of the book. To my wonderful children for their contribution to our learning-by-experience the practical realities of heritage-based intentional parenting through practicing on them. To Krysti, Thayne, Marshyl, Brytt, Bryndi, Nykelle, and our grandchildren, I extend my appreciation and sympathy for being our continuing laboratory subjects. Special thanks go to Jinger and Jennifer, our wonderful daughters-in-law, for their input and advice. And to those readers and parents who follow through on their intentional parenting to establish and perpetuate the heritage-enriched character of their children and grandchildren, I extend my sincere encouragement.

CONTENTS

REMEMBERING
WHO YOU ARE

M Y MOTHER REMINDED ME OFTEN, "REMEMBER who you are!" I always thought that was a strange thing to say. After all, how could I ever forget who I was? Did she think that I was going to have some sort of amnesia? How could anyone forget who he or she was? When I discovered what she really meant, I realized that before a person could forget who he was, he had to first know the answer to the question "Who am I—really?" Throughout my life and career, I have discovered that many youth and adults have never really come to define who they really are or have forgotten the significance and priorities of that realization.

My heritage has been a constant guiding influence in my life. The character of my own family heroes—past and present—continues to remind me of who I should be. These heroes help me know who I really am and what my values, standards, traditions, and character must be to remain congruent to that noble heritage. Drawing from their stories and the influence from my experiences as a youth leader, teacher, parent, and grandparent, I share my insights and heritage-enriching suggestions. My purpose is to help readers discover how they too can be intentional and effective in their efforts to strengthen their family heritage and the character of their children.

Readers will find themselves laughing, crying, and more determined to ensure that the children in their lives establish a strong sense of the legacy of their heritage and its influence on defining their character and values. As you read the stories and learn from the heritage-making principles and projects of these parents, you too will choose to become intentional about establishing and passing on the positive aspects of your legacy.

Thank you for taking the time to read and consider becoming intentional parents who know how to help their children develop heritage-based character.

PREFACE

INTENTIONAL PARENTS SEE THEIR ROLES AS MOTHERS and fathers as a sacred trust to provide for their children's physical, social, emotional, and spiritual needs. They are proactively engaged in intentional parenting to secure the family legacy of values and priorities that will help their children develop clear, character-based identity and self-esteem. To be successful with these priorities, parents need to understand and apply a variety of specific intentional parenting skills, which are introduced in *Securing Your Family Legacy*.

The purpose of the book is to help parents and families become more intentional about helping the children in their lives develop a self-sustaining determination of who they are and how they will live.

Where do the beliefs and priorities that make up the foundations of our children's character come from? How do they develop the standards and values that influence their thinking, choices, and how they treat other human beings? What establishes those character-defining beliefs and values into their subconscious minds? What or who programs the priorities of the "conscious" controls that determine their decisions and actions—their character? How are the priorities programmed? The answers to these important questions can be found in the guiding influence of the family legacy that intentional parents pass on to their children.

Securing Your Family Legacy is a compilation of stories of parents and families who have discovered effective ways to provide that positive character-developing influence to their children. As you read the stories of the various parents and family members, you will learn much more about intentional parenting. You will discover how to increase the positive influence of family values and standards in your home and how to enrich the legacy of your heritage.

We live in an age when unintentional parents and nontraditional families outnumber intentional, traditional two-parent families. It is difficult for loving and family-focused parents to provide for all the physical, emotional, and character development needs of their children. Becoming intentional about guiding the development of the child's character can be doubly difficult when a single parent must be the example, teacher, coach, and mentor.

Ours seems to be an age when even some of the most successful traditional parents spend more energy, focus, and time intentionally planning for their recreation interests, acquisitions, and their portfolio than they do about planning and establishing the values and character of their children. Our children cannot remember and act according to how they are supposed to until they have discovered and embraced the character-identifying principles and standards that define them.

Today's children need the direction of an internal moral compass and the security of established family-centered values, beliefs, standards, and traditions to live safe and successful lives. Children need to know who they really are and what principles and values they and their family stand for. Only when they really know the answer to those questions can they make choices based on those character foundations.

Now is a great time to look back on the lives of our family heroes to find the formula for successful family life. Now is the time to train up our children in the way they should go to find real success and fulfillment. Now is the time to teach and live by the principles that produce lasting happiness and real joy. Now is the time to become an intentional parent focused on establishing the legacy of an intentional family life and heritage.

Securing Your Family Legacy was written to help readers to intentionally "train up [their children] in the way [they] should go" so that "when [they are] old, [they] will not depart from" the character traits defined by that family heritage (Proverbs 22:6). It was written to help all parents identify and combine aspects of the heritage of their parents and grandparents into a legacy of their own. That legacy can help you inspire and encourage your family members to intentionally have lives of purpose, priority, success, and contribution.

INTRODUCTION

A ROYAL HERITAGE

It was a diabolical plan. It was almost foolproof, yet it failed because a child knew the expectations of his heritage. The enemies of the king were not just interested in the elimination of the monarch himself; they wanted to end the monarchy forever! The plan was simple: kidnap the heir and get the young prince to discredit himself, the royal family name, and the heritage and legacy of the throne.

And so the frightened young prince was taken from his home. His captors began their efforts to influence his behavior to get him to violate his royal standards and to destroy his character. The plan was to discredit him by dragging him down to the level of commoner. They would get him to choose their lifestyle of indulgence and immorality. Cunningly, they exposed him to every degrading thing that would disqualify him from his royal birthright.

They offered him a life filled with the things that would rob him of his dignity and his health and make him a slave to worldly appetites. They surrounded him with foul language, lewdness, disrespect, dishonor, and distrust. Their goal was to get him to live contrary to how he was raised and to his royal character and birthright.

After six months of what seemed like constant temptations and pressures to succumb, the young prince still remained true to his principles and values. He rejected all of their unworthy temptations.

Why? How could he? How could any young man reject such inviting temptations? He was away from the eyes and controlling influence of his mother and father and away from friends and the protection of the palace

1

moat, walls, and rules. Yet he was not alone. He was in the good company of his values, standards, and character. His captor could eliminate his family and remove him from the roots of his heritage, but they could not rob him of who he really was.

The young prince was clear about who he was and what his legacy and personal standards required of him. He was honoring a royalty beyond birthright—beyond the royal family heritage. The guiding influence of his parents had helped him establish a personal heritage that did not depend on where he was, who he was with, or the circumstances of the moment. His character rejected the temptation to trade his heritage and personal royalty for the pleasures of the crowd. His parents and his heritage had helped him build a protective internal fence and fortress of character.

When his frustrated captors questioned him about his rejection of their offers and his commitment to his standards, he responded simply, "I cannot do what you ask of me for I was born to be a king."[1]

YOUR ROYAL HERITAGE

The story is purported to be of Louis Charles, second son of the deposed King Louis XVI of France. Yet the story could be about any young man or woman off to college, the military, or on holiday. Away from the eyes and influence of parents and family standards, values, and commitments, each of our young princes and princesses will likely face similar tests. Like the prince, the results of those tests will likely be determined based on the character you have helped to develop and on whether they too know the answer to the question, "Who are you—really?"

THE PEOPLE AND STORIES BEHIND THE CHAPTERS

As you read the stories of the various parents and family members in the following chapters, you will discover much more about intentional living and parenting. You will learn how to increase the character-defining influence of heritage in your home, ensuring that your children know the answer to the question of who they are—really.

Doug is a grandfather and recent cancer survivor whose face-off with death and miraculous recovery leads him to a greater realization of the priceless value of family and how he can help other parents prevent a far worse cancer than his own.

Ann is determined to give her children real family hero role models to replace their fictional TV, comic book, and movie heroes.

Stan and Beth have moved their family into a new home only to discover that more than one kind of fence protects their family and yours.

Jason is a handsome sixteen-year-old teenager facing the typical challenges and choices that come with attending his first major school dance. His mother discovers how her teaching of family values and personal standards influence his choices.

Sarah is a lovely, precocious child whose first day at kindergarten causes her to ask her parents if her name has any important or special meaning.

Sherry has just experienced the death of her beloved grandmother and worries that her toddler son, Billy, will soon forget his great-grandmother. She finds a way to keep those special family memories alive.

Heidi and Jake are fun-loving intentional parents from different family backgrounds who find a creative way to forge their family heritage by turning their house into a heritage-rich home.

Karen is a true professional in about everything she does. She loves the freedom of full-time homemaking and mothering but discovers how to channel her talents and experience into intentional parenting and creating a family heritage.

Kim is the fifty-year-old single lunch lady everyone knows, remembers, and loves. She turns every family gathering into a celebration and feast. She discovers how she can use her newfound computer skills to help build heritage-rich traditions.

Kelly appears to be the perfect mom, wife, and homemaker, and learns how, with only a few positive childhood memories, she can build a powerful family heritage to which she can anchor her children's character.

Marjean is a heritage-minded genealogist who finds much more than ancestors' names and dates. Discovering the stories of lives behind the names reveals priceless treasures of life experience.

Melanie is a busy, young wife and mother who participates in an intentional parenting seminar and rediscovers the power of her dreams and the process of helping her family determine who they can be.

NOTE

1. Vaughn J. Featherstone, "The King's Son," *New Era*, November 1975.

THE CANCER CALL:

Becoming Intentional about Who You Really Are

M Y HAIR WAS COMING BACK, AS SOFT AS DUCK down. My wife and children loved running their fingers through it. The feeling in my fingers and feet were returning too, but it would be awhile before I could shuffle the UNO cards with the grandkids. The other effects of the chemo-induced neuropathy would remind them all about their ordeal and about how close I had come to running out of time. Now with a miraculous recovery, I was focused on fighting a different kind of battle, a different kind of cancer.

My children were all grown, and most of them lived close. They had gathered in the emergency room soon after they got the call. Standing around the curtained gurney, they joked nervously. They had never seen me in a hospital before. They knew I would not be there unless it was serious. But none of us were prepared for the doctor's report.

"The white cell count is over 185,000. We have called for the oncologist."

The oncologist was there in minutes. His pronouncement and answers to the obvious questions were numbing. The cancer was deeply entrenched in the lymph system. It was stage four and high grade.

The prognosis was "A few days, maybe a week or two. With a successful treatment, perhaps two years."

The words stung the family's ears and took their breath away. They stood in stunned silence. No, no—*no!* No way this active, healthy father and grandfather could be at game over!

The game was not over! We would fight this thing together as a family. And fight we did.

The next few days were touch and go. Each day, family members were on their knees and in circles of family prayer, pleading with God for my life to be extended. They were at my bedside to administer the healing balm of faith, encouragement, laughter, and sacred music. I was certain that the blend of their voices was far more powerful than the blend of chemicals in the R-CHOP chemo. With all the family attention, I felt I had been able to attend my own funeral without having to die to get it. Their faithful treatments combined with those of the physicians such that days became weeks. The combined remedy was successful, and I made my way back from death's door and from the edge of eternity. I had come close enough to death to determine that I was far from ready to cross over. I still had too many things I needed to take care of, important things I needed to do. If God would just give me a little more time, I would make those things my priority. I had a story to tell and a greater work to do. I'd like to tell you the rest of my story.

DOUG'S STORY

I was born to be a grandpa! The challenge was that I had to get through most of the family and fathering courses before I could graduate to the grandfathering classes. I passed some of those early classes with good grades but messed up on some of the "good-fathering" pop quizzes that came along the way. And I completely failed a few of the major exams in a couple of the daddy do's-and-don'ts classes.

I didn't realize that some of the fathering courses would overlap into the grandfathering program as much as they have. I did recognize that the advanced classes in great-grandfathering would only have a few students. I am still hoping to get into those senior classes. What I didn't understand was that there would be important lessons in great-great-grandfathering and even great-great-great-grandfathering. These lessons would help me have an important influence on my posterity, even though I would have long since passed on before they arrived to take on my name and heritage. I discovered that grandfathering and great-grandfathering always extends beyond the grave.

It was a darn good thing that all the fathering and grandfathering laboratory specimens (a.k.a. children and grandchildren) that we were given were so good. Lesser-quality subjects would surely have resulted in far poorer grades on my part. Without them, I may have even failed in some of the mission-critical tests of fatherhood and grandfatherhood. All six children and the growing list of daughters-in-law, sons-in-law, and grandchildren have been examined, dissected, prodded, experimented on, and grafted into our less-than-perfect family tree.

In reality, I have to give credit for what good grades I may have received to my lab partner, Judy. She is the major reason we have passed as many of the parenting tests and courses as we have. We are now trying to figure out the more complex formulas in our grandparenting and in-lawing classes. We had pretty much finished up the parenting courses and had a good start in the grandparenting lessons when the wake-up call of my cancer crisis came.

It was also largely due to Judy's amazing partnering that I was able to continue the classes and lab work before the final school bell rang even from what looked like death's bed. Her attention and encouragement has allowed us to progress to some much more challenging coursework in our parenting partnership. I certainly would not want to consider the school of life, mortality, and beyond without her at my side. Thanks to God for Judy, my faithful and loving companion—wife, mother, and grandmother. Judy is truly a helpmate to me.

I have come to view my life as a series of stories. All the stories are intertwined with the stories of other people and families. There are those whose lives and stories have momentarily, temporarily, or consistently affected my own. Some of their stories are triumphs, and some are tragedies. Each story offers its own lessons, meaning, and messages. They are all valuable and contributive. The values I have derived from these experiences and stories have become more significant and precious to me since that fateful day in April 2008, when the story of my lymphatic cancer began.

Until then, I had not fully recognized just how valuable all these stories were to me. Nor did I fully appreciate how important they would be to my family, especially to my grandchildren. The story you are now reading is about how I came to that realization. It is about how I received a miraculous extension to my life. It is about what I am now committed to do with that gift of more storytelling time.

I hope my story will help you rediscover the value of your own stories and family heritage. I hope my story will give you some advantage and help you understand how to build a rich and enduring heritage to influence the character of your children and grandchildren.

Whether yours is a traditional two-parent family, a single-parent family, a combined family, or any other family structure, you don't need to follow me to death's bed to know that family is what matters most; further, that the children, grandchildren, nieces, and nephews of your extended family face an epidemic of personal character and family life crisis—a cancer far more menacing than was mine.

Whoever you are in the heritage of your family, you and your stories matter to your family now and can prove to be far more valuable in the future. You can leave your family a legacy and an inheritance of values, traditions, and character that could save the children of your family and friends from that cancer that destroys character, heritage, and families.

To set the stage, I should share a few of the facts about my family and me. We started our family planning after a whirlwind blind date. I was twenty-one, and Judy was nineteen. She was a city girl from Virginia; I was a farm boy from central Utah. It was her first and both of our last blind dates. Within twenty-four hours of meeting each other, we were discussing the names of our children. I know some readers will find that hard to believe, but it's true. We were engaged in less than twenty-four hours. We never broke the engagement, even though we were 2,500 miles apart for seven of the eleven months before we were married. That is a story worth telling on its own and a miraculous story our children and grandchildren know and cherish, although it is a precedent that presents a number of challenging questions.

Judy came from a deeply religious home in Arlington, Virginia. She was the fourth of five children with two older sisters and an older brother whom she idolized. She was bubbly and energetic and had a clear understanding of who she was, what was expected of her, and what she expected to do with her life. Her values and priorities were absolute. Her father was a faith-filled man of absolute integrity and charity. Her mother, equally faith-founded, was intentional about her influence in the home and the family life, even though her health made much of that influence nontraditional compared to most cookie-baking moms. Her parents' influence on Judy and her value system is perhaps the greatest gift a son-in-law could ever receive. She was clear about the values and character traits she needed to instill into our children. And the example of her parents made that priority an invaluable inheritance to our partnership in parenting.

I was a hardworking farm boy who spent countless hours of bucking hay; picking fruit and vegetables; and working with sheep, cattle, and dairy. I too knew clearly what my parents, community, and God wanted for and from me. I was innately disposed to do good and be good. I was blessed with a brother eleven months younger than me. His association and partnership has been and continues to be a blessing every day of my life. I also have a sister five years younger than me who was and is a joy to both my and my brother's lives. My father was gone from Sunday evening through Friday evening working on various road construction jobs that kept him away from home. My mother was a saint of deep pioneer heritage from the mountains of old Mexico. She was the living example of hospitality, hard work, service, and a childlike simple faith in the goodness and grace of God. From each parent, I came to realize the influence and gift of a legacy and heritage that has guided my life.

We started our first parenting class when baby girl number one joined us fourteen months after our marriage, in June 1974. The first class was admittedly much harder for Judy than it was for me. Now, over forty years later, we have completed so many parenting classes and accumulated countless experiences, memories, and stories of our six children, sons- and daughters-in-law, and thirteen grandchildren. Many of these stories are so amazing that they are hard to believe. They too are true. They too are stories with significant meaning and influence on our posterity.

Then, in April 2008, my story—our story—took an unexpected twist. I was served notice that my story-making time and life were about to end. It was a sudden and completely unexpected crisis.

They called the condition mantle cell lymphoma. Simply stated, it was a rare and aggressive cancer of the lymph system. I was diagnosed at stage four, high grade, and the oncologist's initial prognosis was bleak. I was looking at days, maybe weeks, if they could keep me alive through the night.

Printed words alone cannot express the stark and sudden reminder of mortality's short duration that we experienced that day. The whole thing was surreal. I don't know if anyone can be prepared for a surprise notice of eviction from mortality. I was certainly not prepared for the pain, pleading, pondering, power, and probation that followed that pronouncement. It would take an entire book to tell the full story. I must assure you that I came to know with absolute certainty that there was purpose and a lesson to be learned from my illness. Similarly, I understand that both purpose and obligation came with the life extension I have been given. Part of that obligation includes telling you my story.

On death's bed, a person does a lot of "if only" thinking. "If only" thinking can be sorrowful memories of past "should haves." There are also hopeful yearnings for future "could dos." I learned which kind of "if only" thinking the patient focuses on when facing a potential terminal condition impacts the prognosis for recovery. The thoughts of potential repairs to one's "should haves" brings hope. That hope develops purposeful faith toward future "can dos" and "will dos."

Unless a person is appointed unto death, the positive power of the human heart can give meaning and accelerate healing. This I know for a fact. I know that there can be synergy between all healing treatments, arts, services, and remedies. The combining catalyst is the love, faith, and service of others as well as the healers and God's good grace and power. The greatest healers can be the members of your own family. Mine is a story you can share with those you know who may be having "if only" considerations.

My disease was rare. Cytology identified and verified the displacement of normal genetic linkage in the cancerous lymph cells. Very few cases of this particular cancer had been reported in our state. It was so rare that little information was available to the doctors and to us. My oncologist was great and concerned, yet he couldn't give us much more information than was available on the Internet. I spoke with a few others from around the country who were battling the disease. Their good will and hope was helpful. I discovered that the effects of most cancers are indeed contagious. That is, while they do not infect, they affect every family member and loved one of the patient.

Following my initial hospital stay, I had two subsequent returns to the emergency room that were caused by low blood pressure collapses. In many ways, those stays were more difficult than my initial residence, but in other ways, they were more healing. I was more alert and able to receive the medicine and the voice of quiet healing to be still and know. I needed more pause and patience, and those returns to the hospital provided the needed additional doses. I also needed more time to consider the answers to questions that every terminal patient must face. It is from those questions and the assuring answers that came that have prompted my writing my story and this book.

Some of my most difficult days were not related to slowing the spread of cancer. Rather, they focused on slowing my own busyness. I learned that my world, especially my work and job, was not and should not be the center of my universe. I discovered clearly that the self-assumed importance of my position, presence, and attention to the job mattered far less than I thought. I was surprised to learn that work and life could and did continue with or without me. Further, I learned that so could I. I learned that there was more to life and more in life that awaited my release of less-important things.

I suspect everyone at death's door sheepishly and painfully realizes that we are not as indispensable as we have assumed. We discover that our self-assumed importance and to-dos can wait and that they could have and often should have been made to wait long before our health-imposed slow downs. We usually discover too late that the important things we have been putting off really can't or won't wait. They become the subjects of our "if only" thoughts and tears.

As I lay there in the hospital bed during those sleepless nights, my mind was flooded with questions and realizations about my life. The greatest realizations for me were that people, not things or to-dos, matter most. That *being* is far more important than *doing*, and that all of our lives are all like hourglasses. The top half of the glass is opaque; we can't see how much sand there is. The bottom is clear, and we can see the sand that is still flowing and piling up at the bottom, but we cannot see how much sand is left in the top. The greatest realization for me was that being with those who matter most is the most important and precious use of the sands that are in our hourglasses. This is especially so for the sands left for our intentional parenting and grandparenting.

After I was released from the hospital the first time, I returned to our mountaintop home. A few nights later, I collapsed unconscious to the floor. Getting back to the hospital was itself another miracle. The doctors put me in the ICCU (intensive cardio care unit) and hooked up a blood-gas line to my wrist to give a constant read of my blood pressure and heart activity. As always, Judy was at my side. The doctor was putting something on the chart and looking at the monitor. Suddenly I felt a little strange. I looked up at the doctor only to see a startled look on his face as he dropped the chart board on the bed. The nurse saw his face too as he glanced at the monitor and the alarm went off. My heart had stopped. For a moment, it appeared that the sand in my hourglass had run out.

Then, moments later, just as suddenly as it stopped, it started up again on its own. I guess I had a few more grains of sand in the hourglass after all. I felt little discomfort in spite of the semi-panic of the attending medical team. As my sands of time continued to flow, it became clearer that they would, at least for some additional unspecified time. The doctors were telling us it might be a couple of years, based on the information they had from the meager statistics of others who had survived the disease. But the sands did continue, and so did my focus on what I must do with them.

I began to focus on priorities for my new lease on life. Some obvious have-to-get-done projects took first priority, preparations just in case the sand stopped again.

While I was on the hospital bed, I thought a lot about the people in my life. Of course, family was central to those thoughts. Thanks needed to be given to the many gave support during the crisis of the previous several months. But there were others too. My thoughts turned to those who contributed to my early life. I remembered teachers, neighbors, scouting leaders, clergymen, and family friends. With these thoughts of the important men and women, I wanted to let them know how significant they were to my life. Their contributions to my life mattered, and I needed to express my thanks, whether they needed to hear it or not.

I reflected on my most important relationships and the stories connected to them. Those memories produced deep feelings of gratitude and humility and a yearning to reconnect and recognize those gifts. Remembering and acting on those memories and follow-up impressions have been sweet.

While things were touch and go for me, I felt the need to speak and express my love and gratitude to many. I realized that the next visit of Judy, our children, grandchildren, or friends might be the last opportunity for those important conversations. What should I say? What must I express to them? What was yet unsaid?

I needed to visit with each of my family members. I needed to speak of the love and gratitude and faith and family heritage past and future. I needed to reassure them of their importance and priority and of family ties, time, and love. That yearning continues with compelling urgency.

Like most, I had assumed that loved ones knew they were loved, so I hadn't felt the need to express my love, appreciation, and confidence as deeply or as often enough as I now yearned to do. I hadn't expressed to them clearly or often enough what I believe, value, and cherish. I suspect that procrastinating telling that story and truth is a particularly male failing. Too often, we discover the failing too late to do something about it when either our loved ones or we are gone.

So I scheduled visits with each of my children, family members, and close friends. The visits, memory sharing, feelings, and the words were richly meaningful. The binding glue of our family's shared values, beliefs, and heritage gives reason to hope and believe that our linkage and love will live beyond the sands of time. These experiences have been wonderful. I highly recommend that you experience them yourself. You don't need the excuse of a near-death event to make them a priority. Just don't wait too long to make the connections. The next time my heart should stop, my loved ones will know for sure how I feel and what I know. Please be sure that your loved ones know too, before your sand runs out.

In the hospital, I became aware of the pain and suffering of several other patients and people on the oncology and ICCU floors. They were old and young, men and women. Though their cancers and other serious illnesses were different from mine, their needs and thoughts were similar. Patients suffered from their disease. Others suffered from the pains of loss. There were also those patients who lived but suffered more because of the absence of loved ones who couldn't be there to give their healing love and encouragement. Some suffered even more because loved ones who could have and should have come, didn't. Sad as that was, the greatest pain came from across the hall. It was not the patient but rather the son who should have and could have come sooner but waited too long.

They say that at death's door, your whole life passes before you. I suppose that everyone who teeters between life and death as they stare at the hospital room ceiling wrestles with the same questions: What have I done with my life? How will I be remembered? Who have I really *been*?

Then, when the balance shifts and it looks as though you may yet have some more time, the questions shift: Who *am* I really? Who should I *be* now?

I can attest that, at least for me, the life review and questions became central in those quiet moments when all I could hear was the soft swish sound of the IV pumps. I did review my life in vivid detail. For me, this review was not some unsolicited moving picture. It was a conscious review starting with my earliest memories, moving forward to the last kiss of my loving wife before she left my side and the hospital for the night. I was amazed at how vivid even the oldest memories were and how one memory triggered so many others.

Following my deep reflections, the words to the song "Have I Done Any Good?"[1] ran through my mind again and again. I found myself pondering almost out loud, "What good have I done?" "What will be the legacy I leave to my family and the world?" Perhaps more than at any other time in my life, I learned that how we live and what we leave behind of real value to our posterity are the real measures of a successful life.

My education and professional pursuits focused on youth leadership and outdoor recreation management with a focus on professional Scouting and youth agency work. After short stints with the Boy Scouts of America and Big Brothers Big Sisters, I returned to the college to complete a master's degree in outdoor recreation management with a focus on using outdoor activity as a behavior modification platform for youth and family therapy.

That training and experience landed me in a teaching position at Brigham Young University's Department of Youth Leadership. That teaching experience was a highlight of my life and contributed significantly to the answers to the realization of the importance, value, and power of building and securing family legacies.

I developed and led young adult outdoor adventure programs that utilized the personal character and self-confidence forming experience of these survival and pioneer handcart treks. I supervised the training and coordinating of hundreds of youth leaders and literally thousands of young men and women and youth pastors. The program results were powerful. Many young people experienced life-changing and family life-guiding realizations through these programs.

Then in early 2003 I became acquainted with a new concept that would become a powerful tool for securing the values, beliefs, character traits, standards, and heritage that are the foundations of a family's legacy. The concept is called "storybooking," an idea focused on self-publishing important memories and life stories and experiences of family heroes and their heritage. It was a way to identify and pass on that heritage and family to the rising generation. The impact and influence of the stories for behavior influence was intriguing. I quickly recognized that my interests in youth, family, and values could be served in a business venture that made this storybooking concept available as a powerful intentional parenting tool. So my business partner and I combined our experience and resources and invited others to join us as we formed a digital scrapbooking business we called Heritage Makers. The business focused on helping people capture, preserve, and share the important stories of their lives by combining them with their photos and life values and standards perspectives.

One of the important elements of the storybooking process was helping children come to know the meaning of their names. This was the result of introducing family legacy and heritage congruent character traits in the stories of their family heroes. These stories are inspiring their children and grandchildren to define themselves by their commitment to their values, standards, and character of their parents and ancestors.

Following my bout with cancer, I had a heightened awareness of the importance of my family and of the precarious challenges and threats that my and all families are facing in our time. So many families have members who are becoming disconnected from each other because they do not have a clearly defined set of family values and standards. They have disconnected from any sense of shared family purpose—family legacy. The result is that the righteous influence of family life is being diluted and is dissolving—dying. In cancer terms, this family life and legacy cancer is at stage four and high grade. Simply stated, an epidemic of family life and legacy deterioration can put your children, your family in jeopardy.

Lying in the hospital bed, I wondered about my own intentional parenting and family legacy and if it would transfer to the next generation. What they were facing and would face caused me to read, reread, and ponder the Apostle Paul's prophecy to Timothy regarding the conditions that would be prevalent in the last times, our time. I gained a clearer understanding about the source and impact of the selfish and valueless character traits Paul spoke about. I came to see these traits as both the symptoms and the cause of this debilitating family life illness—this destructive sickness of the souls of families that is spreading like a cancer.

In the Epistle of Paul to Timothy regarding the perilous times that would come in the last days, Paul spoke of that coming time when men would be *lovers of themselves, covetous, boasters, proud, blasphemers,* and *disobedient to parents.* He said they would be *unthankful, unholy, without natural affection, truce-breakers, false accusers, incontinent, fierce,* and *despisers of those that are good.* He warned us that they would be *traitors, heady, high minded, lovers of pleasures more than lovers of God.* They would have *a form of godliness, but would deny His power.* They would *ever be learning yet resisting and never able to come to the knowledge of the truth* as they were *led away with divers lusts* (see 2 Timothy 3:1–6).

The conditions that lead to the perilous times Paul spoke of start with influences that attack a person's character—the immune system of the soul. This sickness lodges in ungrateful hearts and flourishes when surrounded by self-indulging and self-justifying attitudes. It feeds on the addiction to a something-for-nothing mentality. It can quickly infect children who do not understand the relationship between responsibility, accountability, and consequence. These traits and conditions are a threat to the heritage and security of every family's legacy.

The vectors and carcinogens of this disease can be found in profane, life-devaluing, and family-demeaning media, video games, movies, and websites. These influences attack every family member, especially those whose resistance has been weakened through abuse of drugs, alcohol, immorality, and who suffer from healthy family-life malnutrition. Perhaps the most pernicious vector of the character plagues Paul spoke is pornography—in all its forms.

This family life and joy-robbing cancer can attach to all kinds of families. It quickly grows and metastasizes, affecting every family member. Just as tissue cancers affect the breast, lungs, bones, or colon and destroy the whole person, so this family-life cancer in any member, if not treated effectively, can destroy the whole family.

It is my deepest hope that this book will encourage readers to become intentional and successful in developing a clear and aligned family heritage of values, standards, and character. I offer insights and resources for this kind of preventative intentional parenting that can help to remedy and prevent the sickness attacking the security and the strength of families across the world. The intentional parenting recommendations at the conclusion of each chapter can be family lifesavers when they are put into practice.

INTENTIONAL PARENTING—HERITAGE TO STRENGTHEN THE FAMILY LEGACY

"A good man leaveth an inheritance to his children's children . . ." "Hear, ye children, the instruction of a father, and attend to know understanding" (Proverbs 4:1, 13:22)

"And thou shalt teach them diligently unto thy children, and shalt talk of them when thou sittest in thine house, and when thou walkest by the way, and when thou liest down, and when thou risest up." (Deuteronomy 6:7)

Solomon declares that a good man leaves an inheritance to his children and grandchildren. He counsels the children to "hear" the instructions of their fathers. Surely that counsel is to be included as part of the inheritance the fathers will leave with their posterity.

Moses tells the children of Israel that God has commanded them to teach their children his laws and ways to go. His ways and standards were to be taught. Parents were to establish the values in their families that they would live by in the Promised Land. They were to teach these standards of behavior and personal character in their homes at all times. In other words, they were to be reminded of the will and ways of the Lord and their family's commitment and adherence to those ways. This was the inheritance parents were to leave their children.

To understand the instruction of the father (or mother), the children must *hear* it. Before they can hear it, the parent must speak it. Before the parent can speak it, he or she must consider and determine what he or she must teach. In the busyness of the parent's life, it is easy to procrastinate and difficult to find the "right time" for values instruction of the children.

FAMILY HERITAGE CORE COMPONENTS

Parents and grandparents should help their children and grandchildren understand and embrace core family values and beliefs. Reviewing the following list of values and character traits and principles with children and grandchildren at an early age can become the foundation for the children's understanding of the priorities of their family.

VALUES DISCUSSION TOPICS

Discussing the following list of value concepts and character traits with your children can help them understand your family priorities and standards and influence their response to situations that require them to take a stand relative to those principles.

Consider how you feel about these concepts and then discuss them with your children. Remember, a conversation is a two-way process and a discovery process. Invite your children to talk about ideas and concepts with you. One conversation is not enough. Frequently revisiting and restating these concepts will solidify their impact.

I. SOCIAL VALUES AND STANDARDS

Friendships—seeking and making good, like-minded friends with similar values

Work ethic—understanding the value of working hard, excelling at tasks, and being dependable

Integrity—making and living by your word, your bond, and your reputation.

Etiquette—having good manners, being respectful in speech (such as using "please," "thank you," "yes, sir," and "ma'am") and making table, door, and phone manners priorities

Chivalry—for young men, speaking and treating ladies and elders with respect

Grooming—having personal hygiene, grooming, and dress standards to ensure respect and success

Education—developing a professional and employable skill set and being curious and eager to learn

Patriotic—having patriotism, love of country, and a sense of service, civic duty, and contribution

Financial Management, Frugality, and Budget Discipline—earning, managing, saving, and investing to maximize and leverage money, wealth, and the ability to contribute to goodness

Healthy Living—selecting and using foods wisely, exercising, and avoiding harmful substances and bad habits

Recreation—participating in wholesome recreational activities; playing the game well and fairly is more important than winning at any cost.

Culture—appreciating fine arts and music

Ethnic Interest and Culture Appreciation—accepting and appreciating the wealth of ideas and experiences that can flow from ethnic and cultural diversity

Confidence—any worthy goal is attainable through effective planning, hard work, and persistence; dream big and stay focused

Kindness—having a general attitude of kindness and respect toward the interests, feelings, property, and beliefs of others

The Environment—valuing environmental stewardship; being committed to establishing and maintaining a clean and green attitude toward the earth and the community; having the attitude of waste not, want not

II. SPIRITUAL BELIEFS AND PRIORITIES

God—your beliefs in and allegiance to God, Jesus Christ, the Scriptures, church, prayer

Doctrines—the nature of God, His plan for you, Jesus Christ, grace, baptism, the Holy Spirit, canon, repentance, salvation, authority, service, the Sabbath, tithes and offerings and other doctrinal concepts and beliefs and the choice expectations that come with them.

Testimony—your witness with regard to the spiritual dimension, experiences, and personal revelations and priorities of your life—counsel as to how they can have their own testimony and conversion to these spiritual and religious beliefs and values

Morality—your values and standards with respect to dating, physical affection, and intimacy; your belief and stands regarding pornography in all its forms and vehicles

RESULTS

Again, stronger understanding will come from both your conversation and discussions (instruction) and your leadership (example) with your family. Remember: actions speak louder than words. Great heritage-making parents lead their children by example. These parents *take* their children; they don't just *send* off their children on their own. Heritage-minded parents take their children fishing, to church, to the movies, to the theater, to the farm, to the office, and to their knees.

Children who see their fathers and grandfathers respect and treat their mothers and grandmothers with devotion, kindness, and appreciation will have the joy of seeing these same values and behaviors practiced by their children with their spouses. They will be far less likely to see the pain of selfishness and ego-driven self-righteousness in their posterity. Children who live in an environment where they hear their parents express love to each other and to them will hold to that heritage of those loving words and deeds.

As Doug discovered, a rapidly growing societal illness is destroying the foundations and the security of traditional family values like a cancer.

Intentional parenting through proactive communication, instruction, and your life example, can literally save your family's life and heritage. An ounce of prevention, instruction, and heritage-making, is worth far more than a pound of the pain of cure.

LEGACY-SECURING INTENTIONAL PARENTING PROJECT SUGGESTIONS

Family Night—Establish and give parental leadership to regular family night activities and discussions once a week. Have regular family discussions about the positive things each member is doing to build and honor the family name.

Self-Check—Ask yourself these questions: Do my children know my values, beliefs, and standards and how I would expect them to behave regarding our standards? Do my children know who they really are and how to establish and secure that identity? Then act on your answer.

Have the Crucial Conversations—NOW!—Find and make the time and occasions to express to your children/grandchildren your values and standards.

Set the Example—Be certain to always practice what you preach so that your children see a living example of your stated standards, beliefs, principles, values, and priorities. A hypocritical family heritage may be worse than no heritage at all.

I Love You—Children need to hear "I love you" often from their parents and see that in their parents' daily actions. They need to hear the gentle parental laughter and humor of their parents and grandparents to feel content and secure. Regularly express the following eye-to-eye: "I am proud of you and what you are doing with our family name" and "I really love you; you are a family hero."

Love their Moms and Grandmothers—Fathers, tell your children/ grandchildren the story about how you met and fell in love with their mother/grandmother. Tell them why she is so special and how much you admire and love her. The giggles of glee from your little ones and the smiles of understanding and security from the older ones will be wonderful rewards for those moments. Their adopting that behavior when they are older will be yet another powerful contribution to your family legacy.

Pray with and for Them—Let your family, children, grandchildren, and great-grandchildren hear and see you praying for them. Pray in gratitude for them being in your family and pray for their safety, health and success. Pray for the things that are important to them. Teach them to pray by your example and by kneeling with them at their bedsides.

Step Up and Be the Man and the Mom—Dads, be responsible and be available. Give your family the security that you will meet their needs and be the example of hard work, dependability, consistency, and financial responsibility. Take care of the daddy duties—the yard, garbage, car, and whatever you have worked out as your role between you and your spouse. Perhaps nothing is more important for families and our society today than children seeing the example of responsible fathers. The most important influence you can have on your heritage is being a heritage-supporting man and father.

Moms do the most family heritage-making in projects and things that become tools and icons of heritage in the home. Mothers take on the role of heritage-maker and character director, along with the many other duties and roles they perform. Mothers, you can help your children discover their roots. Help them to be really clear about their role as a part of a living family legacy that embraces certain values and priorities. Then help them to identify, explain, and embrace that heritage and legacy. Help them build pride in that sense of who they really are. Sharing the stories of your family legacy is the most valuable intentional parenting goal and service you can provide for your children to protect them against influences that lead to family-life cancer.

Parents, do not wait until a life-threatening illness, yours or theirs, puts you face-to-face with worries or questions about the security of your family legacy before they act. You as parents must work now to establish your family legacy.

NOTE

1. Will L. Thompson, "Have I Done Any Good?" *Hymns*, no. 223.

CHAPTER 2

INTENTIONAL INFLUENCE:

Leveraging Family Heroes

THE INSTRUCTOR HAD ASKED THE CLASS WHO their childhood heroes were. Ann had never really thought about it before. Her memories were more than a little hazy. Ann defined heroes as people who came to the rescue in a crisis. They were women and men who showed up in the nick of time to provide some desperately needed service. It was then that she realized that the difference between most of her childhood heroes and the heroes of her adult life could be summed up in one word—*real*.

Her childhood heroes were largely storybook and TV characters. They were fictitious people and even animals that did good things, but those things were only stories, and she had to laugh a little at the thought of just how important they had seemed to her then. Now her heroes were not fictitious, popular, or famous for their success in life. They were real and they really did come to the rescue—her rescue.

As the group talked, they concluded that real heroes were the people whose example and sacrifice for others changed and improved the world one person at a time. When the instructor asked them to look around the to see if they could see any heroes in their midst, they got very quiet, and tears started to flow. They realized that they did not have to go to the history books or to some far away place to find real heroes. There were plenty of examples of rescuers and real heroes in their own neighborhood and within their own families.

The instructor asked, "Who are your children's heroes?" Another hush came over the room. Ann thought about her kids, Billy and Jenny. Right then, Ann determined that she would turn the minds and hearts of her children to their real heroes.

As she thought about the real heroes in their family, she couldn't help being drawn to the great women in her family. She thought about those women whose stories and influence continued to set the standard for their posterity of lives well lived and of correct priorities. Ann wondered if Billy and Jenny even knew who those women were and why they were real family heroes. She determined that it was time to introduce her children to some of the real heroes in their family. It was time to take the masks off their father and grandfather. These families were not comic book heroes, but they were about to become real storybook heroes.

ANN'S STORY

I knew that Jenny's screaming was contrived for effect. I also knew that particular cry was an attempt to control her brother. So I ignored it and hoped it would go away. It usually did. I also knew that I would be ahead in the war of words if I could let them work it out on their own. But this was the third or fourth round of escalating volume. The war of words had become the war of their world. I figured I had better intercede. I grabbed my superhero cape dishtowel and stepped into the battle. The mission was to save them both from a certain expulsion into the dark side of time out.

"Mom! Mom! Billy hit me!" Jenny yelled in protest.

"Did not!" Billy yelled back.

"Did too!"

"Did NOT!!"

"MOMMMMM!"

"Here we go again!" I said under my breath as I stepped into the toy-strewn living room to the cry for intervention. "Jenny Jones. What on earth are you screaming about?"

"Billy hit me with his sword!"

"Billy Jones, what is going on?"

"Mom, I didn't hit her. I just sliced off her arm."

"Why did you do that?"

"She was bugging me."

"Bugging" is a near capital offense for Jenny's five-year-old, all-boy brother.

"Was not!" Jenny scowled.

"Were too!" Billy barked.

"Jenny, what were you doing?"

"Mom, I was just dancing with Ken. Billy said Ken was Darth Vader and he tried to hit him with his sword."

"It's not a sword; it's a light saber. The force is with me!" Billy waved the toy.

"You already stabbed Barbie!" Jenny whined.

"She was a storm trooper." Billy smirked back.

Now they were ignoring me and moving the argument into full debate.

The phone rang before this Obi Wan Mom could use her Jedi Jones wisdom to bring balance to the forces. I stepped back to the kitchen to answer the phone. The only sound I heard from the battlefield behind me was Jenny's defiant "Told ya!"

I knew I would have about five minutes, if I was lucky, before the next battle would erupt and I would have to return to the front line. I picked up the phone.

"Hello, Ann here."

"Hey, Ann, it's Vicki."

"Hi. What's up?"

Vicki was a good friend and a mom with her own needs for Jedi diplomacy.

"Me, at least for a little while. How's it going on your battle front?"

"Same old, same old. You know, trying to save the family and the living room from the war between Jedi Billy and Barbie Jenny," I said as I picked up another dish from the drainer.

"May the force be with you! Who's winning?"

"We are, I think? But there's sure to be another wave from the dark side any minute. I'm going to have to jump into light speed if I'm going to get the book done."

Vicki was almost as excited and anxious about my storybook as I was.

"How's it coming? I think I am excited about it as you," she declared.

"I am sooo thrilled about it! Mike and his dad are going to just flip out when they get it! You know how Mike practically worships his dad.

This book of his dad's stories is going to pull a few tears from tough Mr. Mike. And I believe it will help me to settle the galactic wars between Jenny and Billy. Their granddad is a real peacemaker. I am hoping his story and his peace-making heroics will rub off."

"I'm sure it will! When is the book going to be printed?"

I had promised Vicki that I'd call her the minute I got it done. The call was her way of reminding me not to forget that she would be my best and "first" critic.

"I've got to get it in on Thursday to have it back for his birthday on the twenty-eighth. I should be finished with the last pictures and edits tomorrow morning. I hope I can keep the galactic peace in place long enough to get to the computer. I really do hope that it will end the war of their worlds or at least get them on the same side."

"Let me know. If it does, I'll get a copy to see if it will work on Bart!"

"I'll let you know. I'm really hoping that it will have an impact on their ideas of who their real heroes are. I think Billy sleeps with his Star Wars action figures and the sword—pardon me—*light saber*. I know Jenny would sleep in the dollhouse with Barbie and Ken if she could figure out how to fit into it!"

"Well, Ann, better those heroes than the ones Bart finds in those crazy video games he's addicted to. Can't wait to see your book! Call me when it's done."

"Will do, and I'll pick you up for the class as soon as Mike gets here to watch the kids. It'll be around six forty."

"Okay, I'll be ready."

Vicki is a neighbor and good friend. Her kids are older, and I'm so glad that I don't have to arbitrate *their* battles. In fact, it's her kids' issues that make me so anxious to end our sibling wars while they are young. Building family unity is not an easy task at any age, but I think the intentional parenting and heritage-making process will lessen our casualties.

We are introducing a group of the ladies at our church to the idea of using family stories to help build family heritage and character for our children this evening. Creating and carrying on family traditions is part of the discussion. Another part is creating real family heroes. That's why I am doing the book for my husband, Mike, about his dad's stories.

Mike is a real hero in so many ways. While he would laugh at that idea, he really is. Oh, he's far from perfect, mind you, but he's a hero, nonetheless. We won't tell him, but his mom and I have been turning him into one. Mike does a lot of heroic things on his own. He braves the snow, wind, and rain—and occasionally the kid's toys—to take the garbage out. He works hard to bring home the bacon, and he's pretty good with all the various daddy duties. But his mom and I are putting him and his dad into their hero "tights" in the stories we tell the kids. Those are the stories that are going into the storybook.

Mike is a middle school teacher. He would say "just a teacher," but he's a really great teacher. At school and at home, he knows how to get the kids' attention and keep their interest. He can make learning really fun. Mike earns those hero points on his own. But his other credentials are what his mom and I call "creative hero-making." Together we are mastering the process. In fact, we're talking about it at the storybooking class.

Vicki and I will be telling the other women how we can incorporate powerful values and priorities into our family stories. Some of them are also doing a family storybook. Some will be putting their stories into binders, others in scrapbooks, and some in storybooks like the one I'm doing. We will be discussing what character traits and values we want to look for in our heroes and how to emphasize them in their stories. Then we'll explain how we simply weave those character strengths and values we want the kids to pick up on into the stories of these super dads and hero granddads. We use real-life events and people as the delivery method for the values, principles, and priorities that are important to us.

I've been collaborating with Mike's mom in writing the story of Mike's dad. Their birthdays are only a couple of weeks apart, so I am giving a copy of the book to Mike for his birthday, and his mom is giving a copy to Mike's dad. But the reality is we are making the storybook for the kids and our future grandkids. Sometimes the heroes of the past can carry more influence than the heroes of the present.

The book is mostly the stories of Mike's dad, but we have included a few stories from Mike's childhood too. The theme of all the stories is "Making the right choices." The childhood stories include bits and pieces about choosing to go to church, being honest, being friendly, being kind to animals, and making other simple good choices. One story is about how Mike's dad always takes care of his things. Believe me, that's a real mark of a hero in this family of clutter and chaos! I keep telling Billy that clutter is from the dark side of the Force. I'm hoping his granddad's story will help him save his toys and clothes from being confiscated by his Battlestar mom.

There's a story from Mike's high school days when he was on the football team and refused to go to a beer-drinking party. And then there's one about his dad telling the truth about scraping the neighbor's car with his bike. The kids are going to love hearing about how their grandpa was the leader of the firemen at his station. I explain what a leader is and how other people follow them to do the right things and make the right choices because they trust the leader. That helps us set the stage to remind the kids that they too can become known as good leaders and heroes.

I also point out how their father and grandfather are alike. They are both committed to making the right choices. Occasionally I remind the younger Jones hero, Mike, that he is our children's hero, but most of the time, he's in perfect character. I remind Billy and Jenny that they are like their dad and granddad and can make those kinds of good choices too. My hope is that the stories will help them deepen their understanding what it means to be a "Jones" hero.

When they are fighting, or do something out of "hero character," I'll use the stories in Grandpa Jones book to remind them of who they are. I will just call Grandpa's stories to the rescue! Anyway, that's the idea we're sharing at the class. There are four of us with similar projects, and my topic is "Turning Grandparents into Family Heroes."

If it sounds a little manipulative, it is. In fact, Mike's mother calls it "creative embellishment of the facts." We purposely leave out the short-comings, unless we can use them to show that even heroes make mistakes sometimes. That's why I say we are hero builders as well as heritage-makers.

We have several other family ancestors with some pretty amazing and heroic stories. I'll be putting them together in my next storybook. Who knows? Maybe I can find one whose name is Ken or Barbie or Skywalker. The heroes stories I am most looking forward to writing are those about the women in our family. We have some incredible grandmothers and aunts whose principles and character will be a treasure and a powerful influence on the family for generations to come. Maybe I'll even tell my own story about how I negotiated peace between the Jedi and Barbie.

Well, that's my story. Wish me luck with my class, and good luck to you with your storybooking as you search for and empower the heroes of your family. And may the force of *storybooking* be with you as you help them define who they really are!

REAL ROLE MODELS—FINDING AND DEFINING YOUR HEROES

"And he shall turn the heart of the fathers to the children, and the heart of the children to their fathers" (Malachi 4:6)

Malachi, the prophet writer of the last book of the Old Testament, refers to the coming of the Lord in the last days in chapter 4. In the fifth verse, he talks about the coming of Elijah the prophet before the coming of the Lord. Then in verse 6 he declares that he will "turn the hearts of the fathers to the children, and the hearts of the children to their fathers."

The key words here are *children, fathers, turn,* and *hearts.* The children (and grandchildren, great-grandchildren, and so on) refer to the posterity of the fathers. The fathers (and mothers) are the parents and progenitors of the children. "Turn to" means to change direction or align, in this case turning to their ways, thinking, and values. The hearts are what are being turned. The heart refers to the core purpose—or central focus—ways, and values of the person. In this verse, the fathers, or ancestors, are looking to the needs of their children—*posterity.* The children's hearts are being drawn to their family members, both living and dead, and then they are turning their hearts to each other, influenced by the spirit of Elijah. This turning of hearts is at the core of heritage-making.

This turning and relinking of hearts is happening all across the world. It is one of the reasons for the tremendous increase in interest in genealogy. The power of the Internet to access huge data resources and records has made the task and the joy of family history research available to everyone. Many of our ancestors' lives and stories are readily accessible at the click of the computer's mouse.

Finding our fathers is more than traditional genealogy of finding names, birth and death dates, and locations for a family pedigree chart. Genealogy is finding the legacy of our family members' lives, values, beliefs, traditions, character, and stories. It is finding out who they really were.

We can find the real heroes of our heritage and publish their stories from the convenience of our home computers. Many families will be lucky enough to have a family historian or genealogist who can help provide information and stories about the fathers and mothers of the family. Intentional parents can look to the experiences of these ancestors to help discover the values, character, traditions, and life contributions and heritage of these family heroes. Finding and turning your attention to the stories of these fathers and mothers is a great adventure and a great intentional-parenting resource. See if you can find the following things about your family heroes.

Discover—When and where he or she was born
Early life stories
Schooling and profession stories
Spouse—meeting, courtship, and marriage, stories
Children's stories
Faith and service stories
Overarching messages about the purpose of their lives

This is foundational information for your family heritage. For millennia past, this form of family record keeping was used to keep the next generation connected to their progenitors and their traditions and values. These records were drawn on cave walls and buildings; written as hieroglyphics on papyrus scrolls, stone tablets, and metal plates; and hand-copied in books to keep the history of the family alive forever.

These early heritage record keepers would be more than amazed at the tools we have to work with today. They would have gladly traded their carving stones and ink brushes for your computer keyboard, mouse, Google, Ancestry.com, and FamilySearch!

Our society keeps family records too. These records are the map and compass that show us where we came from. They remind us of where we are trying to go and what we must do and become to get there. Without the records, we are likely to lose sight of the not only who we came from but also the reason we are here. When we forget whose trail we are trying to follow, we lose our way, wander off the course, and are lost. This is why it is so important for intentional parents to make the connections of the fathers to their children and the children to their fathers.

So we keep records, and they detail and remind us of our heroes and our family heritage. Our heroes' stories become the collective value of the life learning and discoveries of the family. Remembering, even memorizing, their names and a few key bits of information about their lives can secure the value of their experience, character, and life-learning assets to our own emerging family heritage. Talk about these people with your children. Turn their hearts to their stories and to them as real heroes. Tell their stories.

Ask the questions:

"How can our family be more like Grandpa _____?" or
"How can you be like Grandma _____?"

When you see a child following the character example of one of their grandparents, or other family heroes, praise them and make the family heritage connection.

"Johnny, that was a really great thing you did when you _____. That reminded me of what Grandpa _____ would do. He would be very proud of you, and so am I. You are becoming a family hero just like him!"

Even older children need the praise of parents when they act in a way congruent to family heritage and their hero's values.

"Nancy, I noticed that you _____. Thank you for living by our family standards. Your example really helps me to teach the younger children our family heritage and values. It's fun for me to see you becoming one of our family heroes."

Husbands and wives can use the extra encouragement when they get it right as well. Too often we notice and comment when family members get it wrong. We also have to train ourselves to notice and comment when the glass is half full.

"Sweetheart, I noticed that _____. I love it when you provide the example for us to do better with our family heritage-making. Thank you so much."

Be sure to end the compliment with a kiss. Notes in pockets, lunch sacks, under pillows, and on mirrors can also be great reminders and ways to acknowledge the efforts of family members. When someone needs reminding about family heritage, values, and priorities, a little empathy can help the reminder stick.

"Jimmy, I know it's hard sometimes to treat Gail with kindness when she takes one of your toys without asking. Do you think it might help her if we show her an example of how our family gets permission to use each other's things? Maybe we can remind her about Grandma Joy's story."

"Max, I know you understand the family curfew rule, and I know that your friends don't understand our values. They can make it hard to be in on time, but I am really grateful when you call to let me know if you're going to be a little late. That's what Dad does too if he has to be a little late."

The more we can make the practical connection between the heritage of the fathers, their lives, and the family heroes, the more the values will stick.

GETTING THE REAL STORY

You will likely know some of your parents' and grandparents' stories, but not all of them. Ask more focused questions about their early life, struggles, goals, and values. You will find evidence of the values and heritage of *their* grandparents that carry through in their stories.

Going through this exercise may prove to be the most important step in your becoming the heritage-maker in your home. These interviews and searches with your heroes will likely become the subjects of your first family stories. They may be the most revealing and rewarding conversations you will ever have with these family patriarchs and matriarchs. Pick the right time to get them to talk. The right time may be right now. Don't procrastinate these important interviews.

Some wait just a little too long to have these conversations, and the chance is lost as their loved ones pass away Don't let that be you. You might use a lead-in question like these for interviewing family members that are living—

"Dad (or Grandpa), I'm working on a project to identify some of our family's stories and heritage.

Would you spend a little time with me and answer a few questions about your early years?"

Here are some samples of the kind of questions you might ask:

"Can you think of a story or two about what life was like for you when you were in elementary school (or high school)?"

"What were the things that were most important to you back then?"

"If you had to identify just two or three things that were your strongest values and character traits, what would they be?" "Why?"

"What do you remember about your grandfather (or grandmother)? What did he (or she) value most?"

"What have you heard or know about Great-Grandpa (or Grandma) _____?"

"What three things would you say are the most important things about our family?"

"What were some of your most important and fun family traditions?"

Finding out the details of their romance and marriage can be really fun, especially for the ladies.

"Grandpa, tell me about how you first met Grandma and what attracted you to her."

"Dad, why did you decide to marry Mom?"

"What personality traits and values would you say Mom (or Grandma) brought to our family?"

Inviting them to distill the message of their life to just two or three points will be most telling about the family legacy they will leave.

"What would you say are the most important values and character traits you would like to pass on to your grandchildren?"

Having quotes from family heroes about how they feel about values, traditions and their hopes for your family members are powerful fulcrums for leveraging and building your family heritage. What they think, or thought, is as important as how they lived when it comes to the power of third-party reference. The trick is getting them to give you a quote while they are with you and finding an example or statements from them before they pass. Sometimes the dead heroes carry more weight than our living heroes.

GETTING THE "REST OF THE STORIES"

Let's suppose that you are looking for your great-great-grandfather Miles Nibley. You discover that he was born in Edinburgh, Scotland, on June 18, 1811. Is that all you need to know? Not if you are looking for the *roots* of your family heritage and the potential character strengthening stories Miles may contribute to your heritage. Remember, a tree receives strength and stability from its roots. Names and dates may prove where and when he lived, but heritage-makers want to know *how* he lived. We want to understand who he really was and what he valued. Intentional parents want to cut and paste some of his strongest values and standards into their own family heritage and character traits.

What if you cannot find any pictures, journals, or published information? Remember that Miles was likely a product, in part, of the conditions and challenge of life in that area and time. You can extrapolate some of those conditions and assumed life experience by doing a little searching on Google or Wikipedia about life in Edinburgh in the early 1800s. Ancestry.com can also be an invaluable tool for finding at least more of the facts behind their stories.

The further back you go, the more difficult it can be to find personal information. Wherever possible, don't be satisfied with just the facts. Dig a little more. You'll be surprised what asking questions of the older family members, friends, or relatives will reveal. The rest of the story of these "older" fathers can hold the greatest treasures of your family heritage.

LEGACY-SECURING INTENTIONAL PARENTING PROJECT SUGGESTIONS

Basic Genealogy—Create a family tree poster art piece. Many services can help you create this visual reference of who's who in your family history. Ideally, you can produce a family group record starting with your children and reaching back four generations. That is you, your parents, their parents (your grandparents), and their grandparents (your great-grandparents).

The Heart(s) of my Fathers—Create a simple storybook giving the highlights of the lives of each of your parents and grandparents back through your great-grandparents. Give interesting facts and personality traits of these family members.

Heirlooms—Work with family members to identify and secure some relics that once belonged to your ancestors that can be displayed in your home. These heirlooms trigger memories and conversations about your family heritage.

Canvas or Poster Picture—A wall hanging canvas, poster, or framed collage of pictures of an ancestor or group of ancestors can be a reminder about the family heroes and the stories that honor them.

Fun Family Facts—A simple card game can be made using Old Maid, Go Fish, Matching, or basic flash cards that highlight the lives and stories of the family heroes. These can be current family members, including children, as well as ancestors. Make sure to include a picture of the hero. Additional cards can have the name of the family member, the things they like, talents, profession, where they lived, a favorite saying, and something unique about the person. The repetition of the game will help the children learn about the family heroes and help them feel connected.

Family Heritage Day—Create a new holiday called Family Heritage Day. Make a celebration with a party, guests, and a feast to celebrate your unique family. Tell favorite stories about the family heroes. Serve their favorite foods or recipes. Remind each other of the contributions they made to your family heritage.

A Hero Walk—Take family members on a trip to the homes or former residences, cemeteries, or other family interest sites of your family heroes where children can get a hands-on feeling for the persona and life of their ancestor(s). Tell the children about the hero, his or her life, and story. Focus on the positive character traits that make that hero important to your family legacy.

Storytelling—Take the children to meet with a relative who knows the life and stories of a given family hero and have him or her tell the stories. Be sure to emphasize their values and any positive similarities to your children. Visit with a relative who knows the stories of the fathers and mothers.

Pictures—Hang pictures of family heroes in the bedrooms of each of the children. You may choose a particular family hero whose story and life message will be helpful to that child. You can also rotate those pictures occasionally to help establish that story as part of your family heritage.

Bedtime Stories—When you tell your children bedtime stories, pick a story of a family hero and bring that hero to life in the minds of your children. Practice your storytelling skills as you reveal the hero in each of the family members whose stories you tell. Be sure to say something like, "And that is one reason Uncle Paul is one of our family heroes."

3

FAMILY FENCING

Building Internal Family Security

STAN AND BETH HAD BOTH COME FROM STRONG Christian families. Although they didn't talk a lot about it much, their attitudes and ideas about raising the children were generally the same. They hadn't had any really serious issues with the kids, at least not yet. Ted was seven, Tim was five, and at age sixteen months, baby Anny was still perfect. They had enjoyed good neighbors, and the boys had good friends. Now as they moved across town into their new home, they weren't sure what to expect from the neighborhood kids.

Stan had decided to put in his own yard and fence to cut some of the costs of the new home. He was coordinating with the neighbors to make it a joint project. He had suggested that Beth do a little online research about fencing suppliers in the area while he was at work that day. During that search, Beth stumbled onto the article "Fencing the Family." The article intrigued her, so she printed a copy for Stan to read. That's what initiated their discussion that evening.

STAN AND BETH'S STORY

We were so excited about the move to the new house. Excited and a bit overwhelmed. Moving is definitely one of those gird-up-your-loins-and-just-get-it-done jobs! There were so many decisions about what to keep and what to throw away in the move. What still had value and what didn't?

That all came on top of the decisions of what color for the walls, what kind of carpet, what style of fixtures, what kind of tile, what color of stain, what style of knobs, and the list just went on and on. By the time we had packed the moving van and cleaned the old house, I was weary of deciding. I was "decided out"! I was more than willing to let Stan make the decisions on the fence and the yard. Somehow, he had managed to get out of a lot of the other decisions with his "I don't care. You choose" to the colors and fixtures.

Stan knew he had to leave me the right side of the backyard for the flower and vegetable garden. Somehow I knew that getting completely out of the fence project was more than I could hope for. The boys were really excited about helping their dad with the project. Still, when he asked me to find a source for the materials we needed, I reminded him that I chose the drapes and the tile and that it was his turn to choose the fence. As usual, I rolled over and consented to at least check out the fencing resources online.

Do you know how much you can find just by doing a Google search for fence? Don't bother. It was easier just to ask the neighbors. They had already found the answers. I did find something out about fences that neither Fran nor Melody, my next-door neighbors, had come across. It was an article that really got my attention. In spite of my decision weariness, I decided that Stan needed to read the article and that we would have a discussion about it. That's how it all started.

Stan burst through the back door. "Honey, honey, I'm back! Bob and Fred are available over the Memorial Day weekend to put up the fence. What did you find?"

I was reading the "Fencing the Family" article for a second time. "I found a lot of stuff, most of which Melody (the neighbor to the right) had already found. It seems like her husband delegated that job to her too."

"Yeah, Bob said she probably had some good ideas."

"She and Fran have already picked up samples of the vinyl they like. Melody will bring it over when she gets back from the store. It sounds great. So you and the guys are set for memorial weekend?"

"Yep. It'll be good to work with them to get to know the families."

Then I told him, "I found something else that is really interesting I want to show you."

"What is it?"

I didn't want to tell him. I wanted him to read it too. "You'll have to wait till tonight. I want to show it to you."

He didn't answer as he walked to the fridge and then back out to the garage. I know him well enough to know that when I want to have a meaningful discussion, it's better to start when both of our heads are on the pillow.

Melody brought the fence samples over. She was right. They really were perfect for matching the houses and the neighborhood. Better yet, she could get the sale price even before they published it for the holiday. I finished dinner and got Anny to bed while Stan was showing the boys the fence samples and reading their bedtime story.

I had just enough time to get two more boxes unpacked and put away before he finished the story. At the rate I was putting things away, I figured I'd be finished about the time we were ready to move again. Packing and unpacking can be a real pain. For once in the last two weeks, we were both in bed before midnight! I left the "Family Fencing" article on his pillow.

"What's this?" he asked.

"It's the article about fencing I found and I wanted to talk with you about."

"Something about the fence?"

"Well, sort of. It really made sense to me. Read it and tell me what you think."

"Okay, but this is going to cost you."

"Cost me? You already owe me big time!" I reminded him with a smile.

Fencing the Family

There are many different kinds of fences. There are simple white picket fences that divide and define property lines. There are chain-link fences and cedar fences, vinyl fences, block fences, and rock fences. Fences cordon off backyards, divide off garden plots, give structure for growing roses, and give defining character to our property and homes. However, most fences have more important purposes.

Generally, we use fences for one or both of two priorities. These include to define our property lines and to keep some things in and to keep other things out. We want to keep the children in and the neighbor's dog and other uninvited trespassers out.

Farmers and ranchers build barbwire fences to keep their livestock in, on their land, and out of their neighbor's property and to keep the neighbors' livestock off their land. Electric and electronic fences can be used to restrain animals and people from crossing their boundaries. Farmers and ranchers know that they must invest wisely and timely in the building and maintaining their fences.

There are important principles associated with building effective fences. Fencers need to know about the typical and predictable places where animals and people will likely be tempted to break through. Fences must be extra strong and checked often to secure these places. Good fencers know that the corners of the fence will require extra strong bracing because the animals congregate there and will likely press hard against the fence there. Fence line wires must be stretched tight and attached securely to the posts. Effectively spaced and buried posts define the fence line and keep the wires in place to prevent animals from crossing over or breaking through. Strong fences train animals and people not to cross the line.

A "stay" is a small post or twisted wire that is placed in between the main posts to keep wires separated and tight. They help to prevent the animals from sticking their heads through to separate the wire. Animals and people seem to know that where the head goes, the body can follow. Fencers need to understand about heads, attitudes, and thinking. Understanding those thoughts and habits can help the fencer to be successful in building a fence that will provide effective security.

Fences must be checked and maintained regularly to ensure that security. Where there has been a break through, from either side of the fence, an extra post, wire, or brace may need to be put in place to strengthen the location. Sometimes broken or stretched wires need to be reconnected or tightened. Riding the fence, as ranchers call it, ensures that the fence is maintained and that it does its job.

Companies too build fences. These fences are used to prevent people from entering dangerous construction areas and to keep valuable equipment and materials secure from thieves. Retail establishments employ electronic fences and merchandise tags to prevent unpurchased items from leaving the store. Businesses and individuals protect their proprietary trade secrets and intellectual property rights with contracts, trade agreements, and patent fences.

Families need fences too. As it is with farmers and businesses, so it is with families. Parents must be adept at building and maintaining strong and effective fences to protect family members, their valuables, and values. Parents erect fences to keep the toys and children in the yard and out of the street. We use fences as defining and dividing lines for our private property. Fences help us to keep things we want close to us and the things we don't want away. Families too may choose from a variety of fencing systems and options.

Family fences may be built of wood, vinyl, brick, rock, or hedges of shrubs. We can build fences and put signs to limit access to our yards and homes. Groups of families can build fenced and gated communities and place guards to ensure common protection of property and residents. In this way, we can largely eliminate the bulk of uninvited trespassers, criminals, and solicitors from getting to us and to our property, homes, and family. This is how we protect our loved ones and valuables. But how do we protect our treasured values, heritage, and the legacy of the family name and the character of its members? These are our most precious possessions.

Today it takes different kinds of fences and restraints to keep our children within the safe haven of the family security. Intruders come in through the TV and the computer. Blocking these intrusions is equally, if not more, important than fences to block the kids from chasing a ball into the street. Today parents need to understand and employ the security of both external and internal fencing.

Internet filtering systems and TV and movie ratings monitoring tools are virtual fences that can help repel unseen villains. Parental oversight of family member Internet and media choices and use is vital to keep the bad guys and bad stuff out of the home and minds of our children. But what about all the time our children are outside the home and beyond the protecting influence of our voices and our physical and virtual fences? Taller fences, more discriminating filters, locks on the gates, even armed guards are insufficient to provide security when those we love are away from us. Today's growing flood of crime and family value trespassers surround us, come through virtual doors and lurk in areas we used to consider to be secure from such intrusions and intruders.

In today's society many seek to violate and destroy our values. They would break through our fences to get to and entice our children to ignore, cross over, and violate the standards and boundaries of our family beliefs, values, and heritage. These trespassers can penetrate even the strongest physical fences. To deter these sinister characters and influences we must employ another kind of family fence—an internal fence. This fence must also have clear boundaries, deeply planted beliefs, character, and well-placed ethical and moral standards.

Concerned parents must be intentional and timely about

establishing clearly defined lines of appropriate and inappropriate behavior for family members for their internal fences to be effective. We can attach family rules and protective standards to the deeply planted corner posts of their family heritage. We can establish and follow through with regular fence-checking discussions and heritage-strengthening traditions to maintain their fence. Where this critical maintenance is ignored or missing, curious children may stick their heads through or leave the security of its protective boundaries. These departures can take them away from the family and onto the road that leads to departure and violation of their values and standards. Outside the security of these family values, children may enter paths that lead to sorrow, injury, pain, and failure.

Now, more than ever before, parents need to understand the principles of internal fencing to protect their family. Parents can build and strengthen a family heritage fence that can help to secure their precious loved ones and the legacy of the family name, even when they are not at home.

Local fencing contractors and security businesses can provide the latest and most effective external fencing protection information and products. But where can parents find information and resources to build strong and reliable internal fencing for their children? The most effective self-security system parents can erect begins with a clearly defined code of family conduct, honor, and personal character. Parents bring some of these personal character traits and priorities from the legacy of their heritage. Stories of the values, standards, and traditions of heroes from your family ancestors are a great resource for establishing the values and character traits you want to include in the personal character fences of our children.

Heritage-based fences are strongest when parents establish and commit family members to accountability to each other for their family values, standards, and heritage. Children of families who are aligned to the principles and priorities they learn from the stories of their family heroes tend to live by those principles. They are better prepared to rebuff intruders who would have them violate the boundaries of their character.

These are the stories our children need to hear, know, and be able to repeat. The stories of the life lessons and standards of their parents, grandparents, and ancestors can help them to embrace our family heritage. We want our children to embrace the strength and power found in the example of these heroes, which they developed through a lifetime of holding true to their values. Those choices defined who they were and established their character. The stories of the struggles and tragedies and triumphs of their life experiences can help our families remember who they were and what they stood for. They can help our family members remember who they are and how they too should choose to live by that commitment.

These family hero stories, values, and traditions are among the best internal fencing resources we can use to build our family heritage fence and empower our children with the security of a heritage-enriched character. Isn't it time you checked the security of your family fences and enlist the help of your family hero's values and traditions to help secure the safety, success, and legacy of your family heritage?

It took him all of five minutes to read it. I could tell he was impressed too because he didn't make any of his typical snide comments while he was reading. He set it down and gave me that look of "huh, interesting."

"So, what do you think, Mr. Fence-builder?"

"Some good ideas. I think you should build a fence like that too."

"Hold on, mister! That's a fence for both of us to build."

He scowled in mock exasperation. "Okay. Where do *we* start?"

"Just like your fence. We make a list of our family values, heroes' stories, and traditions."

"Okay . . ."

"The traditions are the easy part. We have most of that on the calendar, at least the events. I can make a list of all of them, but traditions are not just events," I observed.

"What else is there? I thought it was birthdays, holidays, vacations, and trips we do every year." He liked those things and always made them a priority.

"Just identifying the traditions and putting them on the calendar doesn't distinguish our family from most other families. A lot of people do fireworks and a picnic on the Fourth of July. Some of them probably burn the hot dogs and burgers too!"

Stan scowled in recognition of the fact and he really did tend to overdo the cooking time and temperature on the family barbecues.

"We all celebrate Christmas with gifts. Most everyone eats turkey for Thanksgiving. Everyone I know celebrates their kids' birthdays with a party and cake and ice cream and gifts. That's traditional for everybody. What makes a tradition for our family is how we celebrate and what we do that makes our events different, unique, and special."

"What, so maybe we shouldn't put up a Christmas tree because everybody else does? That could be good," Stan said with a cheesy and wishful smile.

He was not too excited about pulling out the artificial tree and trying to find the burned-out bulbs on every strand of lights every year.

"No, that's not a good idea. But maybe getting it out and up a week earlier could be," I reminded him.

"No, I think our tradition of two weeks before Christmas works just fine," he retorted.

I knew exactly what he was doing, but he wasn't going to get away with that sneaky renege on his commitment! He had promised to get it out this year on the first of December.

"Nice try, mister, but I have a perfect memory of your promise for getting it up on December 1 this year. You haven't forgotten that little detail, have you?"

"Okay. You can't blame me for trying! So, what do we do to make our traditions different?"

"Well, at Christmas, you read the Christmas story on Christmas Eve. We watch *Mr. Krueger's Christmas* and we let the kids open their gifts from me."

"Yep. But the gifts come before Mr. Krueger. It's always a new pair of pj's. I don't know anybody else who does that. That's a tradition."

"What other family celebrates New Year's Eve?"

"You mean with—"

We grinned and both said simultaneously, "Rook and root beer floats!"

"For birthdays, *you always* take the boys to a movie and out for pizza on the Saturday closest to their birthday. We always fix your fried chicken with homemade mashed potatoes and peas for your birthday."

"Right you are! And on your birthdays *I* always . . ."

". . . bring me flowers and write me a poem and take me out for Mexican food. That's something not every woman gets for her birthday!" That really was *his* birthday tradition for me.

"Not everyone likes Mexican food."

"But I do! And most of our vacations are camping trips. You know, with s'mores and UNO 'til you drop in the tent."

"I like that one!"

That's because somehow he always wins. I quickly reminded him, "So do the boys! And they like the backyard campouts in the tent on the first day of summer with their dad too."

"Yes they do, but that is likely going to have to be somewhere else this year. Unless we put off building the fence until after we get the grass in . . ."

"Uh-uh. I think we'd better follow through with fence first; grass later. The neighbors are already excited about getting that done. Do you agree?"

Stan was right. That backyard camping would have to stay off the tradition list that year. Then Stan reminded me, "Another of the traditions the boys like is shopping with you for back-to-school clothes. That is definitely a mommy tradition."

"And I like it too, when we are finished."

"Okay, so there's a lot more to traditions than just the event. I suspect we could do a lot more about making our traditions different—special."

"Right. Special. This would be a fun conversation with the boys. We could ask them what they like best and what else they would like to do."

"Careful. That could be a loaded question!"

With that Stan turned over, assuming that was the end of our discussion. The more I thought about it and the more we talked about it, the more interested and excited I became. I was not ready for lights out yet.

"What about our values, Stan?" I continued.

"What about them? Are you suggesting that we don't have family values?" he asked with raised eyebrows.

"Of course not! We know what they are, but how well do the boys know them?"

"I don't know. They're pretty darn good kids. Why don't you make a *list* and *ask* them," he suggested.

Stan pulled up the blanket to signal he was ready for me to turn the light *off*. That was a new job for me in the new house. The switch used to be on his side of the bed. The new home had the main switch on my side. The touch lamp that gave us equal access to the chore was still in one of many unpacked boxes in the closet. When I didn't take the hint and turn off the light, he turned back over.

"Is there *more*?"

"You read the article. You know there's more. A lot more."

"Are we going to build the whole family fence tonight?" he moaned.

"Not all of it, but maybe a little more. What do you remember about your family values and standards?"

"We didn't talk a lot about standards. At least not like that. We just sort of knew what they were. Everybody knew what was expected. We knew what our values were," he said, looking up at the ceiling.

"Okay. What were they? And how did everyone come to know them?"

"You know, they're all the standards. Be honest, don't steal, tell the truth, wash behind your ears, brush your teeth, do your homework—that kind of stuff."

"Those are so basic. They don't define our family as being much different."

"Oh, I don't know. How many other dads made their kids brush their teeth up and down for two full minutes!"

"Your dad was a dentist. I suspect that is a standard that all dentists' families have." I had to admit that was a simple but obvious carryover from his family values.

Stan shook his head. "Not just dentists. I see that our boys brush that way, and *I'm* not a dentist."

"I'm not sure if that is a value or a tradition. I'm glad you're keeping that one going. I think they have just about accepted that value as the right way to brush."

"Maybe that *is* the idea. When the things we value become our standards, they are like the posts for the fence."

"Stanley, I like the analogy! So the corners of the fence are like our traditions. Our standards are the posts, and the values are the fencing that runs between them." I was pleased with my analogy and the concept of building a family heritage fence. Stan patted me on the shoulder.

"Now you've got it! I'm sure that you can figure out how putting up the fence around the yard can be that easy." He chuckled.

"Not easy. Not even simple. But I am going to make this a project. I really like the idea of listing what our values and standards are. I want us to talk with the boys about it."

I could tell that I wasn't going to get much further planning either fence that night. But Stan seemed to like the idea of talking with the boys about our family values. That was a good start. He turned over, got up, and turned off the light.

"We should decide who our family's heroes are. Let's talk with the boys about that." I was getting excited about the lists of heritage-fencing tools and materials.

"Okay, we'll do that, but let's let them and our heroes sleep through the list-making tonight. And me too, okay?"

Stan crawled back in bed. I nudged him to his side of the bed and then snuggled up to him.

"You're one good man, and we're going to make a great fence-building team!"

"Uh-huh. Let's work on it in our dreams . . ."

I fell asleep thinking about what my family values had been and what I wanted ours to be. I started a mental list. Like Stan's fencing list, I started thinking about what we needed and where and how we would get it. I knew one of my first calls would be to my mother and my grandmother. I think that this was the night I really became intentional about defining our family heritage.

BUILDING A FAMILY HERITAGE FENCE— INTERNAL FAMILY SECURITY

"And I will make thee unto this people a fenced brazen wall: and they shall fight against thee, but they shall not prevail against thee" (Jeremiah 15:20)

Jeremiah was told that the Lord would make him as a "fenced brazen wall." This description of the protection to Jeremiah was a simile. An external fence or wall would not be there to protect him; rather, he would be the fence and brazen wall. The reference to fenced cities occurs over thirty times in the Old Testament. People of Jeremiah's time recognized the need for protection from the external forces of their enemies.

The scriptures show over and over that these fences around the cities, while imposing, were ineffective to protect their residents who disregarded their heritage. Yet the Lord refers to Jeremiah as a fence that would hold. Jeremiah was *internally fenced* because of his obedience and commitment to the covenants and the laws (values, priorities, traditions, and performances) of his faith and heritage.

We can build the external fences to our yards and walls to our homes. We can make our homes and families as a *fenced city*. We can set the "towers and watchmen" of friends, security cameras, and systems. We can monitor our television and Internet-filtering systems and security to prevent unwanted assailants from entering. But, just as Jeremiah had to leave the security of the fenced city and watchful warnings of his external protections, our family members will also have to leave the protective confines of our "fenced" homes and warning voices. They will need to have that internal, impenetrable fence and brazen wall to filter choices based on their commitments to their family heritage.

Our children and grandchildren can become the very fence that protects them and their family name. Their commitment and adherence to the principles and values of their heritage can help them rebuff the attacks they encounter. This internal fencing of family heritage must be built on principles, attitudes, and commitments that become a brazen wall of character.

THE GATE

Every fenced and walled city, yard, or field has a gate. The gate prevents or allows access and exit. It is the part of the fence that the fence itself is to secure and control. The purpose of the fence is to empower the gate as the filter of what gets in and what goes out. One of the basic purposes of the family is to ensure the security, success, and happiness of each member.

Every family should consider having its own custom vision, mission, and family charter, or gate in the family fence. A written family charter and rules gives children the official and credible behavior expectations for their family. It should include a detailed list of the family's values, standards, and rules as well as a statement about their commitment to their standards and to supporting each other in keeping them. Such a document should be posted at their gate, the door to the home, and referred to often and read regularly. This is a criterion for the gate of the family fence. The gate must be the most secure part of the family fence.

All the family members share the gate-keeping responsibility to keep values and people inside the security of the fence. Gatekeepers are equally committed to not let unwanted values or trespassers in through the gate. When the security of the gate is challenged, all family members call for the official gatekeepers—Mom or Dad—to help secure the gate. When family members discover that some value or person has sneaked in through the fence or gate, they send them away, and, when necessary, they call for help from the other family members.

A family vision, purpose, and mission statement can be simple or complex, long or short. Making it a little legalistic can help make it feel more important to the reader. Here is an example of elements of a family charter mission statement or proclamation.

THE DOE FAMILY MISSION

The declaration—"We, the John and Jane Doe family, do hereby declare that it is our intent, purpose, and sacred mission to . . .

The mission—Secure the health, happiness, and success of each member of our family. We are committed to see that every member of our family has the opportunity to develop talents and to pursue interests to learn important lessons and life skills and to live by our family values.

The values—We value faith in God and live by his teachings and commandments. We value honesty, gratitude, obedience, morality, help-fulness, hard work, and integrity. We value kindness, service, knowledge, education, good music, cleanliness, orderliness, and respect for each other and for others outside the family. We believe in forgiveness and repentance and in being responsible and accountable for our actions and commitments. We believe in laughing and having fun together.

The commitment—We pledge our time, service, support, and sacred honor to help each other to live by our values, standards, and family rules.

The motto—Our motto is "No empty seats at our family's table."

The invitation—We invite everyone in our family and those who know us to share and live by our family standards when they are in our home or presence. This will help us to be true to our family vision and to achieve our family mission.

Signed and dated—[Signatures and date]

CORNER POSTS

The fence around a farmer's pasture is built with strong corners. Its posts are generally larger, planted deeper, and have diagonal and horizontal bracing. Farmers know that corners are where they can expect the greatest pressure on the fence. Animals pressing against the fence trying to get in or out as they follow and test the fence's strength at various places will transfer that pressure along the wire to the corners.

Family heritage fences need strong corners too. The corners of family heritage are the most important and significant beliefs and commitments of the family. These are the virtues, the "absolutes" of family principles and behavior standards. For intentional, heritage-centered families, these are the family's commandments, the "thou shalts" and "thou shalt nots" of the family.

Examples may include:

- **Morality**—live virtuous lives *(as you define it)*.

- **Honesty**—don't lie, cheat, or steal, and obey rules and laws.

- **Faith**—acknowledge God's reality, abiding divine law, reverencing, and seeking God's grace and assistance *(as you understand and define it)*.

- **Respect**—recognize, honor, and appreciate the rights and freedoms of other people.

- **Citizenship**—recognize, respect, honor, and defend those whose rights and freedom are being challenged, threatened, or abused.

- **Education**—developing lifelong learning skills; planning for college; completing and turning in assignments; attending class and being on time; developing talents, and seeking personal excellence.

- **Contribution**—sharing with others and doing one's share; contributing to family and to the good of society; being dependable and hardworking.

- **Responsibility**—being accountable and responsible for your actions and honoring your commitments and obligations.

When family fencing ensures that these corner posts—principles—are set deeply and are braced with rules and consequences, the rest of the heritage fence will be much more secure. It will protect family members from the pain, injury, and disappointments that result when these important corners posts are weak or missing.

Putting these key internal fence posts and braces in place is done with shared communication. It is accomplished by agreement of what our family does and doesn't do. It is important that all family members who share the fence don't climb over it, especially at these corners. Nor should they allow any outsiders to climb over and violate the fence's protective barrier. Climbing over the fence weakens it and encourages others to climb over too.

Because occasionally someone forgets and climbs over the fence, it can become loose and weak. This is why we need to ride (check) the fence line regularly. Ranchers ride the fence to check it and to make sure there are not any holes or breaks in it. When they find places where it has been stretched, weakened, or broken, they fix it *immediately*. Often they will install additional bracing or wire to strengthen the weakened area.

Similarly, security and strength of family fences need to be checked regularly. When a weak location or break is found, it must be repaired quickly and reinforced. Fathers' interviews are an effective way to "ride the fence line" with family members. Casual conversations with children about family values while working or playing together are wonderful fence-checking opportunities.

THE INTERNAL FENCE

Consider the internal fencing metaphor, where individual family members *are* the *fence wires*. The more wires (family members) that are secured to the posts (family values, principles and beliefs), the stronger and more secure the fence will be. We can help our children embrace and connect to family values and rules by discussing and checking their understanding and solid connection to them regularly in informal talks and more formal family gatherings.

These can be simple casual conversations and questions that invite dialogue and thoughtful consideration of their lives and the lives of their friends. Parents can initiate these conversations when driving somewhere with a daughter or son. They can be a wonderful part of a special mommy or daddy-daughter dates, father-son outings, or while moms are making dinner or working in the kitchen or yard. The best place for these conversations is in family council meetings. However, if there has been a breach or a break in a family member's connection to a value post, that discussion should occur as early as possible and always in private.

Here are some lead-in questions to engage your children in conversations about their values, beliefs, and any weaknesses or challenge to their family-heritage fence.

- "Hey, Robby, I appreciate the opportunity to spend a little time with you. What have you been up to lately?"

- "I've been hearing some pretty scary stuff about what our teenagers have to put up with at school. What are you seeing?"

- "Do our family beliefs and values make it hard for you to relate or interact with your friends at school?"

- "Are your values a lot different than your friends'?"

- "Debby, thanks for helping me in the kitchen. It gives me a chance to get caught up with what's going on in your life. What's up?"

- "Millie, is it a good time for us to teach Barbie and Teddy Bear about our family values and rules? Oh good! Maybe some of the other toys should know about our family heritage too. Shall we teach them?"

REPAIRING AND STRENGTHENING THE FENCE

When weaknesses or breaks in the family heritage fence are discovered, prompt repair work can result in even stronger and more effective fencing. The key is to make the security of the family member and the necessary repair work more important than the breach of the fence. Family members must be certain that any violation or breaking of the family's heritage boundary is repairable. They must know that and that they can return and reconnect to the value posts with honor and acceptance. That does not mean that repeated breaches are without consequence and penalties. Violations and repairs do not come without some pain and some cost to that family member.

REPAIR COSTS

The family heritage fence is most effective when there are clear consequences and penalties for crossing it. They should be established and understood at the time the family members agree to the values, rules, and boundaries. Reminding family members regularly about the reasons for the fence and its protective security is preventative maintenance of the fence. So are gentle but firm reminders of the consequences and penalties of climbing over the fence or allowing others to break through. We too must be constantly checking the strength of our family heritage fence line.

When a rancher finds a break in a fence, he may have to move his animals into a different holding pen while the repairs are made. Similarly, time-out corners and grounding are appropriate actions and penalties for fence-breaking. These consequences can also be effective deterrents to fence-crossing.

Fences are all about protection and freedom. They can create total freedom within their bounds. That is, they can keep harmful things and influences out while keeping the values and positive influences close. In this way, fences create freedom from being hurt and freedom to enjoy and have close to you the things you want secured. Whenever the rancher's animals or family members ignore or cross over the fence, they lose that freedom. If an animal continues to break through the fence, the rancher will have to put the animal into a smaller confined area with stronger, more restrictive fences. So it is with family members. Continued violation of family values and rules should be met with more restrictions on freedom. Penalties will also need longer periods in the holding pens of time-out and grounding.

The following Garrett Family Rules for use of the family car by teenage drivers are illustrative.

FAMILY DRIVING RULES

1. Must have valid driver's license.

2. Must have finished Eagle Scout rank (boys) or comparable girls recognition program before they can get license.

3. Must have insurance on the car to drive. Have an A- school grade point average (GPA), and parents will help pay for the insurance premium.

4. With a 3.85 GPA from ninth through eleventh grade, the family will help the teen with a down payment to buy a safe used car for personal use in their senior year of high school.

USE RULES AND VIOLATION PENALTIES

1. Permission to use the car must be given by parents. Violation: 30 days no driving.

2. Permission is based on the purpose for the use and acceptable status of chores and homework completed.

3. Specific explanation of where you are going and when you will be back and strict adherence to agreed-upon return time. Violation: 1–6 weeks no driving.

4. Restrictions of who can be in the car—family and authorized friends only. Violation: 1–6 weeks no driving.

5. The user is responsible for the purchase of the gasoline. If Mom or Dad add errands, they pay for the gas. Violation: Fill the gas tank plus $10 penalty fee.

6. Penalties can be arbitrated by a discussion with Mom and Dad and an explanation in advance.

HANDLING RULE VIOLATIONS—EXAMPLE

Below is an example of a violation and how it was handled.

Jarred was a responsible driver at seventeen. His grades were in line to receive the agreed-upon down payment on a car for his senior year and to have his insurance paid by Mom and Dad. One Saturday in September, there was a back-to-school party Jarred wanted to attend. He cleared the normal permission process to use his mom's car. He was taking two neighbors, who were on the "okay-to-ride list." They were to be back at 10:30 p.m. Jarred took the family "loner" cell phone and everything and everyone was a "go" for a good time.

While at the party, they met another friend, Brad, who needed a ride home. The problem was he was not on the okay-to-ride list. His Mom and Dad were running a present over to his Aunt Joan and would be back about the same time.

Jarred suspected that just dropping him off wouldn't be a problem. Still, he knew the rule. He had to get permission, so he tried to call his Mom back. No luck. She must have left her cell phone home. He tried his Dad's cell, but still no luck. Jarred knew that he was in a predicament.

If he took Brad to his home without permission to be a little later than the 10:30 p.m., he could probably get Brad home and be back to his house. His parents would never know the difference, but then he would have broken the driving rule and one of the basic virtues of the family by *lying*. In less than a second, his mind was weighing all the options. It was awkward for sure. He could wait and keep trying to get his parents on the phone, but he suspected that would get him home later. Jarred finally decided to send his Mom a text message and go ahead and take Brad home. But he was still a little nervous about the decision and knew he would need to have a conversation with his parents about this decision when he got home. He believed that it would be okay. Jarred was extra careful as he drove Brad home. Brad thanked Jarred for the ride.

Jarred parked the car in the garage and was relieved that his Dad's spot was still empty. As he came through the back door, he saw the lights of his parents' car flash across the front window. Now he and his parents would be in an interesting situation. The text message locked him into having a conversation with them. His parents were in a different situation with regard to the family fence. If they just ignored or shrugged it off, they knew that would weaken the fence. They didn't want to make too big a deal about it. After all, Jarred had acted responsibly by trying to call and leaving the text message. Still, the fence had been breached.

Jarred didn't want to get in trouble. His parents didn't want to ignore the violation nor his honest effort to use good judgment under the situation. The resulting conversation was more about the process of dealing with the fence than about its purpose. They called these "spirit of the law versus letter of the law" discussions.

As they walked through the door, Jarred was at the refrigerator getting a glass of milk.

"Jarred, you beat us back! How was the party?"

Mom didn't jump right into the Brad issue.

"It was good—fun. I saw a lot of the guys from Lakeview. I haven't seen them all summer. Did you get my text message?" He figured he was in a better position if he brought it up.

"Uh-huh. Thanks for the heads up. Sorry you couldn't reach me. I left my phone in my purse in the car. So who is this Brad?"

"He's a friend, and I kind of got caught in a situation where it was hard not to drop him off. I hope that was okay."

His mom asked, "Is he a good kid? Should we consider him for the approved list?"

"I don't know him really well, so . . ."

"Well, maybe we ought to meet him sometime and get a feel for him," his dad suggested.

"Yeah, okay. We can do that sometime."

It was Jarred's dad that ended the message with a reference to the fence rules.

"Jarred, letting us know about Brad, even if it was with a text and technically without permission was the responsible thing to do. That let me know that you take the driving rules seriously. It made me proud about how you handled it. That really will help us when we talk about the car rules with your younger brother. He's due for that talk next month."

Fences can facilitate great conversations and build self-esteem and further commitment to the family values and rules when the attitude is set to look for those opportunities. The conversation and experience could have been very different had Jarred felt the need to ignore the rules or lie about what happened.

It was a little thing for sure, but the little things are the building blocks of the big things. In this case, it was the whole family fence that was strengthened, not just the car rules.

FENCES AND FREE WILL

Much of life and parenting is centered on the principle and use of agency, the idea of free will and choice. Children can use their freedom to choose as a justification for not having to be constrained to the rules of family fences. That freedom must be clearly defined by the bounds the family fence sets. Unfortunately, they usually want to ignore the fact that consequences are inseparably connected to the freedom and choices the chooser makes.

Sadly, sometimes children are allowed to make choices that violate rules or laws, and parents or society ignore that breach, or circumvent the consequences and established penalties attached to those rules. In these cases, the child comes to believe that choices and consequences are not connected, let alone inseparable. That false notion of freedom from consequence, or that someone else can and will clean up the mess, leads to ever-increasing acts of irresponsible behavior and rule-breaking.

Parents often wrestle with just how much freedom their children need and should have to develop their ability to choose. That freedom needs to include the freedom to make some less-than-best choices and to learn from them—but also facing the consequences. The key is to manage the fence, rules, and their choices within bounds wherein the child cannot put themselves, or others, at serious risk should they make a poor choice. Successfully balancing freedom of choice and the application of consequence is intentional parenting at its best.

Teaching children about the following principles and building them into the family heritage fence will help to avoid headaches and heartaches. The key is to help them to acknowledge that their choices always come with consequences. Freedom is really a range of options that a person can choose among. All freedoms, or "choices," carry inseparable consequences. Where a choice can be made, the chooser must be able to clearly identify and be willing to accept the associated consequences. Getting good counsel about choices and consequences before you make a choice is the smartest and most mature thing to do.

For children, these kinds of lessons are an ongoing training process, and regular reminders are needed to help them remember:

- "If you choose to eat your vegetables (choice), you can have your dessert (consequence). You can choose not to eat your vegetables, but the consequence is that you won't get dessert. It's your choice."

- "If you choose to clean up your toys (choice) you can go out to play (consequence). You can choose to not pick up your toys, and the consequence is that you cannot go out to play. It's your choice."

- "You can choose to be kind to Linda and continue to play together (choice), or you can choose to be unkind and you can go to your room for time-out (consequence). It's your choice."

- "If you get your chores done (choice), you can have your allowance (consequence). If you don't complete your chores, you will forfeit your allowance. You can choose."

- "When you finish your homework and clean your room (choice), you can go to the movie (consequence). If you don't finish your room and homework in time, you won't be able to go to the movie. The choice is yours."

- "If you keep your commitment to _____, I will _____. If you do not keep your commitment, I won't _____. The choice is yours."

- "If you comply with the contract (choice), you can keep the _____ (consequence). If you do not comply, it will be taken away. If it is repossessed, it will be difficult to get another contract. The choice is yours."

And so on. For most of these principle and choice conversations, we have to remember that age and maturity govern the timing of the discussions and the enforcement of the rules and choice options.

CHOICES AND REWARDS

As the children mature and are better prepared to understand choices and consequences and to act responsibly, we can give greater freedom and range to their choices. We can use *if—then* contracts with children. If—then agreements are like custom rules with a specific choice and consequence for things that are not really family rules but apply to more short-term interests, needs, and learning experiences of the moment. These contract choices further help family members understand the positive nature of consequence for responsible and contributive behavior.

- "Teri, if you clean the laundry room, then you can make a batch of cookies to take with you."

- "Jeff, if you mow the grass and clean the car, then you can drive it to the game.

- "Gary, if we get the garage cleaned before Saturday, then we can go fishing at the lake."

- "Casey, if you get your grades up to a B+ average this semester, then we'll get you the bike."

NO-CHOICE RULES

Some family rules fences come without choices. They are the rules for health and safety of the child and family.

We build fences to keep balls and children out of the street. They do not get to choose to go into the road. We require our children to brush their teeth; they don't get to choose not to. Usually we only need to have a few of these must-do, no-choice rules.

ACKNOWLEDGMENT REWARDS

Not all rewards need to be or should be contractual or cause-and-effect lessons. However, when family members act responsibly and consistently with the principles of good and contributive behavior, surprise rewards can help to deepen commitment to those principles. They can also teach invaluable lessons about the sense of intrinsic worth of personal values. They remind the child that the parent is watching and noticing good behavior as well as errors. When family values become personal values, that aspect of the family heritage fence has been effectively transferred to the next generation. This is when the constructed family fence becomes the child's internal fence, their character. Seeing family members act on principle and in character of beliefs and priorities is a parent's greatest reward.

- "Cathy, can I see you for a moment? I want to tell you that I have really noticed how much you contribute to the peace making in our family, especially with the younger kids. That makes me very proud of you. I want you to have this _____ as a little token of my appreciation and admiration of your peacemaking in our home."

- "Peter, I've noticed that every time you take the car, you return it cleaner than before you took it. I really appreciate that. Here is a little something extra to help with the gas for the next time you need to take it for a date."

- "Cindy, you always do such a good job of setting the table and clearing the dishes. I know that it's your turn to do the dishes tonight, but I would like to do them for you so you can watch _____ as a little thank-you."

And at the breakfast table—

- "Okay, kids, I've noticed that we have not had any violations to the family heritage fence this past week, so I'd say we deserve a trip to the ice cream shop tonight! What do you think?"

No question this intentional proactive family fence-riding and looking for opportunities to reward consistency to family values requires a lot parental commitment.

JUST BECAUSE I LOVE YOU

It is important that parents be careful not to tie all rewards to performance. All of us deserve and need to feel the acceptance of unconditional love. Children need to know they are loved just because they are members of the family and that they belong. Special surprises, regular hugs, love, and acknowledgment are vital.

Little love notes under pillows, in lunch sacks, on mirrors, in drawers, and in pockets and purses are seeds of family and self-esteem. Winks and eyebrow raises that say, "I love you. You're great!" or "You're the best!" and high fives give the family member the feeling of belonging and security of membership and importance. If you want to see the smile of deep and real joy, try giving a simple gift and little note, or homemade card that says:

Not 'cause it's your birthday, nor any special date,

Just because I love you and I didn't want to wait!

These unconditional surprises and reminders that you noticed are examples of pure love and appreciation. They can cover a multitude of parental mistakes. In the hectic rush and challenge of making a living and keeping the house clean and the meals and laundry timely, it is easy to put off and to forget. These simple comments and gestures of loving awareness are important. They are "I love you" reminders that may need to be programmed into the parent priority mind-set. Parents should seek to have these actions become part of their heritage. When they do, they can almost guarantee that they will be passed on to the next generation.

The family heritage fence planning, building, and mending is a process with a purpose. The purpose is to develop responsible personal freedom and security through establishing family heritage-influenced self-governance. The power of the principles, values, and priorities can lead family members to success and joy. We must never make the process more important than the purpose or the people. We must always see challenge and violation of the fence as the opportunity to strengthen it and the offender.

Our homes and family heritage fences are the laboratory for intentional parents to help their children develop the attributes and pass on the legacy of their values, standards, and character.

LEGACY-SECURING INTENTIONAL PARENTING PROJECT SUGGESTIONS

Discuss Heritage Fencing with the Family—Have a family gathering to discuss the concept of a family heritage fence. Explain what a fence is used for and how it has two purposes, namely to hold good things in and keep bad things out. Discuss what kinds of bad things you want to keep out of your family. Discuss what kinds of things you don't want to break into your family and family heritage and steal or diminish your home, family values, or priorities.

Discuss Fencing Materials—Talk with the family and identify what posts, wire, and bracing are needed for your family heritage fence. Make a list of the family's beliefs, values, priorities, principles, rules, and consequences and discuss how these can keep the family safe from intruders and from wandering away from the family heritage.

Map Out the Fence—Make a poster as a visual aid with a drawing of a fence with corner posts, posts, bracing, and stays. Place key words representing the family's values, principles, and rules on the poster next to a post where they go in the fence. This can be especially helpful for young children to understand the concept and how they can help to make their fence strong to protect each other.

Family Charter or Proclamation—Make a formal family charter or proclamation that declares and explains the family's vision, mission, beliefs, and values. It can be a "We believe in being . . ." document. Involve all family members in a discussion of what the values are and why they are important and help to define your family. Have someone take notes and compliment the ideas and contribution of family members. You may need to guide and wordsmith ideas and suggestions from small children. When the child reaches eight years of age and can recite or fully discuss its meanings, have them sign the document.

Ride the Fence Regularly—Review the values and beliefs each month in a family council meeting (ride the fence) to see how the family is doing and how the fence is holding up. Talk about adding stays in the fence in weak areas.

Awards—Create value medals or mini traveling trophies to be awarded to the family member who most exemplified that particular key family value during the month. Reevaluate and present the awards to another family member each month. Be sure to have enough, such that each family member will get one for the month.

I Saw You Cards—Make and use special "I Saw You" cards. These are simple compliment cards a child can come and ask for to give to a family member whose behavior exemplified a family value that day. The observer signs and gives the card to the family member. Allow only one or two cards per observer a day to maintain the significance and power of this recognition system.

Add Stays—When you find a value or rule being abused regularly, add a "stay" to the fence. The stay is an extra consequence for violation or even an extra rule to strengthen that portion of the fence.

Family Logo or Crest—Design a family logo, icon, or crest that incorporates family values and can be used in various family visual reminders.

Family Icons—Make a family crest values flag, values "fence signs," clothing items, or other wall hanging or decoration items as visual triggers for family values.

4

FAMILY VALUES AND PERSONAL CHARACTER

Before It Is Too Late

JASON RYAN WAS NOT THE MOST POPULAR YOUNG man in the eleventh grade, but he was definitely on the list to be considered. The junior prom was girls' choice that year, and his wavy black hair atop an athletic 5'10" physique definitely made him a prime target. He didn't have a steady girlfriend, but his sources indicated that several girls were talking about asking him to go. This would be his first formal date. While she was trying to conceal her excitement and anticipation of this milestone event, Jason's mother saw this as a crossroad and as a test of her intentional parenting of the family's values and the successful transfer of the family legacy.

Waiting for some girl to ask him on the date was sort of exciting, but to be cool, Jason would have to really downplay his interest with the other guys. Truth was, they were all worried about who might or might not ask them too. There were several girls that he wouldn't mind going with. Jason just figured it was who got to him first.

Dating was off for him until he was sixteen, and steady dating was totally off-limits. So he was a relative newcomer to the whole dating scene.

Jason's family had pretty strict dating standards compared to the peers he associated with at school. Most of his buddies respected the situation, although several took the opportunity to chide him about it. Many of them were experienced with the boy-girl thing by the time Jason turned sixteen. He knew enough about some of their previous dating activities to be glad that he was left out.

Jason would have had plenty of opportunities, but the word was out that he couldn't date until he was sixteen. That kept most of his girlfriends just that—girls that were friends. He told his buddies he had more girl-friends than all of them put together. He worried a bit that his "nice guy" reputation might get in his way now that he was of age and ready to take on the adventure of real dates and maybe a real girlfriend.

Two weeks before the dance, Jason had still not been asked, but rumor was that most of the girls were asking their wannabe dates that weekend. Sure enough, Thursday night when Jason got home from his job at the local Food Plus Market, there was a balloon bouquet with a card on his bed. The idea that some girl had invaded the privacy of his bedroom, his personal sanctuary, was a little frustrating. He made a token complaint to his mother, who had facilitated the delivery.

Mrs. Ryan stood in the doorway, waiting for him to open the card. Jason looked back at her with that look of "Mom! Please! A little privacy here!" After all, she already *knew* who brought the balloons. She sighed and took the hint.

JASON'S STORY: HIS OR HIS MOTHER'S TEST?

Mrs. Ryan leaned back and relented, "Okay, okay. But you're going to be surprised."

He swung his door shut in mock protest. Jason actually had a great relationship with his Mom—with all of his family for that matter. But being the oldest, he had to exert some appearance of dominance. He pulled the card from the balloon bouquet. Inside the envelope, a mysterious note read—

Dear Mr. Jason Ryan,

You are hereby requested to accompany me to the West High School Jr. Prom on Saturday, April 20. To discover the details of this proposed date, you must pop the red balloon and find the clue to our afternoon activity.

P.S. You must respond back by Monday evening at 10:00 p.m., or the date is off.

That was it? That is what the entire card said? There was no indication of who it was from. Jason ran down the stairs with the red balloon in tow and hollered, "Mom! Mom! Who brought it?"

Jason got a pencil from the drawer and proceeded to pop the balloon. The resulting *pop* sound startled his Mom.

"Hey, was that called for?"

"Exactly!" Jason responded as he pulled a tightly rolled note from the exploded balloon. The typed note read:

If you like doing things outdoors, you will probably like my plans for our date. If you like good company, you'll like it better. If you like me, you're bound to have a great time. To find out more, call Rossio's and order a small pizza delivered to your home tonight with these ingredients: ⅓ Pepperoni, ⅓ Anchovy, and ⅓ Mushroom.

"Not again! There's no name! It doesn't say who it is! Look at this."

Jason handed his mom the clue and grabbed another pair of his socks. Mrs. Ryan read the note.

"Looks like we're having pizza for dinner," she said with a grin.

"Funny, Mom. It's a personal size pizza, and who would ever eat anchovies anyway?"

"Right. *Well . . .* since I only knew *one* of the three girls, I guess I will have to give you her name. It was Marilyn Sorensen."

"Marilyn? No way! She's been going steady with Grant Wilson all year. They are, like a thing. There's no way it's her!"

By now, Jason was getting a little heated with the whole mystery.

"Seems to me that you better order your pizza," his mother suggested.

Jason looked up the number and made the call.

"Hello? Yes. I'd like to order a small pizza, to be delivered. Right. I want it divided with three different toppings."

"Okay, what is it you want on it?" the voice asked.

Jason gave the order, "One-third pepperoni, one-third anchovy, and one-third mushroom."

The man on the other end paused. "Oh yes, this is a special pizza and it's free! That is if you want it delivered to 235 West Overton Street?"

Jason responded, "Right, that's my address. How did you know that? *You* must be in on it too!"

Jason hung up the phone. He didn't know whether to laugh or to be mad. His mom threw a towel to him.

"Here, make yourself useful until your pizza comes." She threw him several dishtowels to fold.

Jason flopped down on the couch and interrogated his mother while she folded the rest of the towels. By the time the laundry was folded, he was convinced that his mom really didn't know the other girls.

It was almost exactly thirty minutes when the doorbell rang. A wiry redheaded kid gave him the pizza and waited expectantly for a tip. Jason gave him a dollar, and the kid ran off. He opened the box and nearly dumped it on the living room floor. Inside the box he found the pizza and a small pepperoncini. That was all. Jason shook his head.

"So where's the information?" His mom looked inside the box.

"Hey, if you're not going to eat that, I'll take a piece," she offered.

Jason pulled the small slice of the anchovy section of the pizza out to give to his mom and noticed the corner of a small envelope tucked under the pizza. It was like the small card that came with the balloons. He pulled the envelope out from under the pizza and handed the box to his Mom. Inside, the small card read:

Details for the date are in the blue balloon.

Jason dashed back up to his room and with a little effort managed to pop the blue balloon just as his mom got to the door with a piece of the pepperoni pizza.

"Hey, I'll trade you," she offered.

He waved her off as he unfolded the note.

Dress warm. Pick up at 10:00 a.m. for a picnic at the lake. Then we have reservations at Rubio's for dinner before the dance and then to Iceberg for dessert after. Oh, yes, we'll have a few surprises too. To accept the date, pop the green balloon and follow the instructions by Saturday at 3:00 p.m.

P.S. Your pizza is the key to my name . . .

Jason read the note twice and shook his head.

"The note says that the answer is in the pizza. I hope I didn't eat the answer!" she said, putting her hand over her mouth.

Jason got a desperate look and went back to the kitchen and the pizza box. There were still two slices. He looked again and again for a hidden note, writing, or something, but nothing showed up.

"This is nuts!" he said as he shut the lid for the third time. "This whole tradition of asking is so lame!"

"Okay, honey, what exactly did the note say?"

Jason pulled the note from his pocket again and read the P. S. "It says, 'Your pizza is the key to my name.'"

"Well, that's it, Jason. It's the pizza, not the box it came in!"

Jason gave his mom a look of unbelief at that suggestion. And then got a quizzical look as he stared at the pizza.

He opened the box again and stared at the remaining pieces. One piece of mushroom, one of pepperoni, and both the pieces of anchovy looked back up at him, but offered no hints.

Mrs. Ryan got a piece of paper and pen and wrote the words *pepperoni*, *anchovy* and *mushroom*. She was about to write *cheese* when Jason interrupted her by blurting out, "No way! No flippin' way!" He then began to laugh as he flopped back onto the couch. "Pam—it's Pam. That's it!" And he laughed again.

"I don't get it. How do you get Pam?" his Mom asked with a puzzled look.

"It's Pam. See: (P) for pepperoni, (A) for anchovy, and (M) for mushroom. It's *Pam*!"

"Okay, but who's Pam? Pam who?" she queried.

Jason looked up and said, "Pam . . . Pam . . . Pam . . . Oh, heck! I don't remember her last name!"

Suddenly, Jason jumped up and bounded back to his bedroom for the green balloon. He couldn't remember her name, but he did remember that she was cute and he thought probably a little—maybe a lot—out of his league. He popped the balloon. The note fell to the floor.

I'll be at my cousin's place on Saturday morning. You can call me there.

"Great! At least I don't have to try to look up her number without a last name," he said, as his mom reappeared.

"So I take it you're going to accept?"

Jason smiled. "Unless I get a better offer tonight."

But he really couldn't think of someone better to go with. This would be interesting. He took the last piece of pepperoni pizza and settled in the easy chair to talk to Grant about Pam.

He called Pam and accepted the date with one condition. He was saving the anchovy pizza for her. Pam laughed, and the date was on.

The morning of the prom, Jason mowed the lawn and dropped his little brother off at his Boy Scout meeting. Then he went to pick up the wrist corsage his mother made him order. He couldn't convince his mom that most boys didn't get flowers for girls these days, especially on a girl-ask-guy date. He loved his mom and capitulated even though he was feeling the need to exert his independence.

Jason had debated his mother on a lot of things lately. It seemed to her that he wanted to exert his independence a little too soon and little too strongly. He was trying to fit in more at school and regularly challenged her opinion of what he should and shouldn't do. She was trying to give him some space but wanted him to stay focused on and committed to his family values and rules. Mrs. Ryan suggested that he order a tux, but he protested that nobody was going to do that at this dance. It was to be more casual—jeans, an untucked dress shirt, and maybe a tie. Jason offered to clean the garage and the car to use it for the date. He was a good driver, and his dad agreed to the deal. His dad wished he could be there to see his son off on his first big dance date, but he would be out of town on a business trip that weekend.

"So it's a deal, Dad? I'll clean the garage and car and I can use the car for the date?"

His dad gave him that "yes, but" look. "Okay, son, but you will likely need to clean the kids' cracker mess out of the backseat. And, remember . . ."

"I know dad—seat belts, mirrors, gas, and prayer."

That was the family checklist for trips in the car. It had been drilled into him and the other kids since before he could remember. More often than not, the kids were the ones who reminded their *parents* about the car rules. Jason was particularly good at remembering, especially the mirror thing. After he backed over Amie's trike, he determined that his own rule was—seat belt, mirrors, gas, prayer, and mirrors *again*.

The plan was to pick up Grant, Cory, and Cory's date a little after 10:00 a.m. They would meet the others kids, including Jason's date, at the lake. They were taking a picnic up to Lookout Ridge, the most prominent point above the lake. Jason knew Grant and Cory, but the other two guys, Don Murray and Brian Masterson, were from the other high school. Their dates were Marilyn's friends. Jason knew the other two girls from his history class. He was glad that his date wasn't one of them. They were cute and popular, but they hung out with some of the more wild kids at school, unlike Jason.

They had a great time, except when Brian brought out the beer. Jason just said, "No thanks." That was a little awkward, but they didn't make a big deal about it. He learned a lot more about Pam as they were hiking to the ridge and eating.

Jason was glad she didn't take the beer, but he wondered if she would have if he had not been there. He really wanted to know why she had asked him to the dance in the first place. Maybe he would ask her at the dance.

He dropped the group off at 5:30 p.m. at Grant's and headed home to clean up for the dance. He flew through the front door and bounded up the stairs, almost ignoring his mother at the kitchen door.

"Well, looks like you had a good time," she called after him.

Jason came back to the top of the stairs and looked down at her. "Oh, yeah, it was great."

"And . . . ?" she questioned.

"We had a good time. I've got to go get ready for the dance."

Jason wanted to tell her about the beer and his refusal, but he thought better about it. That would probably just make her worry about whom he was with. He'd tell her the whole story the next day.

It had seemed a little odd to Mrs. Ryan that students from a rival school would be going to Jason's school prom. When she asked a neighbor about the practice, she had been assured the schools had arranged for the crossover participation for the event. Nevertheless, she was just a bit concerned about this date. Even though Jason had been a little testy of late, she knew he was a good kid, but she didn't know the other kids and was a little apprehensive about their standards or values.

This was Jason's first date, and though he wouldn't know it, it was pretty important to her too. She was nervous, just like Jason, but for different reasons. This was sort of a field-testing of Jason's social skills and his understanding of his family values and standards, which could and likely would be challenged on this night.

Jason looked in the mirror one last time and adjusted his tie before he ran back to grab the keys. Like all juniors, he felt it was terrible that he didn't have a car of his own. At least he should have his own set of keys. The good thing was the family suburban had enough room to take all eight of them. He agreed to pick up Don and Brian after he picked up Pam. Then they would pick up their dates and meet Grant and Marilyn at the restaurant.

"Bye! I'm gone!" he called as he headed toward the door.

"Not so fast, mister!" his mom called back as she came in from the patio. "Let's see this sharp young man!"

Jason dutifully turned around and made a token bow.

"Looks good, Jason. Looks *good*! Do you have your flower?"

Jason had almost forgotten. "Oh, shoot! Thanks, Mom."

He ran to the refrigerator and grabbed the gold box with the white carnation wristlet. He had paid for it. He might as well give it to her, even if the other guys didn't have one for their dates.

"Remember who you are, and I will be looking for a report when you get back. Remember the clock," his mom said as he gave her a token kiss on the cheek and bounded off the porch.

Jason was just glad that she had extended the normal curfew to 1:00 a.m. for this special event. That was sort of the family rule—10:00 p.m. on school nights, midnight on weekends, and 1:00 a.m. on special occasions.

"Okay, Mom, I won't forget!" he called as he jumped into "Tilly the Tank" as they called the Suburban.

"Are you sure you haven't forgotten her name again? Now, what is it again?"

"Pam. Pam Harding, Mom. I haven't forgotten it. See you later."

"Remember to be back *here* by 1:00 a.m."

"I know, I know! Bye. Love you."

The "love you" was automatic for all the Ryan family when one of them was leaving the home. She loved that family tradition.

His mother followed Jason to the door and watched as he drove off in the Suburban. As she shut the door, she had another one of those *Mom moments*.

Wasn't it just yesterday that . . . she thought, reflecting on how fast he was growing up. He was leaving the security of the family and home, but he was taking with him the expectations of the family legacy and extended security of his mother's prayers. Prayer is no doubt the most important and frequently used intentional parenting tool.

Jason's debating and challenging attitude had increased over the past year. He had not wanted to do some of the things the family had planned. And normally, he wanted to hang out with his friends more. They were generally good kids too, but tonight he would be with kids she didn't know, and she was feeling a little uneasy. Jason was doing okay in school, and she knew he was just going through growing pains. He was a good kid—she *knew* that. He was just growing up too fast and that had put a little strain on their relationship. She was sure that these growing pains were always a shared condition between mother and son. But tonight, Jason wasn't feeling her angst.

Jason pulled up in front of Pam's house and went to the door. Pam's younger sister answered the knock.

"She's coming. You could have just honked, you know!"

Jason felt a little awkward waiting for Pam. He kind of expected her dad or mom to come to the door to check him out. That's what would happen at his place. Her mom did emerge from the kitchen and introduced herself just as Pam came down the stairs from the second level. Pam had on a purple taffeta dress with a waist-length sweater.

"Hi, you look great," said Jason. She did look a lot different than she had last fall at her birthday party. "Nice dress," Jason repeated the compliment.

"Thanks! You look great too."

"You two have fun. Pam, remember, no shellfish."

"Okay, Mom. Bye."

"Bye."

Jason figured that their family was a little less formal than his was after all, even though they lived in a much bigger house. It was a ritzy neighborhood compared to his.

In the car, Jason asked Pam, "So what was that deal about shellfish?"

"Oh, I'm allergic to shellfish. I have to remember to avoid things like shrimp and clams and stuff like that, but I can eat fish," she explained."

"Good, because the anchovy pizza is in the backseat waiting for you," Jason teased.

Pam gave him a mock slug but looked back just to make sure he was kidding. They chitchatted while Pam directed him to Don and Brian's place. It didn't surprise him that Brian carried a twisted paper bag that was obviously covering some sort of alcohol. But it did make him uncomfortable that they were transporting it in his mom's car. At least Brian didn't open it in the car.

They picked up the other girls and Jason let them all out while he parked the car. They were waiting for him inside the hostess area. Jason had never eaten at Rubio's before, but it was supposed to be good food and not too pricey. That was good because the deal was that the boys buy dinner and the girls pay for the prom tickets and pictures.

Dinner was good. Jason got ravioli, Pam got another pasta dish, and the others all got lasagna. Brian and Don acted a little strange, but generally they were okay. It was obvious at the lake and in the conversation at the restaurant that his companions were more than a little familiar with their girls. That made Jason feel a little more awkward around Pam.

Grant and Marilyn had been together for so long that their relationship seemed less showy and forward. But then Pam was Grant's cousin and maybe he was on his best behavior because of that. Pam was pleasant but was definitely more forward than most of the other girls Jason had dated—all four of them. That too made him feel a little more awkward.

After dinner, they got back in the Suburban and headed for the school. They were only going to stay for a few dances and then get pictures. While Jason was driving, Brian brought out his sack-wrapped bottle and handed it to Don. It was clear to Jason that he was about to be liable for driving with an open container.

"Hey, hey! This is my mom's car, and I'm driving. Put that away!" His words startled even him.

"Oh, do we have an issue here?" Brian mocked and laughed as he put the bottle back into the bag.

The girls laughed too, but Jason could tell they were put out with him. Then Jason felt weird and didn't know what to say. Pam broke the silence by asking if the gold box Jason had set between the seats and forgotten was for her.

"Oh, yeah. It's for you," Jason sheepishly replied. He had forgotten about the box, and none of the other guys had given their dates flowers.

She opened the box. "It's beautiful! Thanks, Jason," she said as she put the corsage on her wrist.

He smiled as Pam turned around to show it to the other girls in the back. They "oohed" and "ahhed." That made him feel even weirder, because Don, Brian, and Grant hadn't given flowers to their dates. Jason already wished that *they* had driven themselves.

They arrived at the school and parked the car. As Jason walked up to the school, he felt important having a girl from another high school as his date. He knew that Pam was a popular girl whom several of his classmates would recognize.

The music and decorations added to the excitement. Although Jason was not a good dancer, he was okay. So the fact that they talked with other couples and sat around more than they danced was just fine with him. They were only there an hour or so when Brian and Don got antsy to go. It was about 9:30 p.m. when Grant got their attention and nodded toward the door.

Jason had a good time, but he was a little surprised that the evening was going to end so soon. They gathered up the girls who were chatting away with some of the other girls from Pam's side of town. Jason noticed that several of them and their dates followed them out. Then he noticed several of the jocks from his school and their dates were close on their heels. Because he didn't normally associate much with that group, he wasn't sure if these were friends or foes. They were all laughing and he heard one of them holler to Grant as he got in a car, "See you over there!"

As far as Jason knew, the plan was to go out for ice cream to end the date. He soon learned that there had been a change of plans, or that he was not in on the real plan. Once they were in the Suburban, Jason looked questioningly at Pam as she proceeded to tell him the *rest* of the "plan."

"We're invited to join some of my friends at a really neat house over in Brook Meadows. I'll tell you how to get there."

One of the girls in the back added, "This is so cool! They have an enormous pool and the house is like worth millions!"

Don added, "Oh darn, I forgot my suit." The girls laughed.

Jason asked, "Whose place is it?"

Pam responded, "I don't think you know him. He graduated a couple of years ago. His name is Collin Richens. His parents travel a lot, and he is home this weekend from ASU. He was the guy with Dana Huet. You know her?"

Jason knew who she was, all right! She was one of the most popular girls in the senior class. She had a reputation of being pretty loose with the guys. It was usually in the locker room where he heard about her.

In spite of the reputation, it did sound like an exciting after-the-dance get-together. Jason felt a rush as they pulled up in front of the two-story mansion. The patio lights were on behind the six-foot privacy fence that enclosed the entire backyard. The yard backed up to the river. Immaculate flower beds and trees lined the walk to the back gate. The music was blaring and there were already about thirty kids around the pool.

Several of Pam's friends came over to greet her as they walked up to the pool. She introduced them to Jason. It was exciting, but somehow he felt like he shouldn't really be there. It only took a few minutes for that feeling to grow. The poolside tables were covered with munchies and a keg of beer, some kids were dancing, and about a half dozen kids were already in the pool. As they walked by, Brian gave Jason a pretend shove toward the water. Then he stopped at the table with the large punch bowl. The cases of soft drinks and a stack of six packs had caught his attention.

Brian looked around as if to sneak something and then pulled the bottle from his paper bag. Jason couldn't see exactly what it was, but it was obviously alcohol. Brian had poured half the bottle into the punch before one of the girls grabbed his arm.

"Hey, that's enough!" she scolded. Then grinning, she added, "Save some for later!"

Brian raised his eyebrows and smiled as he tucked the bottle back into the sack and under his arm. Then he ladled out a glass for him and his date. He turned to Jason and held it up to him with a questioning look.

Jason smiled and shook his head. "No thanks."

Just then Pam tapped him and said, "Jason, this is my friend Collin. This is his place. Isn't it great!" Jason turned to see a handsome blond kid who looked much older than Pam had indicated.

"Hi. Glad to meet you, Jason."

"Yeah, me too. Thanks for inviting us over," Jason responded.

"No problem. Make yourself at home. The folks aren't here so we have the whole place to ourselves all night. Hey, Pam, come on over. I want to introduce you to couple of my friends from ASU."

Pam turned and looked at Jason as if to get permission to leave him. Jason smiled and nodded toward Collin. As Pam walked away, Gary grabbed Jason's arm. Gary was about as out of place at this place as Jason, probably even more so.

"Jace, you've gotta see this! Come on!"

Jason followed Gary and a couple others he had gathered to the back of the house. People were coming and going in and out of the patio doors. Inside, Jason could see why Gary was anxious to show him the house. It was amazing!

Several guys were playing pool on a huge ornate billiard table. Several others had plopped down in front of an enormous entertainment center. As Jason glanced at it, the scene on the screen made him blush. Gary pulled at him to go over to a grand staircase. A couple was coming down, laughing as the girl fluffed her hair and winked at him. At the top of the stairs, Gary pointed down the trophy-lined hallway with eight bedrooms and a large library room at the end of the hall. He pushed Jason toward the trophies.

"Jason, this is Randy Richens's place! This is his house!"

Jason was clueless.

"Randy Richens. The tennis player!" Gary continued.

Jason's look let Gary know he still didn't get it. Gary was one of the other school's top tennis players. He must have figured everyone else knew the who's-who in tennis.

"He's like the best tennis player the state ever put out! He's awesome!"

Jason just nodded in agreement, but his attention was drawn toward the library.

It didn't take a detective to know what was going on in there. Two girls and a guy Jason didn't know came out wiping their noses and gave Jason a "go on in" look. Just then, Jason heard Pam's voice.

"There you are! Some place, huh?"

Jason turned to see Pam walking toward him. He smiled and nodded, "I'd say!"

"Come on. I want you to meet some of my other friends."

As they turned to go down the stairs, a bedroom door swung open, and a couple came out. Pam knew the girl who gave her a wide-eyed smile as she adjusted her dress. Jason followed Pam. Halfway down the stairs the large grandfather clock at the top of the stairs chimed midnight.

Jason thought, *Oh, great! I have to leave here in half an hour if I'm going to be back home by my curfew at one. How am I going to tell Pam and the others that I have to go home to Mommy?*

A group had gathered in the entertainment area, and Collin was talking to the group.

"Okay, thank you! You're welcome here. Just don't break anything, and let's keep the noise down. The neighbors across the street are a little anti-party. There is a donation bowl on the piano to contribute for the refreshments—about five bucks a head ought to do it. Anybody who wants the *good stuff* will have to arrange his or her own deals. Any of you who want to hit the pool or hot tub, there are suits in the patio dressing room, for any of you who need them."

Several laughed, and Pam nudged Jason. He felt his face flush.

Collin continued, "If any of you are interested in a little card game, we're going to set up in the library upstairs."

Grant, Brian, and their dates had joined them by then.

"Okay, gang, what's it going to be? A little dip in the pool to start, a tour of the house, or some refreshments?" Brian asked.

Marilyn pulled at Grant, "We've got to see the basement. There's another party going on down there."

"Count me in!" Brian added.

Dennis quipped, "Let's see. Behind me is the pool, the basement—for who *knows* what—or the upstairs adventure that is about to begin."

"I've got news for you, buddy. The upstairs adventure already started!" Brian informed him. His date jabbed him in the ribs. Looking at Jason, Brian continued,

"So, what'll it be, *Mr. Ryan?*"

Pam looked at him with a "Whatever. I'm game" smile.

Jason was torn. This was all so new and exciting, yet he felt it was all a little too much of a forbidden adventure. Somehow, he could feel the Suburban calling to him, or was it his curfew or his mother? Pam tugged again and smiled while she turned toward the basement stairs. He thought about calling his mom to get some leeway, but it wasn't just the time that was at issue with his conscience. The whole situation was an attack on his standards and character. He glanced again at his watch. 11:20 p.m. He waited for the heckling to begin. Moments of truth are never convenient.

At home, Kate Ryan turned over in her bed. She couldn't sleep and glanced at the clock, *again*—12:30 a.m. She strained to hear the anticipated car. She turned and looked at the dim light on the ceiling. *It's late*, she thought. Kate hoped and prayed that it was not *too* late.

This was a telling time for the investment she and her husband had been making to prepare their oldest son, and the other family members, to hold on to the values and standards of family legacy. She knew that this test of just how strongly Jason believed in those values was going to be a challenge. It was a test of how effective Kate had been as an intentional parent and heritage-maker in her home. She closed her eyes and prayed again.

When the lights crossed the curtains, briefly illuminating the ceiling, she opened her eyes. A few moments later, she heard a door open and the sound of keys being slipped onto the hook on the wall.

"Back, Mom! Talk in the morning. Night."

His quiet voice offered no apology, nor excuse. He didn't need one. He and his mother would sleep well tonight.

FAMILY VALUES—BUILDING CHARACTER COMMITMENT

"Train up a child in the way he should go: and when he is old, he will not depart from it." (Proverbs 22:6)

The proverb implies that while our children are young, they may stray away from the way they should go. They may become prodigals to the ways of the family, the community, the church, and the Lord. The consolation is the assurance that if children are trained up in the right way, they will not depart or will at least return to the right way.

Let's begin with some consideration of "the way he should go." What is the way? Biblically, the way was the way of the Lord as defined in the law of Moses. That was the set of rules and values that all Israelite families were to abide by. The traditions of the fathers, the celebrations, feasts, and commandments were the way they should go. That way was a well-defined straight and narrow path. It was written, reviewed, and remembered—even memorized. It included the traditions, teachings, rites, and ordinances of the law. The *way* they were to go was the heritage of Abraham's, Isaac's and Jacob's families and all the tribes of Israel.

Similarly, the "way" we teach our family to go can be seen as our family heritage—our straight and narrow way. First, we have to know those "ways" before we can teach them. That is why we need to connect to our family heroes and their legacy and why we need to clearly determine which values, beliefs, and traditions we will incorporate into our way.

The Israelites had the way, the law, and the prophets in scrolls and books. Part of their required way included daily reading, memorizing, discussing, and even debating the meaning of the law. This was the process of ensuring the continuation of the adherence to the law, their way.

Unfortunately, by New Testament times, this process for remembering the law had become more important than the law itself. In essence, the means had become the ends. The rules and rituals for remembering the law and its purpose had become the law. Jesus spent much of his time pointing out these failings of the scribes and Pharisees, who were more committed to the process than the purpose. They were committed to the outward observance for the public recognition rather than the internal observance for the acknowledgment of God.

We too need to have the tools, books, and reminders of our family heritage. However, we must make sure these tools and their creation and prominence do not become more important that the heritage they are intended to "train." We must remember the means for training and what its purposes are.

Of course, the child referred to in the proverb symbolizes every member of our family. We see many families today subscribing to the idea of training babies even before birth. For example, a growing number of families play the music of the great composers and musicians while the baby is in the womb. These "ways" of great music can be experienced and have influence before the child is born. Similarly, more and more parents are training babies in basic reading skills with flash cards and educational videos long before they can speak. The results are astounding.

The fact is that the child is being trained constantly by the example of the people around them, especially their family members. How they respond to and treat each other become early and powerful lessons about their "family's way."

The tone of voice, touching and loving looks, and orderliness and calmness of the home, all train the child in what is acceptable and not acceptable. Formal explanations and teaching about the family's rules, heritage, and priorities comes as the child develops the ability to focus, interact, and communicate. It is then that the trainer can explain and clarify questions about the way they should go.

Parents have the primary responsibility of training children. However, other family members can and should help in the process, but parents must not delegate nor leave this role to anyone else. While training is a shared parental responsibility, the lessons about family heritage and character development fall largely to the mother. Because more and more mothers need to work outside the home, the training must come in bits and pieces.

Quality family training time must be seen as a mother's highest priority. The task is daunting when you consider the competition for her time and the attention and demands from all family members. The growing pressure for the time and attention of the child from schools and friends can pull children away from home and family activities. This makes the training task even more challenging, especially for teens. Teenagers must contend with the value-defining voices of friends, TV, Internet, radio, school, and the media. All of these voices want to "train" our children in the way they should think and go.

Ours is an age when family values are being assailed on every side. All members of the family are being enticed to cross over their heritage fence and bring unwanted values and voices into their lives and living rooms.

There is precious little time and opportunity for formal discussions and training in the home. Parents must rely much more heavily on mini-lessons and learning tools and reminders to help them establish family values. In biblical times, children were surrounded by symbols to remind them about "the way." Symbols were on doorposts, on the walls, mantles and the most prominent places in the home. The symbols were included in their clothing and ornaments. These symbols were reminders and mental triggers for the values they were learning and embracing.

What are the value symbols our children see in our homes? What do they hear in the powerful voices that come from our prominently placed "training tools"—the TV and computers. We should consider the focus and power of these training influences and reminders in our homes. Clearly they can be used to remind us and to strengthen or weaken our family values and standards.

We must not let the messages and reminders of the "way to go and the way to be" of the world blind and deafen our children to our family ways. Isn't it time to surround your children with the values, traditions and priorities of family heroes—your family heritage?

THE WAY TO GO

Conversations and interactions that contrast the family "way to go" with the world's ways can help children draw clear distinctions of character expectations. Discussions about what would be the right way and the wrong way to go in certain situations can help prepare children to respond appropriately when similar situations arise. Parents can use questions where they suggest a situation and ask, "If you were in this condition, how would you use our family heritage and principles to make things right or better?"

Every culture has its own lingo that helps it to define and differentiate itself from other cultures and groups. The words we use to describe our family's "way to go" can help us to establish our unique heritage and "family culture." This family language becomes a way children can remind each other of their way of being.

As you weave the words and concepts of family values into conversations with the children, they become familiar with and comfortable using them. They will incorporate them into their thoughts, attitudes, and conversations. Consider the following value vocabulary list to see how you can intentionally engage your family in an intentional parenting discussion to establish what your family's attitudes and standards are regarding the concepts these words suggest.

VALUE, BELIEFS, AND STANDARDS WORD RESOURCE LIST

Abundant _____

Accountable _____

Active _____

Adventure _____

Ancestors _____

Belong _____

Brave _____

Character _____

Charity _____

Chastity _____

Cheerful _____

Clean _____

Committed _____

Compassion _____

Confident _____

Contribute _____

Courage _____

Courteous _____

Creative _____

Dependable _____

Devoted _____

Dignity _____

Disciple _____

Discipline _____

Dreams _____

Duty _____

Efficient _____

Empathy _____

Endure _____

Faith _____

Family _____

Fit _____

Friend _____

Frugal _____

Generous _____

Gracious _____

Grateful _____

Happy _____

Harmony _____

Healthy _____

Heritage _____

Herocs _____

Holy _____

Honesty _____

Hopeful _____

Hospitality _____

Humility _____

Humor _____

Independence _____

Inspiration _____

Integrity _____

Intelligence _____

Intimacy _____

Joy _____

Justice _____

Kind _____

Knowledge _____

Leader _____

Liberty _____

Love _____

Meek _____

Modest _____

Neat _____

Obedient _____

Optimistic _____

Orderly _____

Patient _____

Persistent _____

Prepared _____

Pride _____

Promise _____

Punctual _____

Pure _____

Reliable _____

Respect _____

Responsible _____

Reverence _____

Sacred _____

Sacrifice _____

Spirit _____

Sympathy _____

Tidy _____

Thankful _____

Thoughtful _____

Timely _____

True _____

Trustworthy _____

Truthful _____

Unity _____

Values _____

Virtue _____

Wisdom _____

Worthy _____

LABELING

When children violate family standards or values through misbehavior, parents must be careful not to label the child as the behavior. The problem is that when a parent or other person of assumed authority connects the child and the behavior as "their way of being," it can program that negative behavior expectation into the child's mind. The child hears and begins to think, *I am that way; that behavior is my way of being.*

When children take on the label as a truth about themselves, they can see that label as their life script. This branding can lead to acting out those negative life script behaviors, because it is their role and they are supposed to, even expected to "behave that way."

Parents can intentionally respond to and reprove a child when they are "out of character" and they can give "in-character approval" without adding the negative effects of labeling. When the child misbehaves or acts out of character to family values and rules, the parent can say something like—

- "Johnny, when you are unkind to Christine, it makes me feel so _____ (sad is better than angry). Being that way with your sister is not like the hero you are in our family. You are usually so kind to her. Being unkind is not how a _____ (your family hero name) should be, is it?"

Compared to—

• "Johnny, stop that! You are so unkind!"

If the parent says, "Johnny, you are so unkind!" Johnny hears "*I am* unkind." Even the self-programming thought of "I am" can deepen the attachment to the behavior.

Conversely, you can use positive labels to reinforce positive traits.

• "Johnny, you are so kind. When you share your toys with Chris, it makes me feel so happy that you act that way. When you show that kind of love for your sister it makes our home more peaceful and calm."

Johnny hears "I am kind."

This positive "I am" programming can be a powerful learning exercise. You can have the child say, "I am _____ (kind, thoughtful, organized, helpful, and so on)" for every character trait you want to incorporate into your family heritage. Have the child say the words "I am" and add the value in a strong (louder and more intense than normal) voice several times with increased conviction and volume. After which you say, "Yes, Johnny, that is how you are!"

This simple explanation of the meaning of your values and including it as part of family heritage will pay huge dividends. It is an intentional, proactive way to build the child's character and train him or her up in "the way they should go."

This programming of expectations based on principles of family heritage builds that internal fence and attitudes that will influence the decisions children make. When you see them do it, be sure to compliment them, saying, "Way to go!"

When peer pressure is strong and the feeling of independence is high, your children, especially teens, may not act in harmony with their values and heritage. But as the proverb says, once fully trained in the way to go, when the children are "old"er, they will return and not depart from it.

LEGACY-SECURING INTENTIONAL PARENTING PROJECT SUGGESTIONS

The List—Make a list of the values and character traits and explanations you want to incorporate and emphasize in your family heritage as the way you go. Have a heritage conversation with your children about the words and their meanings.

Value Cards Game—Make a set of value flash cards. You can put the value word on one side and the meaning on the other side. Be sure to relate the value to any family heroes who are exemplary of that trait. Then play various flashcard and matching games with them.

I Spy—Establish "Hero Watch" days where each family member is looking out or "spying" for evidence of other family members living a family value or "way of being." At the dinner table, have them share their discoveries of the good things they noticed.

Heritage Stars Poster—Make a sticker poster with the child's name at the top and key value words down the left side. Have boxes for stickers or stars to the right of the words for each time you see the child do something that reflects a family value. Have family members watch for positive examples among family members and opportunities for awarding a sticker or star.

Story Time—Write/tell a story about the child using as many of the values in it as you can. End the story with something like—"And that is why we are so proud of _____ because he/she is so _____, _____ (and so on for all the values in the story).

I'm Thinking Game—Play the game of "I am thinking of a value that _____" (give the definition) and have the child guess the value.

I Am Award—Create a poster, plaque, or trophy for key values or for those you are working on with a place to put the names of family members who achieve the required recognition. They can be traveling awards that the child keeps in his or her room until the next family meeting to pass the awards onto a new achiever. Be sure to have enough awards to have each child get one at the meeting. One or two can be generic enough to make sure that no child is left out of the awards.

Child Presentations—Hold a family sharing time where each child gets to prepare and give a talk or tell a story about a value that he or she is working on.

My Hero Cards—Make and send a value card through the mail to the child acknowledging the value they have exhibited. Add a love note and offer encouragement to work on a value he or she may be having trouble with.

5

NOT JUST A NAME

The Making of the Meaning

SARAH KNEW EVERYTHING THAT A BRIGHT-EYED, energetic five-year old should know—and maybe a little more. She knew her colors, her phone number, and her address. She knew how to write her name and could recite the alphabet, although sometimes she had to resort to singing it to get the letters all in order. At least she did until a recent move.

Sarah knew how to be safe too. She was safe in the car, crossing the street, going to the store with her mother, and playing with her friends. She knew how to be safe around the stove, around knives, and especially with her bike. She could make her bed, put her clothes away, and brush her hair and teeth—but sometimes she had to be reminded about that. Sarah knew how to behave in Sunday School and how to pray. She was proud of that. Her mom, Rebecca, told her she prayed like a big girl. That is because she was a big girl now.

Sarah was average in height and above average in intelligence. She had to be! How else could she have so many questions that defied her mother's ability to answer the first one before two or three more questions came? She was happy and full of energy and her life and her world were expanding rapidly.

It seemed incredible to her parents that Sarah was growing up so fast! From bassinet to car seat, from crib to playpen, from stroller to walker, from wagon to tricycle, and now, from training wheels to two wheels—it was all happening so fast!

Sarah was flying through life! Rebecca wished that she could slow that clock and the calendar down. It was obvious that it was running far too slow for Sarah but far too fast for her mother. Even so, sometimes with all that busyness and growing, Sarah did manage to find time to be bored—just a little. They both were dealing with so much to do and so little time to get it all in. There were precious few moments when Rebecca could apply the intentional parenting that could help Sarah determine who she really was.

The family had recently moved across town to a new home, but it wasn't the move that was foremost on Sarah's mind. Sarah had turned five years old. Her world was about to expand exponentially. She was going to school for the first time! After all, she was a big girl now and had been practicing going to school and doing her homework and even teaching the class of her dolls and teddy bear. Even the family dog was inducted into her fantasy classroom and lessons on occasion. Now she was fully ready for the real thing.

Sarah talked to her grandfather on the phone the day before school started. She explained all about going to school and what it was going to be like. She told him that her school was the Brad Mason Elementary School. She said everyone told her mom that it was the best school. Sarah was so excited about going and belonging to the Brad Mason School! The school's name, stories, and reputation made her feel important.

SARAH'S STORY AS TOLD BY HER MOM

Sarah, our second daughter, is a bit precocious and can be a little intense when she is focused on something. And she was definitely focused on starting school. She is always excited and full of energy! My mother continues to remind me to enjoy this time because all too soon this little girl's exuberance will be replaced with teenage drama.

Typical of that excitement, two days before school started, Sarah asked me to help her lay out all her school clothes on the toy box so she could pick the perfect outfit for her first day. After the evaluation, she hung up a light blue shirt, knee-length shorts, and a thin red sweater on the front of the closet so she would not forget what she had decided to wear. After all, girls had to look just right for her first day at kindergarten! Everyone would remember her because she was the new girl with the red sweater and polka-dot hair ribbon. She could hardly wait to meet her teacher, Mrs. Johnson, and the other kids.

The night before school started, Sarah couldn't make up her mind whether to go to bed early or stay up a little later. She didn't know which would bring morning faster. She really did have a hard time getting to sleep just thinking about all of it.

I asked her if she was nervous about starting school, even though she was not the nervous type. Sarah is friendly and outgoing, even if she is a little smaller than most kids her age. I'm not sure that she even knew what nervous meant. Her response revealed her excitement to get to school and learn all the things that school was about.

"Mom, will you let me read to you when I get home tonight?" she asked in positive anticipation. Sarah had been practicing her words, basic phonics, and reading skills, and was sure she would have it mastered by the time she got home.

"Sure, sweetheart, we can read together again tonight."

"No, Mom! I want to read to you, not you read to me! I am in school now, so I can do it!" I laughed and assured Sarah that she could read to me when she got home.

I walked her into Mrs. Johnson's kindergarten room just before 9:00 a.m. Sarah got just a little antsy and held my hand a little tighter as we opened the door. The moment Sarah saw the desks, play area, book-shelves, blackboards, the other children, and Mrs. Johnson, the excitement melted any uneasiness.

Mrs. Johnson greeted her. "Good morning, Sarah. Welcome to our class! We are happy that you are going to be with us this year."

Sarah nodded and let go of my hand. Then her full attention went to several other children, who were already playing with the giant blocks and puppets.

"Go ahead, Sarah. You can go over and play with the other children," Mrs. Johnson encouraged.

Sarah looked up at me with a little bit of hesitation. "Go ahead, Sarah. I need to talk with Mrs. Johnson for a minute, but I'll come and say good-bye before I leave."

Sarah walked slowly toward the other kids but was quickly absorbed in the adventure of stacking the blocks and talking with the other children as I greeted Mrs. Johnson.

After I finished talking with her teacher, I walked over to say good-bye.

At that point it was me who was just a little anxious, and I wondered how Sarah would do when I left her.

I stepped over to say good-bye. "Hey, looks like you met some new friends!"

Sarah nodded and pulled herself away long enough to give me a hug.

"I'll be back to pick you up after school. Are you okay?"

Sarah was more than okay! She had lived her whole life for this day! She pulled her red sweater down, waved me off, and ran back to the puppets and friends.

"Okay, I'll see you later!" The first day of school is always harder on moms than the kids.

The other children came in over the next few minutes before Mrs. Johnson rang a little bell to get their attention. They all gathered on the carpet in a circle around Mrs. Johnson's chair. Sarah had not had enough time with blocks and puppets to get all the wiggles out. Several of the children fidgeted and raised their hands repeatedly while Mrs. Johnson welcomed them and explained what it meant to be a student and how they were to be to make the class would work.

She said that at school they have rules, that everybody obeys the rules, and that the rules would help everyone to be safe and happy. Some school rules were just like the rules they had at home with their family and some were just for school. They would talk about the rules every day for the rest of the week to help the children remember and understand what they were supposed to do and not to do. It was all serious and interesting to Sarah. She was especially interested in the rules about snack time, rest time, and toy time!

Then Mrs. Johnson said they were going to get acquainted with each other. That meant that they were going to tell each other about themselves. Mrs. Johnson started by telling the students that she was a grandma and that she lived in the country away from the city. She loved animals. That made Sarah happy because she loved animals too. Mrs. Johnson liked to read books and go to the theater. She said the theater was different than the movies. But the most important thing Mrs. Johnson said was that she already knew she was going to love each of the students and was excited to get to know them and be their teacher.

Mrs. Johnson asked a little blond boy to be the first one in the circle to introduce himself to the class and tell them who he was. Mrs. Johnson asked him to tell them what his name was.

He said, "Mark. Mark Ward."

"And what do you like to do, Mark?" asked Mrs. Johnson.

"I like to play with my dog, and I like pizza, and I like root beer, but I don't like peas and broccoli."

"Tell us about your family."

Mark paused for a moment before Mrs. Johnson asked, "Do you have any brothers or sisters?"

Mark nodded and told the class that he had a brother and a sister—John and Meagan—but he was the oldest in his family, and they didn't go to school.

Next it was a dark-headed girl with a ponytail who introduced herself. Her name was Maria Rojoflores. It was a hard name to say and harder to remember. Mrs. Johnson had the class try to say it. Everyone could say Mark Ward, and they could remember Maria, but her other name was hard to say.

Mrs. Johnson had Maria say her name again very slowly.

"Maria R-o-j-o-f-l-o-r-e-s."

"Once more," her teacher asked.

"My name is M-a-r-i-a R-o-j-o-f-l-o-r-e-s."

"Okay, children, let's try again."

"M-a-r-i-a R-o-j-o-f-l-o-r-e-s," they repeated slowly.

It was still too hard, and all the children laughed, including Maria.

"Well, we'll have to work on the last name. It is a beautiful name, Maria. Do you know what it means?

Maria nodded. "Maria is the name of a saint—that's a very important person," she said. "My other name, Rojoflores, means a red flower."

Sarah could remember red flower much easier than her name.

They went around the circle and when they got to Charley Adams II, Mrs. Johnson explained that II meant that Charley was named after his dad or grandpa. Charley said it was his grandpa and that he had that name because his grandpa was such an important person and that meant Charley was an important person too.

Sarah was next. "My name is Sarah Hales, but I don't know what it means."

Mrs. Johnson caught a tone of concern in Sarah's response and explained to the children.

"That's okay, Sarah. Some names don't mean anything except the name."

Sarah nodded and answered her teacher's questions about what she liked and about her family and explained that she had just moved to her new house. Sarah kept thinking about her name and if it meant something. Maybe it didn't. Somehow that didn't feel right, even though most of the other kids didn't know the meaning of their names either.

Play time, snack time, and reading time were fun, even though Sarah was disappointed that Mrs. Johnson did all the reading and didn't teach them how to read. But she was happy and excited that the story was really good. Sarah was in school, and that was all that mattered, even if her name didn't.

When I came back to the classroom to get Sarah, I met some of the other children's parents. There was an obvious common sense of pride in the children's faces as they came out of the school doors. I think all of us mothers had our own sense of pride too. On the way home, I asked Sarah to tell me all about school and what they did.

Sarah excitedly told me about the story Mrs. Johnson had started reading and how excited she was to hear more the next day. She told me about the puppet show they did at playtime. *That* was her favorite thing!

When I asked about the new friends she had made, Sarah told me about Mark, Kendra, Jamis, and Shelly, and then she mentioned Maria and got quiet. I glanced down at her as we came to a stop at an intersection. Sarah seemed deep in thought and looked a little troubled.

"What is it, Sarah? Did you have a problem with Maria?"

Sarah looked up and responded, "No, Mommy. She is nice. I like her. I can't say her other name; it's too hard, but it means 'red flower.'"

I could tell something was still bothering Sarah.

The light changed, and we drove on with Sarah gazing out the window. We hadn't gone far when Sarah turned to me and asked, "Mommy, does my name mean something?"

The question hit me oddly, but I could see that Sarah was serious. "What do you mean, sweetie?" I asked.

"You know, my other name, Hales? Does it mean something? Mommy, your name is Rebecca Hales. Does your name mean something?"

I was getting the gist of the question but didn't quite know how to respond.

"Well, Sarah, I don't really know if it means something. 'Hales' is Daddy's last name, and when we got married, I got his name too. Now I am a Hales, and when you were born, you got the name Hales too!"

Sarah looked at me and nodded but still looked disappointed.

"Maybe it does mean something. We can find out. Let's ask Daddy tonight."

"I hope it does mean something. Maybe it's something important!" Sarah said, almost pleading.

The question was now becoming significant for me too. I began to wonder if there was any significance to our family surname. I even wondered about my name—Rebecca.

"Sarah, I don't know, but we'll find out. Maybe it's a secret. Maybe it does mean something important. We'll ask Daddy about it when he gets home."

Sarah smiled. Even if Mrs. Johnson said some names don't have to mean anything, Sarah wanted to have a name that meant something pretty like "red flower" or important like "Brad Mason." She was just sure that her name did mean something. I silently prayed for help in finding the meaning of her name.

I continued to think about it. Did names have meanings? Did our family name have a meaning? I knew a little about our family history and where the name came from. I had even seen some advertising about family crests and saw a book at the library about names when we were trying to decide what to name Kody, our son. Somehow, I too felt that a name should mean or stand for something—*but what?*

Jeff, my husband, came through the front door with his usual jovial spirit.

"Ready or not, the Tickle Monster is here. You shall be caught!"

It was a game the kids loved to play with him. They didn't call it hide-and-seek; that would have made it like everybody else's game. Their game was "The Tickle Monster Game." They had about thirty seconds to find a hiding place before Jeff, the Tickle Monster, started looking for them. Their squeals of glee usually gave away their hiding places. Once he found them, they had ten seconds to try and find another hiding place.

When they were found the second time, they had to go to the living room couch. That was Tickle Monster Prison. They couldn't get out until they had told Jeff about their day. They had other Daddy games, but this was their favorite. Sometimes he started it, and sometimes they watched for him to pull into the driveway and then they would hide and it was my duty to inform Jeff that the game was on!

I wondered how many other dads had similar games they played when they came home. I had heard friends complain about their husbands dropping onto the couch with the TV remote or newspaper or heading to the computer to check the news. It made me all the more grateful that I had a husband who valued his time with the kids. That was a blessing.

The game distracted Sarah from her name issue for the moment. When the Tickle Monster found the children the second time, he had the right to tickle them relentlessly until the hiders could get to the security of the couch. When the last child was found, the kids turned on him for a thirty-second Pile-on-the-Monster that ended with uncontrollable laughter and pure joy.

"Okay, okay! You win!" Jeff muttered in mock protest of his outnumbered capture.

They plopped down in the couch, and I joined them for our traditional day-in-review reports. Afton and Kody told about their first day at school, and then Jeff turned to Sarah.

"And you, my sneaky little hider! How was your first day at school, Sarah?"

Normally Sarah could and would go on and on about her day with journalistic details. Her reports were a report on every toy, TV program, and friend who came to play. Now that she was in school, I knew we were in for a daily state-of-the-school and Sarah brief.

"Really fun, Daddy! I like Mrs. Johnson. She's nice and she lives in the country and has two grandbabies and she likes animals. And there are lots of kids in my class and they are nice and . . ."

I saw it coming. I knew that her mind had just reconnected to the "what does my name mean" conversation.

"Daddy, can you tell me about my name?"

The question caught Jeff totally off guard, and, without context, he didn't know quite what she meant. I stepped into the rescue to buy a little time and to prime Jeff for the discussion.

"Sarah, how about if we talk about names after we get the dinner on the table. Would that be okay?"

She hesitated a little and then smiled with the assurance that we would talk about it.

"I need some help setting the table and getting the water and bread ready. Afton, the table. Kody, water and bread. And, Sarah, will you help me finish the salad? But first, everybody to the bathroom to wash up!"

They scurried off, and I cued Jeff on the conversation with Sarah about the meaning of her name. He raised his eyebrows in a pondering gesture, and nodded as I headed back to the kitchen. Jeff went into the den and got on the computer.

After the blessing on the food and the first round of passing and serving, Jeff jumped into the conversation.

"Sarah, mom tells me you had an interesting discussion with your class today about names."

"Uh-huh, and Daddy, I told them that I didn't know what my name means. What does it mean, Daddy? Doesn't my name mean something? Mrs. Johnson said some names don't mean anything, but some names mean something. Does my name mean something?"

"Well, Sarah Hales, I just happen to know that your name is very important. In fact, just to be sure, I went and looked on the computer to see what it means. The computer tells me that your name, Sarah, comes from England. Do you know where that is?"

Sarah nodded her head and then shook it. After a brief geography lesson, Jeff continued.

"It says that there are several meanings to the name Sarah. It says Sarah means 'lady of royal standing, like a princess.'"

Jeff played up the importance and continued. "It also said that your name has a meaning of 'secret place or special garden.'"

Sarah beamed, and of course Afton and Kody wanted to know what the computer said about their names. Jeff hadn't had time to check that out but promised that after dinner, they could see what it said. Sarah seemed satisfied, if not just a little puffed up.

Jeff added, "Sarah, your name also has some special heritage meaning too." Sarah looked puzzled. Jeff continued.

"Your name, Sarah Hales, has some of the meaning of Mom's family name, my family name, and your grandparents' names too. Sarah was the middle name of Mom's grandmother. She was your namesake. That means you were named after her. She was a really great lady and important to our family. My grandmother Sarah was a real saint. Just saying her name around family members brought a rush of comments about how they missed her and about what a wonderful person, mother, aunt, and grandma she was."

Sarah could be proud that her name carried all that meaning and importance too. I knew that I had some important work to do in telling Sarah more about her great-grandmother. I had simply not taken that opportunity. I would make it an important priority to get the pictures and stories together to help Sarah relate to this important member of our family heritage.

Jeff continued, "When someone who knows us or finds out that you are Sarah Hales, the daughter of Rebecca Hales, and great-granddaughter of Lydia Sarah Frandson, they automatically think that you must be like them. Because we have the same last name, how we act will give people an idea about the meaning of our name. That's why it is so important for us to take good care of our names. We never want to have people think badly of us or our other family members who share our name because of what they hear us say or how they see us act."

What Jeff said next was amazing, and I wish I could have recorded it! There had to be some inspiration behind it. I'll bet I've shared it with a half a dozen of my friends since then. I'll try to get it as close as I can to what he said.

"You know, kids, what somebody's name means is more about what they make it mean. It's more about what they do and how they act than about what anybody else, including the computer, says about it. So, Afton, what do you want your name to mean?"

She shrugged her shoulders and gave us a typical short answer. "Good . . . smart . . . I guess."

"Okay. So what if I said 'Afton' means good and smart girl. Would that make a difference in the way you act?"

"I don't know. Maybe," she said, a little more drawn in between bites of meatloaf.

"Big K, how about you? If you could make up the meaning of Kody, what would it be?"

He shrugged his shoulders.

"What if your name meant big and strong helper?" His smile was answer enough. Jeff continued. "I'll bet you would always be using your muscles to help mom and your friends."

"Who has the right to say what your name means?" Jeff asked as he looked around at all of us. This time Afton spoke up.

"You do."

"What do you mean, 'you do'? Do you mean 'you' as in 'Afton' has the right to tell us what her name means, or 'you' as in Daddy has the right to tell people what 'Afton' means?"

"You," she said again.

"So, if I said 'Afton' means honorable sister and friend, what would you do?"

"Be a good sister and friend," Afton said in her best big-girl voice.

Jeff smiled. "Why?"

"Because that's what my name would mean and how I should be," Afton reasoned.

"What if somebody acted different than what their name meant? What would people believe most, what they said their name meant or how they acted?"

"How they acted," Kody piped in, and Jeff continued.

"I think you're right, Kody. So what you *do* is more about giving your name its meaning than what somebody says it means, right?"

All three nodded in agreement. I wanted to chip in, but Jeff was on a roll, and I wanted to see where he was going to take it. I was amazed at the kids focus on the topic. He was going to continue, but first he had to have another helping of potatoes.

"So, I have an idea. If Afton is right, then we will choose to be what our names mean. And we can choose what we want our names to mean. What if we all decide what we want our names to mean and then we can be that way and people will know the meaning of our names?"

The kids nodded, but I was afraid the idea was a little over their heads. Jeff continued.

"Okay, I say my name, Jeff Hales, means happy, honest, and kind. How do I have to be for other people to know and say Jeff Hales is happy, honest, and kind?"

I was ready to jump in this time.

"You just have to be how you are because you are happy and honest and kind and smart and—"

"Wait a minute! I didn't say I was smart."

"No, but you are and that's how you act so I say you are smart too!"

All the kids agreed and laughed.

"I think this is a good thing to talk about in our Sunday family time. What do you think?"

His question brought nods of approval from the kids and ended our first of many family discussions about the meaning of our names. The result of the evolution of that discussion had given us some powerful tools to help our children connect their names, values, and behaviors together. It has also become an important element in our family heritage story.

That conversation led to the adoption of one of the lines in our family pledge, "We live up to the promise of our family name. As Haleses, we are honorable to our promises and truthful in our words. We always do our best because that is what it means to be a Hales."

Sarah was concerned that first day at school because she was afraid that her name didn't mean anything. Now she says proudly, "I am Sarah Hales, and that means I am honest, kind, and helpful." Jeff's off-the-cuff conversation has become a key to our family heritage-making.

Sarah's question became a quest to give real meaning to our names—even if I had to make up the meaning myself. Making the meaning was what led me to become a heritage-maker and to help our children see that their names, who they really are, are the same as the character they exhibit in their lives.

THE NAME CHARACTER CONNECTION— FINDING AND MAKING MEANING

"A good name is rather to be chosen than great riches, and loving favor rather than silver and gold." (Proverbs 22:1)

"What is in a name?" So asks Juliet in Shakespeare's *Romeo and Juliet.* Her suggestion that "the rose would smell as sweet by any other name"[1] may hold true for the flower, but what of the name of a child? Does, or can, the implied meaning of a name, or association of the name with a namesake, have an influence on behavior? Is a name just a label to be used to identify the person? If, as the scripture suggests, a good name is to be chosen, from what list and qualifications should parents select the name? What makes a name good?

Is the good name referred to a given name or the family surname or both? Can or does their surname influence how a child will think, act, and choose? Certainly the story of the young son of King Louis XVI, prince of France, cited in the introduction would suggest that birthright and name could have an influence.

We wonder, "Why am I as I am?" The parent can choose the name of a relative, friend, or famous person as a way to honor that person. The name of a favorite character from the Bible or a novel might be selected. Parents can choose a name that is highly unusual or even create a name they have never heard before. Some combine names to create a new name.

Most parents may not have considered the potential influence of the source of the child's name. They can, however, help the child to build positive meaning to the name just as Jeff and Rebecca did.

THE MAKING OF THE MEANING

Intentional parents tell the story of the name and build the royalty of its genesis, history, and importance. If it is a relative's name, heritage-maker parents promote the values, character, and contributions associated with the name. Then they write the story down and tell it to the child regularly. Why write it? When it is in print, it adds to the credibility and power of the story.

Intentional parents teach and remind their children about their namesakes to help them develop similar attitudes and values that will influence their choices. They compliment the child for even the smallest adherence to those values and choices associated with the meaning of their name. Intentional parents, grandparents, and families can be highly proactive about training up the child and use the positive labeling of their name to do so.

Sarah's parents used the Internet to discover that one of the meanings associated with the name Sarah was "princess." But far more important and powerful are the meanings Sarah's parents helped her create for the meaning of her name.

SURNAMES—ROYAL BIRTH

In some cultures, the family name follows the matriarchal line of the family. The names of Johnson, Jenson, Larson, Morrison come from an association with the father's given name. They are the "son" of John, Jens, Lars, or Morris. In these cases, the association of the child to the reputation of the parent carries the identity and reputation of the father. These names were then applied to grandchildren and the entire family line.

One prominent western leader relates how in a dream his grandfather, for whom he had been named, appeared to him and asked, "What have you done with my name?" Because he had been raised to view his grandfather as a great man, a hero with specific beliefs and virtues, he had been taught and always considered what his grandfather would have done if he were in a like situation? So he honored the name and added honor to it. In the dream, he was able to respond, "I have never done anything with your name of which you need be ashamed."[2]

Children may also take on a name associated to identity with a sport team, club, or church group. These affiliations often come with a creed or pledge that define acceptable behavior as a member of that group. For many, the most important association outside the family is that of taking on the name of Christ as a Christian. That church and religious name association will have family-centric values that will strengthen home and family.

Parents and grandparents should consider that by their life experience, choices, and character, they are contributing "name meaning" to their posterity. The family surname is the identifying label of their family heritage and it will carry on beyond the child's life.

In some cases, a parent doesn't have the initial opportunity to give the child their name, as in an adoption. In these and other cases where the name came without intentional meaning and positive character association, the parent can help the child craft the meaning.

We can make, as well as choose, a "good name." We can give them more than great riches of gold and silver. We can give them the "loving favor" of a good name. Do not feel guilty if you are getting a late start in considering the naming process. Now that you are becoming aware of how you can use the power of name association, you can add meaning and significance to their names. You can enhance the meaning of the child's and your family name intentionally.

LEGACY-SECURING INTENTIONAL PARENTING PROJECT SUGGESTIONS

Name Foundations—Search out the etymology of your family name. Check on Google for meaning of the name. Ask relatives about it to find if there is more, historically or anecdotally, available to you to include in your name.

Hero Names—Make a list of family heroes whose names you might want to consider for future children's names or nicknames. Identify a few stories from their lives that would exemplify the significant values and virtues that you want associated with the name.

My Hero Book—Create a simple storybook about the child's name. Create the story around the character, talents, and values you want the child to "live into" and associate them with the child's name. The story should be about how they save the day when Mom or Dad or other family members or friends needed their special character powers of being helpful, honest, hardworking, and so on.

Name Celebration—Have a special name celebration and conversation with your children to recognize how the standards and values they live by make you proud of them. Help them understand that the way they live and the choices they make bring honor to their name and the family name.

Hero-in-the-Making—Create a storybook journal for the child in which you chronicle with a picture and the story of each time they choose to honor and contribute to the family heritage. For each inclusion (monthly, quarterly, or annually), write the story of the child's experiences that give honor to that child and the family name.

Name Plaque—Put a name plaque on their bedroom door. For example, "Johnny Doe—Doe family hero"

Brag—When you have relatives or guests around, be sure to allow your children hear you praise their positive behaviors and express how proud you are of how they are great examples of living out your family name. Have an intentional conversation about the child on the phone with a family member or friend who will give a positive response back to the child about your bragging. Then report their comments to the child. This third-party validation is powerful.

Name Crest or Plaque—Create and hang a name crest or plaque that incorporates the values, words, and icons you want associated with the child's or family name. Involve your child in the project.

Hero T-Shirt—Create a T-shirt with a simple superhero-like insignia with the child's initials in it. Tell the child that when he or she is going to do something important in their home that needs to draw on their superhero power they can wear the T-shirt. For example, doing extra chores or perhaps helping a family member complete a special assignment. Help the child know he or she must be careful not to do anything that would damage their hero image while he or she is wearing the shirt. You will be amazed how this shirt will influence intentional hero behavior.

NOTES

1.   William Shakespeare, *Romeo and Juliet*, act 2, scene 2, lines, 43–44, shakespearermit.edu/romeo_juliet/full.html.

2.   George Albert Smith, "Your Good Name," *Improvement Era*, March 1947, 139.

6

A STORYBOOK GRANDMA

Continuing Her Loving Influence

SHERRY LOOKED DOWN LONGINGLY ONCE MORE into the saintly but silent face of her grandmother. She was the perfect storybook Grandma! Now she was gone. Gone were the visits, phone calls, cards, gifts, and hugs, and the magical twinkle of her eyes. Gone were the custard pies, the perfect gravy, and the divinity candy. Most of all, gone was her smile with its constant gentle understanding and encouragement. Gone was that deep and abiding look of knowing. Gone was the deep comfort of her lap and her hugs.

Sherry shuddered at the cold chill and tears that were forming and falling onto her cheeks. It wasn't fair! Why now? Why her? She had always been there for Sherry, but now all that was left were memories. But they were such sweet memories. Grandma's counsel, indeed her life, had always had a powerful influence on how Sherry felt about things and the choices she made. She was a great listener and a wise and loving counselor. Her stories always seemed to make Sherry want to be better, like her grandmother—kind and fun.

Memories flooded over her as Sherry remembered the image of her grandmother's outstretched arms. Oh, how she loved those warm, comforting, enfolding hugs. The gentle squeeze was like a secret message of love and understanding. Sherry loved the walks in the garden and the stories. Oh, the stories, especially her stories about her and Grandpa Jim. Now they were both gone—her inspiring grandparents and their stories of family, life, and heritage.

The knots in Sherry's stomach and throat tightened as they closed the lid to the casket. Billy tightened his three-year-old grip. Sherry glanced down at her precious son's puzzled look. Would he remember this perfect grandma—his great-grandma? He'd had so little time with her. Billy may not remember her embracing love or her wonderful stories.

What would he remember? Sherry would always remember the stories of adventures of the old days and the old ways. Grandma was such a great storyteller. Now Sherry would be the keeper of these precious reminders of her grandma and her heritage. She would make sure Billy had his great-grandma's stories, even if he didn't have her. Bringing Billy to see her grandma was Sherry's gift and joy. But the visits had been too infrequent. Now, on his last visit, as Sherry held him up to see her, Billy whispered sweetly, "Gamma Lilly sleeping now."

SHERRY'S STORY

The days after the funeral were busier than ever. Maybe I made sure of that to avoid the tears when I thought about Grandma Reese. Being busy seemed to make life move on and helped me deal better with the pain of loss. Thanksgiving came, and we used Grandma Reese's gravy recipe and her special gravy bowl and ladle, but the gravy just wasn't quite the same.

At the family Christmas party, Mom used Grandma Lilly's divinity candy recipe, but it too wasn't the same. Someone asked who had taken one of Grandma's quilts. I glanced over at the old rocking chair. It was there, but Grandma was gone, and I was lost in her memory again. Someone asked for another piece of pie and jolted me back to the party. Then I was off to the kitchen and consumed again with the present.

At our family reunion in the park that summer, the conversation turned to Grandma Lilly once again. We talked about what we missed most. It was interesting that all of us missed her deep intelligence, quick wit, and her ability to stretch a dollar. But what we missed most was that incredible ability to see positive options to almost every situation and her deep and abiding faith. Grandma's faith was the center of her life. Many of her stories involved how she and Grandpa Jim had come to know and trust in God. Hers was a simple yet profound faith that everything would work out with God's will. Oh, how I wished my own faith could be that simple and that strong! I had leaned heavily on Grandma's faith and confidence.

I loved hearing her read from the Bible. Better yet, I loved how she could tell me the Bible stories I loved. She always made them so exciting, real, and meaningful. It was like Grandma Reese actually knew Moses and King David and Jesus. Another thing about Grandma was how she always reminded us to have a family prayer before we returned home from a visit. Grandma lived by her faith, and that faith had become the seed of my own convictions. I really missed her spirit and her spirituality, but I still leaned solidly on her faith. That faith had become a family legacy— my legacy—and in turn, it would become Billy's legacy.

Then one of my cousins asked about some of Grandma's photos. She was looking for copies of pictures with her and Grandma and Grandpa Reese. My mother kept the box that had the pictures Grandma had saved, but she hadn't got them out since the funeral. I laughed inside at the rush of memories I had around that old box and the times Grandma told me the stories connected to the pictures and about the places and people in them.

My cousin's query reminded me that there were some pictures of Grandma that I wanted too. I knew that my brother wouldn't have much interest in the box of pictures. I also knew that, like my mother, I would likely be the heir apparent for the box of Grandma's pictures, along with all the hand-me-down pictures of the rest of the family. But before that future day came, I would have to go through the pictures just to be sure that I got the ones I really wanted to be certain to keep so that part of our family heritage was lovingly passed along to future generations.

As I thought about those pictures, I realized that not only were many of my childhood memories captured in those pictures but also the people in my life. Those pictures were chapters in the family legacy. They were the evidence of stories we all loved, stories that, like the pictures, were fading. Suddenly I wanted to see those pictures, hear those stories, and remember the times, places, and people who were hidden in the pictures in that box. As I thought about it, I realized that the pictures without the stories they were connected to were likely to become worthless. I did not want to let that happen.

Spurred by my cousin's question about the pictures she was looking for, I cornered Mom and told her that I wanted to come by and look through the box of Grandma's pictures. Mom's response left me a little shaken.

"Okay, honey, but I'll have to remember where we put them."

Where she put them! How could she not know exactly where she put them? They must be put up in a safe place! They were priceless!

"Mom, what do you mean? Don't you know where they are?"

"Oh, Sherry, I am sure they are here somewhere. They were in the garage with some of her other stuff we moved out of the attic, but your father has cleaned things up out there, and I'm not sure where he put them."

I panicked. Not in Dad's garage! Dad was notorious for losing and throwing things away. He wouldn't have—he couldn't!

I left Billy with Mom and dashed off to find Dad. Making my way through the darting kids, dodge ball, and Frisbee-flinging relatives, I found him predictably sitting with some of the other men, telling the stories of some hunting adventure they relived at every reunion. I excused my interruption of their hunt, but right then my hunt couldn't wait.

"Dad, do you know what happened to Grandma's box of pictures? Mom said it was in the garage but that you might have moved things around." I waited with an obvious look of desperation while he thought about it for a moment.

"Well, Sherry, I don't remember seeing a box of pictures. Do you remember what it looked like?"

My heart almost sank. Remember? How could I forget! How could anyone in the family forget that box and its precious contents!

"Dad, you know, it's that old sewing machine box—remember? The thick grey box with granddad's old work belt around it?"

I had peered into that box dozens of times with Grandma for addresses on old Christmas and birthday cards and to look for pictures Grandma needed to give someone. I could never forget that box and the memories of Grandma Reese that it held.

"Oh, right. I remember. It's on top of the green cabinet next to my tool chest in the back of the garage."

A flood of relief brought a deep sigh, and I turned to dash back to Mom and Billy with a determination to rescue the box from certain displacement or destruction.

"Thanks, Dad. Good luck with the hunting!"

I got back to Mom, who had already forgotten the discussion of pictures and was helping Billy with yet another sugar cookie. I barely rescued them both from the temptation of another piece of Aunt Margie's caramel fudge.

"Mom, Grandma's box is still there. Dad says it's in the garage. Can I come over tomorrow to check it out? Would you mind watching Billy while I go through the pictures?"

"Okay. That'll work.

"Great! I'll be by in the morning."

The next morning, while I was dressing Billy to get him ready, I asked him, "Do you want to go with me to Grandma's to get some pictures?"

Billy always wants to go to Grandma's, she always makes it her mission to spoil him, and he loves digging through the things in our old toy box with her. He nodded, and we were off to the rescue.

"We are going to go find some of Mamma's pictures. Can you remember Mamma Reese, Billy?" I asked and watched for any indication of recognition.

His blank look and hesitant response startled me. Could he have forgotten her so quickly?

"Remember Mamma?"

That was the term we used to distinguish my mother, his Grandma Jane, from Grandma Reese. This time he nodded, but I was not convinced that he really remembered her and felt some urgency to reestablish the memories before they faded even more. I would show him some of the pictures of him as a baby with her and tell him stories about his great-grandmother. I knew that without the pictures and the stories, the memories and the influence would fade more, and not just for Billy.

I thought about the last time I was with Grandma Reese looking through her pictures. Suddenly, I became aware that I could almost smell Grandma's gardenia-scented perfume. It was a memory with a fragrance! That was incredible to me! The last time I was looking in the box had to be two, three, maybe four years ago. As I thought about it, I realized it had been a lot longer than that. Time passes *so* fast! *Too* fast.

As soon as we arrived, I left Billy in the capable and spoiling arms of my mother and went immediately to the garage. I glanced up to the top of the green cabinet where Dad had said he had put the box—it was not there. My heart sunk.

"Mom! The box isn't there! Dad said—" Before I could finish my sentence, Mom was at the garage door, Billy in tow.

"Sherry, your dad got it down this morning. He put it over there on the workbench for you."

I picked up the box and was surprised at how much it weighed. I put the box on the kitchen table and untied the old work belt that Grandma used to hold the box closed and together after Grandpa Jim had passed. Even the belt held the keys to countless stories of Grandpa Jim's work and life.

It was a magical moment for me.

Inside the box were three rubber-banded bundles of old letters. One was Grandpa Jim's letters to Grandma while he was away in the service. One was her letters to him. They were organized by date. That was so like my grandma! There were treasures that somehow I would definitely make time to read in the weeks to come!

The third bundle was a variety of cards and letters from aunts and uncles and cousins. I set the bundles aside and peered in at the stacks of rubber-banded photos and a single photo album. The album was a collection of old black-and-white photos that Grandma received from her mother. I didn't know many of the people in the photos, but they were important to someone in our extended family. Taking them out of the binder would be tricky. No wonder the box seemed so heavy. I thought there must be a thousand pictures! As it turns out, there were *far* more than that. I found out there are about one hundred pictures per stacked inch of pictures!

The next two hours were like an emotional ride in a time machine. Exploring the treasured photos and trying to remember and discover the memories associated with them was a real adventure. Billy and Mom seemed totally happy to let me absorb myself in the box. I was amazed at how old some of the pictures were and how recent others were. I felt a little guilty, again, for not having done some sort of scrapbook for Grandma with these pictures. I guess I really wasn't all that crafty, or maybe I just never had or made the time. Once Mom and I talked about doing a scrapbook, but we just never got around to it.

Grandma Lilly had organized the pictures into family groups. Many of them were of distant cousins and family members, friends, and acquaintances that I did not know. When I asked Mom about them, even she only knew a few of the faces and places. We decided we would try to pass those photos on to other family members at the next gathering of the whole family.

As I pulled up the bundle with the familiar pink lace bow, I felt like a kid again. These were our pictures! I remembered the feeling of excitement I had sitting on Grandmother's lap looking at and putting newly collected pictures in that pink lace family bundle. There were pictures of my mother's wedding, family vacations, and of my brother and me with our grandparents through the years. It was like a quick review of many of the most important events of my life.

It was amazing! It was an adventure that made me feel warm and secure, even though the lump in my throat came again and again as I looked and thought about Grandma Reese. The pictures made me remember and miss her even more.

Mother brought me a sandwich and drink for lunch. She sat down beside me while Billy played under the table with one of my brother's old toy trucks that he had scavenged from the toy box. Mom looked at some of the items I had placed on the table.

"My goodness! I had forgotten that she had all of these things!"

"I know! It's amazing, isn't it! Mom, do you have this many pictures in our box?"

"Oh my, yes, I'll bet I do—probably more. Your father was always taking pictures of you kids, don't you remember?"

It was true. During my early years, Dad had been the one to bring and use the camera, *all* the time. It had always seemed to be such a bother to stop and take pictures when I just wanted to run off and play and see things. In recent years, he had left that job mostly to Mom. Now I've taken on that role for my own family.

As we looked through the pictures, we laughed and cried as we remembered the stories behind each photograph. But we were both surprised at how many of the details we had forgotten or just didn't know. Like the photos themselves, the memories were fading, and, for some of the pictures, the memories were simply blank.

I found a picture of Billy as a new baby on Grandma Reese's lap. I pulled that one out and pulled Billy up beside me to show him the picture. I wanted to tell him all about his great-grandmother, but the picture just couldn't compete with the storybook he was looking at on the floor. I guess that's when I started to get it—the idea that storybooks were more powerful than pictures. That became a significant moment for me in my journey to becoming my family's heritage-maker. It was a powerful lesson in the power of storybooks for transferring heritage and character.

It was not the right time to tell Billy about all the incredible things I had learned from my grandmother. I wanted to tell him and I would. I had to! Somehow, the telling of the stories always pulled Grandma back. I could not let her stories die too. Billy just had to know Grandma Reese! He *had* to! I sensed that telling Billy about her kept her memories and influence alive for all of us.

By the time we had gone through the box, I had found forty or fifty pictures that were precious proof of the memories of Grandma and Grandpa Reese. These were our family treasures. I would get them scanned and uploaded to my computer. Honestly, I wasn't sure exactly what I would do with them then.

In looking through the pictures, we found that two-thirds of the photos, cards, and letters really needed to be given to other members of the family. I put those in another box for mother to give to her sister, Aunt Ruth, the next time she saw her. She would distribute them to that side of the family. When I tied the box back up, I asked, "Where should I put the box, Mom?"

I obviously did not want to return the box to the former precarious perch on the green cabinet, or to potential accidental destruction or loss if they went back to Dad's workbench.

"Oh, honey, I don't know. Maybe we can combine them with our pictures in the chest in the attic. Better yet, why don't you just take them? You are the one in the family that will want to do something with them. Heaven knows your brother won't want that job! Besides, you'll end up with all our family pictures sooner or later, anyway."

I knew that was true. Eventually it would fall to me to take the pictures and the job of the family *picture keeper*. I just didn't think it would be so soon. I had already become the family *picture taker*. While I didn't know what I would do with these family treasures, I felt good about taking Grandma's pictures to a more secure place than Dad's garage. I didn't want to see them tucked away in the attic with all the other stuff that was destined to eventually end up at the Good Will Store or to be tossed out.

So I agreed and put the box in the trunk of the car. I cleared the lunch dishes with Mom, talking all the time about some of the recently reopened memories of Grandma and my own early life. Then, much to

Billy's objection, I gathered up his toys, put on his coat and hat, and took Billy off to do the rest of our errands.

When we got back home, I decided that I would put the box of pictures at the top of the hall closet. That is where we put our family pictures immediately after they are brought from the photo finisher.

Then time flew by. A full four years later, at Billy's eighth birthday, my memories of Grandma Reese's pictures were jogged again. Several of the extended family members joined us in the celebration. Jerry, one of my favorite cousins, was in town and came by for cake and ice cream. We hadn't seen Jerry for a couple of years. As he handed Billy his gift, Jerry said, "Good grief, Sherry! He looks just like Grandpa Jim! He even has that half dimple in his left cheek!"

We had all previously noticed the marked similarity.

Jerry continued, "Do you still have a copy of that picture with your dad and Grandpa Jim at the lake? You know, that close-up one with their cheesy grins? Take a look at that one and you'll see what I mean!"

I was sure I had seen that picture—it was in the box. As I went to the closet and looked up at the box, the image of my grandmother and grandfather came back to mind, but this time I could not smell her perfume, and I felt a little sad and guilty.

I discovered something important that day as I retrieved the box to find the picture. Tucked away in the top of the closet, the pictures may not have been lost, but the memories associated with them, my memories, had continued to fade. Billy knew less, not more, about his great-grandmother and he knew even less about Grandpa Jim. Now, on his eighth birthday, I realized that my memories were fading too.

I had indeed become the family picture keeper, but I was letting my family heroes and their memories continue to fade. Because the pictures were the records and reminders of my family's stories I was effectively the family story keeper too. In one sense, I was doing my job well, keeping the pictures safe, yet I was failing to keep the stories and their significance to our family heritage from being lost.

As I pulled the box down, I suddenly felt Grandma beside me. The feeling was so real that it nearly took my breath away. It was as if she was there trying to tell me something. She was in the box, in the pictures, in the stories. She had waited long enough. It was time for me to do something about it. This time I wasn't going to put the box back until I did something to reintroduce Grandma Lilly and Grandpa Jim to Billy *and* to me!

That night after Billy was in bed, I started writing the story that would give Billy his great-grandma and great-grandpa. That night, I spent time again with Grandma and Grandpa Reese in their memories and stories.

GRANDMOTHER'S INFLUENCE—STORIES THAT LIVE BEYOND THE GRAVE

"Who can find a virtuous woman? For her price is far above rubies. . . Her children arise up, and call her blessed . . ." (Proverbs 31:10, 28)

Sherry's quest to reconnect to the life of her grandmother is common those who have loved, lost, or know they will soon lose the sustaining hugs and love of a grandmother. If you ask the grandmother what, above all else, she wants her children and grandchildren to retain and cherish of her life for the future, it will not be the contents of her jewelry box, some old knickknacks, trinkets, quilts, or dishes. Grandmothers want to leave an inheritance of the legacy of their lives. These are the jewels that matter most to these virtuous women of our heritage. Their life lessons, memories, and stories are truly more precious than rubies to their posterity.

Grandmothers' jewels are found in the treasure chest of their life experiences. They are passed on to her posterity through the legacy of her stories. Wherever possible, we should seek to gather the stories directly from our grandparents before they are gone. Often, they forget to write down their stories, remember the details, or realize that time is running out for them to put their memories and life counsel jewels in a safe place where they will not be lost to their posterity. Don't let them forget. Don't you forget!

BRIDGING THE GENERATION GAP

Paul traces the faith of his trusted companion and fellow disciple Timothy back to his mother and grandmother: "When I call to remembrance the unfeigned faith that is in thee, which dwelt first in thy grandmother Lois, and thy mother Eunice; and I am persuaded that in thee also" (2 Timothy 1:5).

Clearly, Sherry's grandmother was one of those virtuous women. We talk about the widening generation gap. We speak of generation X and Y, and in other ways, segregate and separate the children from the thinking, priorities, and values of their parents and grandparents. We hear that they, the older generations, don't understand. We see the younger generations embracing language, interests, music, movies, games, and activities that are incongruent with those of their grandparents and their heritage.

Is it because we have not done an effective job of established the connection and bridge between the values, standards, and beliefs of our generations? Have we overlooked and undervalued the importance of the heritage of our grandparents? It is true that this current generation's world is different from that which their grandparents or even we, their parents, were raised. Yet for many of us, at least for a while, we all live in the same world, some even in the same homes. Many families wrestle with the conflicting values and priorities that create the so-called generation gap. The goal of the intentional parent is to bridge those gaps. The life, love, and influence of grandparents, living and passed, can help in the bridge building and value crossing.

Grandparents are the most celebrated of family heroes. Maybe it's because they get to dote on us when we are young. Grandparents are there to hug, have sleepovers, give us presents, and take us to the movies and to the ice cream shop. Theirs is the privilege to spoil us, and theirs is the responsibility to give us an inheritance of life lessons, values, standards, and the other elements of family heritage.

Grandpas know how important it is to have fun, to work hard, and to laugh at ourselves. They know where the best places are to hike and where the fish are most likely biting. Grandpas know how important it is for grandsons to have adventures and they know how to create them. They even know some of the things granddaughters need to know too. But Grandmas know more.

Grandmas teach their girls how to knit and cook, feed the chickens, pick the flowers, and listen to stories. They can read to us or tell us stories that hold our attention better than a movie. Grandmas don't look at their watches and clocks as often as moms and dads do. They have the time— for a while.

Grandmothers always have or make time to send cards, to play games, and to listen. They are expert listeners. Grandmothers talk to us about how we are and what we are doing. They help us to know how we should behave and who we should become.

Added to their spoiling duties, grandparents are safety nets for parents. They calm us when our children are sick and when they, or we, make yet another parenting error. Grandparents have Band-Aids for parenting accidents. They can help to take some of the "ouch" out of parenting.

Perhaps the most important thing about grandparents is their love. The love of a grandparent has magical healing powers. They know that "this too shall pass." Their homes are often the emergency room for heavy hearts, perplexed minds, and frustrated adolescents. They are the X-ray technologists that can see what is really happening in the lives and hearts of their grandchildren. They know how to fix broken hearts. From the experiences, stories, and virtue of their lives comes the balm and the glue of family heritage.

THE STORIES THAT MATTER MOST

If you are lucky enough to have access to a grandparents' journal or a life story, you will often find that they have presorted what they believe to be the most important stories of their lives. Autobiographical stories may be more of a history and chronology of their lives than a description of their treasures and the map to the family-heritage treasure chest. If they are deceased and did not leave written stories, you may need to become the biographer. Whether you are searching through their writing or drawing from your own and others' memories of them, you can look for their jewels. You can find the treasure of their lives, the treasure that will make your life and that of your posterity richer.

If you have the luxury of interviewing a living grandmother, you are among the lucky ones. The process can be a simple interview of the grandparent. Start by setting and keeping the appointment. The interview can be conducted by phone, but it will be infinitely more valuable to do it in person. Be prepared to spend at least three to four hours with her. One story will trigger memories of many other stories and they all have their jewel lessons. Take a laptop, iPad, or notebook and pen. Depending on their age and alertness, you may need to break up the interview into several shorter visits.

When you interview grandparents to capture their life legacy, ask about the values, character, virtues, and traditions that they were true to. Ask about the major trials, tragedies, and triumphs of their lives. Ask about how they treated each other and their family and friends. Ask about their faith and their commitment to service, charity, and church.

When asking about hobbies and interests, get deeper into what they did with the fruits of their hobbies. Seek to find the contributions they sought to make from their time and talents. Ask them if they had to describe themselves with just three words they would hope to be remembered for, what would those words be and why.

Once you have responses to your questions, you can start putting the story together. It can be a really fun process as you weave your grandmother's answers into a story that will take on the pattern of her experiences and the theme of her priorities. You can do it from the interviewer's voice, or in first person as your experience and the story of your interviewing her. You may also be able to put it in her voice by weaving her answers into her own story.

Where you can, find pictures associated with her stories and put them in a book. With today's technology, it is easy to scan and upload the pictures to your computer for incorporating them into the layout of your book. You can do a simple manuscript printing directly from your computer. Then you can put it in a binder with soft or hard binding. You can make photocopies or use a professional publishing service. Several good choices are available online. The great thing about these services is that you can print multiple copies. You can be assured that as relatives get word about or see a copy of your "grandma book project," there will be many who will want copies of their own.

In this way, you will be mining your grandparents' stories for the jewels, not just the facts. You will be capturing and securing their life essence. Your efforts cannot bring them back to life when they are gone, but they can bring their stories new life, meaning, and value. You can turn them into superheroes whose real powers are to save the day of their grandchildren and great-grandchildren, even for their posterity yet unborn.

Remember in time that most mothers become grandmothers and fathers grandfathers. So don't forget about the importance of *your* story, you mothers and grandmothers to be. Don't wait until you are a grandparent to start capturing your stories and life lessons for your grandchildren, and theirs.

LEGACY-SECURING INTENTIONAL PARENTING PROJECT SUGGESTIONS

Involvement—Make your grandparents an active part of your family. Help your children to spend as much quality time with their grandparents as possible. Invest in their presence and relationship. Generate a yearning in the children to spend more time with their grandparents. Make it a reward for them to have special dates with Grandma and Grandpa, sleepovers, and celebrations. Take plenty of pictures of grandparents with the grandchildren.

Empower the Grandparents—Talk often and with high respect and gratitude for the grandparents as family heroes. Tell the children that their grandparents are real family heroes. Give them evidence of how they live by their values, service, and contribution. Tell values stories that begin with "I remember when Grandma . . . or Grandpa . . ."

Pictures and Wall Hangings—Hang framed pictures of the grandparents and display pictures of them with the grandchildren in the home and children's bedrooms. Show pictures and tell the stories of the special events of their grandparents' lives.

Heirlooms—Work with your grandparents to establish a special heirloom gift and associate the item with a special value, belief, service, achievement, or commitment of the child. It can be a locket or necklace for the girls, or perhaps a compass, pocketknife, or watch for the boys.

Teaching—Facilitate conversations with your grandparents about family heritage and history and what it means to be a member of the family with their name. When they live at a distance, use cards and letters. Use the phone, Skype, text, emails, or other communication tools to make and keep regular contact between grandparents and grandchildren. Don't let a generation gap develop or widen as a result from of too infrequent contact.

Storybook(s)—Create a grandparent storybook or scrapbook with stories and expressions of their values, standards, and traditions. Help the children come to know them for who they are or were, what they stand or stood for, and what they hope or hoped for their posterity.

Celebrations—Establish a "Grandparent's Day" celebration and do special things to honor, remember and be with grandparents. Use these days to review the ideas around the family heritage. Be sure to have them tell their stories. Parents, remind family members of how [child] is so good about remembering that value. Have the children share what they remember and love and remember most about the grandparents, especially those who cannot attend or who have passed away. Serve a grandparent's favorite treat to celebrate their many and varied contributions to your family and heritage.

Room Reminders—Work with Grandparents to prepare and give a plaque, or decoration for each child's room that includes the family name to symbolize the continuance of the heritage from grandparents to grandchildren.

Audio—Make an audio recording of the grandparent giving a brief life sketch and sharing their values and aspirations for their posterity. Where possible, make copies and have them add a personal message about their love and hopes for each child.

Favorite Sayings—Find out the grandparent's favorite saying or motto. Make a wall art item with the sayings, or a set of Christmas tree or other holiday ornaments of each grandparent with their picture and favorite saying.

7

TALKING WALLS

Turning Houses into Homes

THEY ARE AN UNCOMMON COUPLE. OH, THEY HAVE a lot in common, but it's the uncommon things about them that make their story interesting and important for intentional parents. Jake is tall, lean, and a manly man by anyone's standards. Heidi is petite, pretty, and friendly. They make a handsome couple and great parents if you ask their three happy, healthy, and always hungry children. One of the uncommon things about them is that they know how to turn a house into a home, a heritage- and character-rich home.

Jake is a builder. He provides for and plays with his family but wishes he could reverse the amount of time he spends on the job and the amount he has to be with his wife and children. Jake does love his fishing. He tells everyone that Heidi is the best catch he ever made. She responds that she will forever be grateful that she got hooked up with him.

While Jake is a house builder, Heidi is a homemaker. She has the uncanny ability to turn a perfectly framed wall into an amazing work of art, warmth, and celebration of their family heritage and legacy. You have heard the old adage, "If these walls could talk." Well, Heidi's walls *can* and *do* talk. They tell the stories not only of what has happened within the walls but what happens to the Murdock family outside the walls as well. They tell the stories of where and from whom they have come and where and with whom they are going. They are a record of the Murdock family legacy.

Heidi's walls are not her only homemaking skill. Jake says he builds big things, and she makes little things. Jake is the first to admit that it's the little things that matter most in the Murdock home. Jake has pounded the nails, and Heidi has pounded the computer keyboard. Jake has hung the windows and the doors for his family to look out onto the world and to come in from it. Heidi has hung framed pictures and craft projects to remind the family of what they have seen, where they have been, and who they are and what they can become. And that is what makes the difference. They have made a family who knows and is surrounded with reminders of who they are.

Theirs, like most families' heritage, is a work in progress. The conversations and occasional disagreements about their developing heritage and family legacy bring them back to the need for unity as a cornerstone or "load-bearing wall," as Jake would say. With this somewhat evolving blueprint of how they want their family values to be built, Heidi goes forward with making the house fit the plan that reminds them of that heritage.

Heidi's story is about how they are building and securing their family legacy. It is about how she has been able to make her walls tell the story of their family priorities and values. It is about what makes Heidi's house a home. Her story is real, and her system is really helpful for intentional parents who want to surround their children with the priorities and celebrations of their family legacy.

HEIDI'S STORY—*THE BUILDER, THE BAKER, THE HERITAGE-MAKER*

Do you face the issues of too little too late, not enough soon enough, and finding what you lost yesterday while looking for what you misplaced today? It's nice to know that I am not alone. As Jake says, "We are fishing in the same hole."

Do you ever wish you could just stop the clock and maybe turn back the calendar? Do your kids seem to be growing up faster than you can keep up? Is there always more month than money at your house? Did your personal to-do list for today get overfilled weeks ago? Do you sometimes feel guilty about not doing more to turn your house into a home?

If you can relate to these challenges, then we have a lot in common, and we have something to talk about. It's about turning chaos into cute. Creating cute things is my way of coping, and I can assure you that you don't have to be an artist to create something that fits my definition of "cute."

Let me start out telling you about my list. I'll bet much of it is just like yours. It usually starts out with getting the kids up at 6:30 a.m. That is, if they haven't reversed the order and gotten me up much earlier. Then it's breakfast with a repeat reminder that oatmeal is better for us than some sugar-frosted, cartoon-promoted cereal. Packing Jake's lunch comes next, and if I am *really* with it, I've started and have a load of laundry going at the same time.

On my best days, I read a verse or two out loud from the scriptures while my family gobbles and gulps. Although I'm not sure they can hear when their mouths are open to talk or to eat, often at the same time! But I try anyway. Then it's finding the keys to the jeep for Jake, bus time for Matt, and Sesame Street for Lexy. Next it's socks and pants out of the washer into the dryer and towels out of the hamper and into the washer. I think we mothers really have discovered the secret to perpetual motion—laundry!

Then it's time to clear the table of the breakfast mess and refill the tabletop with the socks to sort. While my hands are doing that, my shoulder holds the phone while I arrange a play date for Lexy and a ride to Cub Scouts for Matt. Oh, and my feet gather the remaining bits and pieces of breakfast that somehow made their way to the floor under the table. No wonder my socks are as dirty as Matt's!

Oh, yes, I almost forgot. Matt's hamster cage needs the chips changed, and I'll try to get to that today because I didn't get to it yesterday, but I suspect it will have to wait until tomorrow—again. Does any of this sound familiar?

Anyway, then it's on with the systematic search for the mysterious lair of the socks monster in hopes of finding the missing mates. Then it's socks and shirts to the bedrooms, towels and sheets to the linen closet, and hope that I don't meet myself coming around the corner. Whew! And all of that in my first hour and a half! Still, the clock keeps ticking. Sesame Street is over soon, and Lexy will be letting me know that she is "so bored" because she simply has "nothing to do."

I remind her that she had color books and crayons yet to conquer! "Remember, Matt's birthday is in two days. You wanted to make him a card."

She responds, "Okay! But remember, Mommy, we have to bake the cupcakes for his party and you said I can put on the sprinkles."

"Yes, you can Lexy. We are going to do that tomorrow." That is, if I can ever get through today.

With Lexy cuddled up on the couch with her coloring book, I'm ready for a little creativity on the computer. Remember, "cute" is how I cope! It is the creative crafty kid in me. I guess it is my crayons and coloring book.

I know I only have an hour at best to finish Matt's birthday project. This is how I deal with the rush of my routine. It is how I turn our house into our home in just an hour or two, here and there, where I can sandwich it in.

I used to be a scrapbooker. Was that ever a trick! Talk about chaos and magnification of a mess! I loved the craft and the cute, but I just couldn't get enough time or space. When I found a little time, it took most of it to set up and clean up. I ended up doing most of my scrapbooking late and then later at night. That robbed me of either important family time or of much needed sleep time. Usually both!

Thank goodness for digital crafting! Now I can do a lot of my cute stuff without a lot of setup and cleanup. It's only a click-on and click-off for most of my homemaking and sanity-saving breaks. I still add some of the more scrapbook-like, tactile, cute things to my projects to give them the depth and frill I can't quite get with the computer.

Ours is an overlapping partnership of building and baking and heritage-making. I think the results are pretty amazing. I am running out of room on the walls and shelves, dressers and doors in the rooms to hang and put my home and heritage-making projects. Thankfully there is still plenty of room in the bookshelf for my storybooking projects. Although I may have to have Jake build me another shelf to handle the continuing chronicles of the Murdock family heritage.

I thought you might be interested in a virtual tour of our house to give you a little better idea about how I use my heritage- and character-building projects as intentional parenting tools. We try to craft heritage and character reminders into every room. We capture the stories and pictures of people and events of our families' activities and progress. We incorporate them into the decor of our home so we can celebrate the memories and be surrounded by their influence.

It's a little like some of Jake's fish stories. The fish seem to get bigger, and the trips all the better each time he tells the story. The pictures and stories I put in the annual family storybook help me to keep "the fish and the stories" alive.

Those memories help to lighten the load on days when there are fewer hours than the to-do list requires and more stress than we think we can handle. Most important, they remind us of how much we love each other and how much we love doing things together.

Now before we start the whirlwind tour, you must know that I insist that you understand that what I have crafted is not craft for craft's sake. I will be anxious for you to understand that there is a well-planned ulterior motive behind each project. They are not just cute; they are the evidence of our intentional focus on parenting and heritage-making and character development. They are projects with a purpose—not just creative crafts.

With that understanding, let me show you how I make my walls talk. As you walk up to our door, you will see the Murdock family flag, complete with the family crest. No the crest didn't originate in the fifteenth century or some distant medieval castle or court. It came from a conversation Jake and I had around our kitchen table about the times we live in and what we want the Murdock family to be known for.

I drew up a little crest design with some emblems of a few of our important family values and standards. I got some heavy-duty white nylon fabric and transferred the design. Then we used some fabric markers, and the kids colored in a few of the sections of the design.

It's a little tight in the entry, so I only have room for one project on the wall and a couple on the wall table. So here on the wall is the family picture. Getting all of us together and focused on the camera was a real chore. After a dozen or so tries, we got this one. We had it printed on canvas. I love the unframed, three-dimensional look that makes it pop out from the wall so well.

Here on the wall table is a project I did with some wooden blocks. They are made from six-inch pieces of 2"x4" wood scraps from one of Jake's framing projects. I had six blocks to design. I put one message on each surface so we could change up the messages occasionally.

Message one is the six words that represent our family core values—charity, integrity, service, faith, freedom, and fun. You can guess who was responsible for the last word. The set of words for the other side are favorite family quotes including:

- *"Onward, upward, together"*—Judy Babbel, my grandmother

- *"Pursuing our dreams keeps us young"*—Jason J. Murdock, Jake's great-grandpa

- *"Do it now"*—Spencer W. Kimball, one of our former church leaders

- *"Kindness always begins with me"*—Anonymous

- *"Stand up and stand out for what you stand for"* —Doug Cloward, a family friend

- *"Carry on"*—Kris Lee, a relative

I made up the text design pages on the computer and printed them on stiff paper, cut out the statements, and glued them on the blocks. It's amazing to me how many visitors take the time to read each of these blocks and ask about them. They have started a lot of interesting conversations about our family's values and our intentional parenting efforts.

Okay, next is the den, around the corner to the left. On the wall facing the desk we have a framed document of "The Family: A Proclamation to the World." Around the document, I have placed a bunch of small family pictures, maybe fifteen or twenty 2"x2"photos. The document is a proclamation of our beliefs about the purpose of families.

The back wall has a big mirror, and I put some vinyl lettering on it with one of our favorite sayings: "The family that prays and plays together, stays together." Then there is our bookshelf. Each year I do a family album or storybook to chronicle the adventures and family progress of the year. These little books are meaningful to us because they each feature members of our family! I create a page or two every month or so about whatever we've just done that month. Then at the year's end, the finishing touches of the book are pretty simple and it's not a huge project. Of the entire heritage-making projects I do, this is probably the most important and well used. In fact, it has become the tradition that celebrates our traditions.

Our living room is small too. We have only one wall for me to hang family heritage pieces on. So I started out with a small grouping in the center of the wall of our wedding pictures and a little framed story and poem about our special day in the center of the wall. I used vinyl wall lettering to create the caption: "Jake and Heidi—In the beginning . . ." There are a lot of creative things you can do with vinyl lettering.

Then I added a group of kids' pictures under the heading ". . . and then came Matt, Lexy, and Katy." They each have a baby picture, one of their first birthday, and then one of our most recent pictures of them. These family heritage reminders were so easy and are so meaningful.

Over on the other side we had room for our family charter and our family pedigree chart on the other side of the curio. You could probably have guessed that the curio was a Jake project. It's filled with a bunch of heritage enriching mementos of our family vacations and adventures. It also has some of our favorite greeting cards. We make our own cards and display some of the ones we really like in the curio. We're probably the only family you'll ever meet that keeps a copy of the Christmas cards we send out on display all year long!

The family charter is our own creation. We started writing it shortly after we got married and have revised it several times over the years. It is a statement of our commitment to each other and declaration of our values and standards as a family. We read it out loud with the family as a tradition to start each of our family night gatherings.

The family tree chart is fun too. Of course, it is surrounded with pictures of our relatives. There are several online programs that you can use to complete and print out your own family pedigree chart. It really lets you see how your family fits into the family line.

You might wonder what kind of family heritage and home-making projects there could be in the kitchen. The best! Remember, I'm the baker so here are a couple of the Murdock family cookbooks on the counter. The big one is a collection of all our extended family's favorite recipes. I made that for a Christmas gift two years ago. It was great! One gift, sixteen copies, covered both families. It's not just the recipes alone that make a family recipe book so valuable. We added pictures, descriptions, and the story of the origin of the recipes. They are cute and so fun.

Over on the refrigerator, we have magnets crafted by the kids and me. This is where we put reminders, notes, pictures, kids' art, wedding and shower announcements, and Jake's latest fish photo. They're simple and fun.

With all the cupboards, we only have a little area left by the door to the garage and I have to share it with the phone. Here is where I put one of our most important family heritage projects and resources—the family calendar. I started that tradition three years ago, and I'm glad our extended families love them. They are the perfect Christmas gifts too!

When you look closely at the calendar, you will also see that each month focuses on a mini story of a family hero. Sometimes it's an old timer; sometimes it's one of the kids. The kids love the recognition the calendar gives them for their successes in school, sports, and service. So that's the kitchen. Heading down the hallway to the bedrooms, we pass the Murdock wall of fame, the "Rogue Gallery" as Jake calls it.

Our Wall of Fame is where we hang pictures of our ancestors, our important family friends, and immediate family. We made up some simple wood frames for the pictures and I printed the photos out on the computer so I could add the names and information about the pictures. We change the relatives' family group pictures when they give us an updated photo. The best part of our Wall of Fame is the Personal Progress Board. Jake made the 2'x3' framed corkboard. There's a section for each member of the family, plus an extra section that is currently blank—just in case we add a caboose one of these days. No, that's not an announcement, so please don't start a rumor!

There is a constant flow of things the kids want to post. The really important things I scan and save digitally in their online folders. That makes it a lot easier to get rid of the old stuff without the kids feeling like we didn't like it or it wasn't important. They know we've saved it in their folder on the computer, so it's okay when it's time to take it down to make room for the next important thing. My mother had a box for us kids with all our stuff in it. We called it our "Treasures of Trash." I'll bet that you probably had something like that too!

Next up, the kids' rooms.

Matt is all boy. So we have all the typical boy's room stuff. The sports-themed wallpaper, the basketball hoop laundry hamper (for some unknown reason he hasn't gotten the swish shot for his dirty socks yet!) and we have the Matt Box his dad made for his toys. The first family heritage project is the framed picture I made for him on his fifth birthday with his first big fish.

There are two pictures and a message between them. One of the pictures is a print of a painting by Greg Olsen of Jesus with a little boy called *In His Light*. It is amazing. The bottom picture is of Matt, Jake, and me sitting on a rock at the river. It's one of those "I can't believe it turned out so well!" shots. Jake asked some fisherman who was walking by to take the picture. Boy, did he catch a trophy picture for us! It is priceless, so we mounted it!

The other project I wanted to tell you about is on his nightstand. It's a small storybook titled *Matthew J. Murdock*. He's about worn it out. I gave it to him when he was two. It's the story of Matt's birth. It starts out with a picture of Jake and one of me. The story on that page is simply—*"One time a girl and a boy fell in love."*

The next page has a picture of us at the wedding. The story continues. *"They got married and wanted to have a baby to share their love. They prayed and asked God to send a baby to make them a family."*

The pages that follow include pictures of my big tummy, Lexy's arrival at the hospital, her early days, months and up to her first year. The story line is simple and expresses our excitement, anticipation and great joy in her arrival and joining our family. It makes her feel wanted, and an important part of the family. It confirms our intentionality in having her. It reminds her that she is intentional and loved. I simply can not tell you how much this little book means to her. It is her favorite bedtime storybook and I often find her looking through it on her own. When she can read I suspect it will continue its heritage and legacy enriching power in her life.

The rest of Matt's book. It's just a few more pages of pictures of Matt with his grandparents, his baby blessing, his first fishing trip with his dad and the last one is one is of Matt and Lexy when we brought her home from the hospital.

I cannot tell you how important this little book has been to Matt! He was two when he got it and it has been his favorite bedtime story. The look on his face, his giggles and pointing to the pictures, especially my big belly is pure joy. I still find him looking through and reading his book on his own. I believe the book is having an impact on his desire to do what is right and live up to who the book says he is. What would any mom be willing to pay for a book that could do that for her kids?

Lexy's room is similar but with girly pink and purple and frilly lace curtains and no fish! It has a cute doll house Jake built for her, which I got to decorate and was like a little kid painting and furnishing it. She has a similar framed wall poster like Matt, but her picture of Christ is with a little girl called *Forever and Ever* by the same artist, Greg Olsen.

Lexy's book follows a similar flow and it's a near everyday read for her. It tells me opportunities to tell her things like:

"See, Lexy, that's just like what your book says. You are always so helpful." Or *"Lexy, is that the kind of girl your book says you are."*

This is another example of how we are applying intentional parenting to help develop their character.

Lexy has the bigger of the two kid's bedrooms because she shares it with baby Katy's crib, at least for now. I am still working on Katy's projects. I just need to find a little more time but who doesn't? It isn't a race; it really is intentional parent for me to work on it.

Only one more stop—*our* room. This is the one place for me in our home where I can go and the world has to stay out. This is where most of my family intentional parenting thinking and planning takes place. Often it is late at night or in the early waking hours when Jake and I can talk and think out loud about what we can do to influence the character and heritage development of the kids and the family. Several projects and interesting things I've made are hung around the room and placed on the headboard shelves. But the biggest and most important is the framed picture poster on the wall facing the bed. It has a large picture of us at our wedding. It is a close-up of us looking at each other. You know—the dreamy, goose-bumpy kind? It's my favorite. Maybe not Jake's, but then I made it so I got to choose!

The picture is great, but the text is what makes the project important. Once shortly after we were engaged and Jake was off on a trip, he sent me a letter. It was a sweet expression of his love and commitment and about the kind of husband he promised to be. It was a tearjerker for sure! In fact, I suggested to him that it was like his vows to me. He had sent me a lot of sweet notes and letters before we were married. When I was packing up some things just before we married, I came across it again and decided I would write my vows to him in a letter. So I did. It took me most of the night to get them just like I wanted. He was going on a day fishing trip with his dad and brothers just before we were to be married, so I took the opportunity to have his roommate slip it into his fishing fly vest pocket. Then I started to worry and wished I had made a copy of it.

His older brother tells the story of Jake finding and reading the letter better than Jake tells it. He said Jake cried as if he had lost the biggest fish of his life. He kept the letter too! So I tweaked the letters just a bit to form the text of our vows to each other, and now they hang over the bed. Our letters and vows remind us of what is most important in our lives; then they watch over us as we sleep. I'd tell you what our vows say, but I think I'll keep that personal. And, to be fully honest, there have been a couple of days when I really needed to be reminded. Probably Jake has had a few of those days too.

The other thing I wanted to share with you is my treasure. It's Jake's first book for me. He titled it *How Do I Love Thee?* I know it's a little cheesy, but it is precious to me. He used every letter of the alphabet to describe a reason he loves me. I'll give you a little sample of what he wrote.

"A is for *Angel* because you are heaven sent.

"B is for—" you guessed it—"*Baker*" and he blames *me* for his weight gain (as if *he* could gain an ounce!)

"C for *Cute*, because you are the cutest girl I ever knew." I know it's sappy, but it is still fun!

"D is for *Dreamer*." That one fits in more ways than one.

"E is *Eternity* because that's how long we'll be together."

"F is for—" no, *not* fish—"*Fun*"—the details are a real laugh! And so on.

Whenever I get a little down on myself, I can get a real pick-me-up from this well-worn little book, and I remember that at least I have Jake fooled! If he thinks I'm okay, then I am okay. I believe what he and his book tell me.

You know who really loves this book, almost as much as me? Lexy does! She'll come into the bedroom, grab the book, and hold it out to me. We have a great mommy-daughter read and laugh together. This little book assures Lexy that she too is secure because of her dad's love for me. It is so sweet and really powerful. I wish every husband and every wife would take the time to think through and write the alphabet of their love for each other. It would make a big difference. I know it has for me and for several of our friends who have taken the suggestion.

I started off my story by asking if your life was busy and hectic like mine, and if you could relate to my time-cramped routine life. It's a fact—we are *all* busy. Even people who aren't doing anything are busy doing it!

I want to assure you—if my story and our home has inspired you even a little to do something to celebrate and strengthen your family and heritage, you can do it. You can find and make a little time here and there to work on, one intentional-parenting project at a time. Believe me, it's always a work in process, with only occasional moments of completion. But for me, it is always a labor of love and fulfillment.

These little investments with the past and your present family activities, memories, and parenting will pay off huge dividends in your family's future. Please, do not let time, inexperience, or being a self-proclaimed "cute-klutz," as one of my friends calls her lack of craftiness, dissuade you from being intentional about turning your house into *your* home. You can turn a house, apartment, or a tent, if necessary, into a home that celebrates and nourishes the love of your family. You too can teach your walls to talk! If you listen carefully, they are already calling you to get started creating a few of these reminders and teachers of your family character and heritage.

TEACHING YOUR WALLS TO TALK— SAVORING THE MOMENTS

"Lo, children are an heritage of the Lord: and the fruit of the womb is his reward." (Psalm 127:3)

"And ye shall teach them your children, speaking of them when thou sittest in thine house, and when thou walkest by the way, when thou liest down, and when thou risest up. And thou shalt write them upon the door posts of thine house, and upon thy gates." (Deuteronomy 11:19–20)

This scripture reminds us that our children are "an heritage from the Lord" and a reward from him. Celebrating that reward and caring for that gift of family heritage is the role and the priority of *intentional parenting*.

The scripture continues and reminds us that we must teach our children in our homes. We must also teach them when we walk with them, put them to bed, and when we wake them up. It tells us as did the law of Moses that we should write our family heritage and values and rules on the doorposts and on our gates. The principles are just as, if not more, important now so.

Fathers provide for the support, and mothers provide largely for the teaching and caring of the children. Central to that teaching and care is nurturing them in the admonition of the Lord. Surrounding them with the evidence of their significance, importance, and the standards of righteous family living can be a challenging yet joy-filled task.

The ancients were commanded to write the laws of God on the doors of homes. They had candlesticks, burnt incense, scripture scrolls, and other religious decorations and reminders of who they were as the children of Israel. They were surrounded with evidence of their identity, and the importance of and commitments to keeping the laws and ordinances of their God and family.

Our homes can be made to be a constant reminder of who we are and what is expected of us. Our homes can be a place of refuge and a place of learning, celebrating, and praying. Our walls, pictures, shelves, and decorations can become reminders of what we teach and the values and standards we believe in. They can also be the refuge from the outer storms of conflict and confusion. The voices in the home can be soft and the images uplifting to help us celebrate our achievements and progress toward our earthly and eternal goals.

Ours is the opportunity to bring heritage home. As Heidi advises, it doesn't have to be all at once. Being surrounded with reminders of our family heritage is a way of living. We can add a little at a time as we build our legacies of heritage. How we decorate our homes and what we talk about, watch, read, and listen to in our home can either invite or offend the spirit of family love and family values.

SAFE PLACES

Children need safe places. When they play dodge ball, they have a designated safety zone. They use guarded crosswalks and fenced playgrounds at school. The safest and most welcoming place should be their homes.

Sadly, some children are latchkey kids, kept in houses or rooms that are not homes. These children return from a less-than-secure school and community environment to a house that is empty of parents and of reminders of family love, unity, and heritage. They live without the surroundings and evidence of truly belonging. They are not welcomed home by the happy voices of a loving parent and the warm décor of the love they share as a family. They live without the self-assuring and securing evidence of family values, traditions, and belonging.

For children to feel safe and secure in their homes, they need the presence of four things:

- A loving voice to welcome them.

- The assurance and evidence that the family is secure in its love and commitment.

- To know that they are missed and prayed for when they are away.

- To know that there is always a feeling of celebration when they return—an open door to love and support, even if they are returning with marred character.

TALKING WALLS

We all have walls, and they can either be silent or we can teach them to talk and to tell our stories as Heidi does. Family pictures, stories, and decorations are a wonderful start. Christmas and changeable holiday decorations can give warmth and joy and heritage to the home. These things say a lot about your family and your home. Holiday and other family-appropriate music can literally come from the speakers and sound systems attached to the walls reverberating the voices and spirit of the season throughout your home.

Music is a powerful tool to set the tone and teach the values and standards of your family heritage. It can also promote the opposite. Sadly, it can create discord, disharmony, and conflict. Pick the music that is played in your home wisely. You do have the right, even the duty, to protect your family from the voices and messages of so-called musicians who promote anti-family attitudes and feelings.

With the growing prevalence of flat-screen TVs, they too become talking walls. What we allow to be viewed and used as "background noise" and voices *is* vitally important for each parent to filter and censure. Our talking walls can help to set the tone of peace and cooperation in our homes or destroy them. They can separate our homes from the voices and noise of the outside world. Conversely, *if* uncontrolled, they can bring in, magnify, and exaggerate the growing discordant and antifamily voices and standards so present today in the world. Intentional parents must be wise in setting the standards of what we let our home's walls speak—audibly and visually. With today's technology, our home computers can send our TVs self-made videos and slides with messages of love, joy, values, and heritage—intentionally. These can be invaluable intentional parenting skills and projects.

THE POWER OF THE ENVIRONMENT

Your walls not only can talk, but it also has a heart with its own rhythms, pace, and beat. Your home has feelings and emotions that it emits and reflects. Your home has a spirit of its own. That spirit is programmed by the voices it hears and the feelings and emotions it absorbs. Have you been in some homes where the feeling is sweet and calm and serene—peaceful and inviting? How about homes that are loud, dark, filled with agitation and discord? Which home do you want? Do you know how to control the heartbeat of your home?

Sometimes the spirit and energy of people in the home can dampen the positive energy. For others, their energy may calm and soothe the home. What and whom we allow into our home and what influence we allow them to bring is a factor on how effective we can make our homes to be filled with the influence of our values and family heritage. Sometimes children's friends need to be reminded, *"We don't talk that way, or act or play that way, or use those words, or watch that show, or listen to that music, or do that or be that way in our home."*

It is wise to request or require others who enter your home to keep your rules to maintain your special home environment, feeling, and family heritage. We build fences and walls to keep unwanted influences out. We use soft voices and fill our ears with uplifting music and put heroes' pictures, stories, and family heritage on our walls and shelves to bring the influences we want in. We have and hang the flag of our country and our own family icons to share our convictions and allegiance to our country and our family.

The most important element of the environment of the home is the soft and calming voice of the mother. The most powerful and securing aspect of the home is the presence and leadership of a strong and committed father. These are the most vital aspects of making your house into a home—a heritage-rich home.

LEGACY-SECURING INTENTIONAL PARENTING PROJECT SUGGESTIONS

Be There—It is a prerequisite for every heritage home that parents are committed to being there whenever children leave or return to the home. In some cases where the parent(s) have to work, additional training and rules may help to provide much needed security and serenity. Love notes and messages that extend love, confidence, and reminders of the children's duties and options should greet children when parents can't.

Dedicate Your Home—This can be a simple ceremony where a prayer is offered requesting divine protection and the Lord's spirit to abide in your home. It can be a reading of a statement of purpose and dedication where you define the values and rules of conduct in your home and have family members raise their hands or stand to accept the dedication. It can be as formal as you want it to be. The purpose is twofold. The first purpose is to make a statement and agreement among family members as to how you are going to treat your home, treat each other, and treat guests who come into your home. The second purpose is to secure the blessings of Providence to help you turn your house into your home.

Mark the Entry—Either with a family flag, like the Murdocks used, a special welcome mat, or some plaque or other way to mark the threshold of where the world stops and your home, security, and rules begin. This is the place your safe zone starts.

Fill the Air—Have calming, family-friendly music playing. Try Classical, Baroque, soft classic rock, or ambient instrumental music for a peaceful, creative atmosphere. You can alternate other music that you like, but you will find that the most powerful homemaking sounds are likely to be classical. That music can stimulate a more quiet and cooperative presence in the home. Want more powerful music in your home? Sing. Yes, sing. Nobody cares if you don't have the voices of the latest pop singing groups. Just sing with your family and laugh about your singing. Encourage youngsters to sing and develop musical talents to warm your home. Singing and family music are wonderful tools for building memories of family heritage in your home. You can fill the air with a warm aroma from scented candles, potpourri, or fresh baked goodies. The warm, spicy, home-baked fragrance will bring thoughts of Grandma, holidays, and simply joy to your home.

Cover the Walls—Just as Heidi did, add family images, stories, and crafts that help to define and celebrate the family and its heritage. This is one of the important ways you will turn the house into your home and teach your walls to talk. How you decorate your home will speak to its family and their guests. You can teach your walls to remind you of how you want your family to feel about each other and their family heritage.

Plant a Garden—Children love to plant and see things grow. Planting a family vegetable or flower garden can be a wonderful addition to family time, work, and fun together. Give each child his or her own row to plant. Let them choose what they want to grow. Take pictures and chronicle the planting, watering, cultivating, and harvesting activities. Tree planting can also be a wonderful heritage-enriching addition to your home and yard, if you have the space and assume that you will be in the home for several years. You will likely spend far more for the garden than is justified in the harvest of the vegetables and flowers, but the return on the investment of family time and learning in the family heritage is invaluable.

Personalize Your Home—Name and talk to and about your home. Sound crazy? Try it. I am not talking about a name like you would give a dog or a car. Your home is a castle, a kingdom. Think Camelot, Arvonia, Celeste, or Mageenia, or Chateau de Jones. You can use simply Mansion or even Homey. The idea is that what you call your home adds to its separate and unique identity. Once you give it a name, talk to it. Treat your home like a family member. It will be a great listener and you may be amazed at how it talks back to you and what it may have to say. You will have the advantage of telling the kids, "I'm sure our home is happy (or not happy) when you (or we) treat her that way.

Play Together—Be sure to have a rich supply of board, card, and sports games as part of the heritage of your home. It is true that the family that plays together stays together. There is great value in learning to play by the rules, winning and losing graciously and the joy of the game above the joy of the win. So much of game playing now is focused on one-on-one electronic competition and involves warring and fighting and mayhem. That kind of play does not involve the kind of personal interactions, communication, and laughing that are so valuable to heritage-making lessons of the family board and card games of the past. Learning to laugh at and with your opponents, having fun, and building relationships through playing is becoming a lost art. Don't forget about the parlor, table tennis, croquet and ball games that bring family and friends together. Certainly there are some wonderful family and group electronic activities available on Nintendo Wii and other gaming platforms. Time to dust off the board game boxes and gather around the table to laugh and converse one with another.

Teach and Extend Hospitality—The Apostle Paul refers to the virtues of hospitality in his letters to Titus, Timothy, Peter and the Romans' churches (Romans 12:13; Titus 1:8; 1 Peter 4:9; 1 Timothy 3:2). Teaching our children to be hospitable and to enjoy serving people in their home is a heritage-building tradition of great value. Dinner parties where children learn to help prepare the home, table, meal, and to serve and cleanup are perfect training experiences for them to use good manners and laudable conversation as they are developing the attitude and the skills of hospitality.

8

HERITAGE-MAKING

Worth Your Time and Your Talent

KAREN WAS A TRUE PROFESSIONAL. EVERYTHING she did was professional, not perfect but professional. What's the difference? Well, to hear her explain it, "Professionals are responsible and dependable, on time and on target. They know what is expected, they evaluate, they commit, and they deliver." That pretty well sums up how Karen lived her life.

It was that professional attitude that had gotten Karen the grades, the scholarship, into the best school, the right interviews, the perfect job, and finally the great salary. It was that professional attitude and discipline that got her the reputation, the promotion, the assignment, and the opportunity to meet and work with Rick. Then it was Rick who got her. He got her to say yes, then got her the ring, got her to be so happy, and got her the house. And together they got their first son. Then it was Timmy—Timothy J. Martin, to be professionally correct—who got Karen to decide that it was time to stop being a professional, at least for the time being.

KAREN'S STORY

The ride had been great. I was successful, happy, and had learned a lot. Perhaps the most important thing I had learned was that success, in the workplace, usually comes at a high price and sacrifice to your personal life. For a woman to continue to succeed in the corporate world, most of us have to choose between family and job. From my perspective, there just didn't seem to be enough time to give what was needed to do both, with a truly professional focus.

One or the other had to take second place. I had seen it so often. The competition and struggle to climb up the corporate ladder had to come first if you were going to get to the top and stay there. There just wasn't time for much of anything else.

I attended a meeting once in my early college days, and the speaker made a strong impression on me. He quoted another educator, David McKay, who had stated, "No other success in life can compensate for failure in the home."[1] That really stuck with me. Still does. I had always equated real success with home and family. My apartment was not my home. It never would be. Talk of family always brought up an internal struggle between my professional self and that other maternal self that I knew was looking to emerge from the holding pattern. However, at that point, I was on the fast track toward a career that most women could only wish for. I had dreamed about it and that dream was coming true.

I was not married and had no prospects, and quite frankly I was happily consumed in my professional pursuits. A successful family and home life would come later, after my success in the workplace had been secured. And so I pursued, competed, sacrificed, and achieved. I was pretty successful and happy. Or so I thought.

Then I met Rick. That's when the equation for success quickly changed. When we decided to get married, settle down, and buy a home, the maternal me started seriously competing with the professional me. When Timmy came on the scene and changed us from a couple to a family, I was ready for the full transition. From the first time I held Timmy in my arms, I became clear about the difference between the joy of my profession and the joy of my motherhood. So I left the workplace; rather, I changed its location. I became a professional mom. I joined the at-home workforce.

I had friends who chose to continue to work and do the balancing act with childcare and homemaking. For some of them, the economics of the home and family's needs simply did not allow them the choice to leave the workplace. Others simply needed the workplace for their own sense of value, growth, and contribution. I understood all that. After all, I was the professional. Thankfully, I did not have to work for either of those reasons. Rick was a successful attorney and was more than happy to support my choice to be a valued stay-at-home mom.

I will admit it took a little time getting used to not feeling the demands and busyness of the business and the importance of my professional contributions. The transition to being a professional mom gave me a much deeper sense of satisfaction and a greater appreciation for my own mother—for all mothers. I would never again think, much less say, "just a stay-at-home mom" or "just a housewife." I was intent on being every bit as professional in my mothering as I had been about the other aspects of my life and career.

When Timmy was three, I began feeling that there was something missing in my professional mothering. I wasn't sure exactly what it was, but I knew that I needed to be more intentional about our play together and my parenting. I was reading books on parenting and child development, but I wanted something more to weld Timmy, Rick, and me into a stronger family. We weren't having problems or anything like that. I just wanted to be more, well, professional and intentional about my approach. I wanted Timmy to be clear that there was no place like home and that our family was special.

We wanted more children, but the stork must have forgotten our address because he just wasn't delivering. By the time Timmy turned five and was in school, I was even more concerned about preparing Timmy for his life outside of the home and away from our watchful eyes and protective arms. I guess every mom feels that way, especially about her first child. Timmy was my first priority, and helping him develop the life skills and successful character traits was job one. That was proving to be a real challenge to find tools to help me to do that professionally.

I checked out a few ideas, but I was looking for something tangible that really set us apart as a family. We were building on some of the fun family hobbies and traditions Rick and I had enjoyed in our own families. As we sorted through and established more of our own family identity, I realized we were really building a heritage of our own. The patterns and values of the past were important, but so were the new unique aspects of the Rick and Karen Martin family.

We were both active in our church and community. I worked in the children's program, and Rick worked with the youth ministry. The service and social connections at church were also aspects of our intentional family life priorities. We had friends, but I wouldn't call them really close friends. That was largely because our family focus was not quite what they had in mind. They were good people, but they had their own professional lives and priorities, so we just didn't get together much socially.

Then, one night while I was thinking about what was missing, I told Rick I was feeling a little empty. I told him I thought I needed a little more training. He suggested that maybe I was feeling a little empty-nest syndrome now that Timmy was going to kindergarten. That could have been part of it. Then I asked Rick a self-revealing question.

"Hey, babe. Are we doing enough for Timmy?"

He looked at me with an evaluating squint. "What do you mean? Does he need something?"

"Oh, no. I mean, I don't think so. I just have been feeling like I am supposed to be doing something more, well, important to help him be more ready for school and life."

Rick rolled over in bed and observed, "We've talked about this before, several times. Your professional side is showing through again. Maybe its you that needs something. Maybe a hobby or a part-time job is what the doctor would order."

"No, not a hobby. That's to frivolous. I need to be doing something that matters. Something that I can be more effective as a parent, as a mom. Do you know what I mean?"

Rick looked puzzled and shook his head. "Must be a girl or a mom thing." He rolled his eyes, and I hit him with a pillow. I knew he was kidding. He is a really sensitive guy.

"I'm serious, Rick! I'm going to find something I can do that will make me a better mom. I mean, I need something that lets me stretch me a bit. Maybe it is that I need to be a little more professional about my mothering. Is that okay with you?"

That was a loaded question and Rick new it. "Sure, honey. Whatever you want. Just don't turn Timmy into a guinea pig. And don't forget that you are a great mother, wife, and lover, Mrs. Richard Martin. Speaking of lover . . ."

He gave me one of those sweet little pecks on my cheek that was his way of saying good night and rolled over to his side of the bed. I switched the light off and rolled back over to cuddle with him. But I kept thinking about what it was I was really looking for that would provide training and resources for becoming more intentional and professional about my parenting.

I was lying there thinking about the possibilities when I heard Timmy cough and whimper. I slipped out of bed and into his room. He had kicked his covers off and was cold. I covered him up, and as I bent over to kiss his cheek, I remembered once again why I was a retired professional.

Turning to go back to bed, I knocked over a stack of storybooks on Timmy's nightstand. I loved reading to Timmy! That was one of my favorite things each afternoon. It was my special time with him. Rick got the bedtime-story shift, and not even Monday night football could pull him away from that treasured daddy duty! Timmy always wanted Rick to tell him the stories about when he was a little boy. And he loved hearing me tell him about when he was a baby and about his Grandpa and Grandma Martin and Uncle Paul and Uncle John.

I paused a moment before I shut Timmy's door, and the thought slipped into my mind from that meeting years before. *"No other success in life can compensate for failure in the home."* I certainly didn't want to see failure in our home. I wanted the success in the home that I know I was committed to and capable of creating. I just needed a few good ideas.

A couple of weeks later when I was picking Timmy up from school, Timmy's teacher, Mrs. Sorensen, handed me a notice and invitation to a "getting to know you" program the class was having the next week. She reminded me that Timmy was supposed to bring one of his favorite things to tell about. It could be a toy, book, or really anything. She shuddered a bit when she said she hoped no one had a pet snake this year! I got a good laugh out of her story about the little boy who brought his snake the year before. I assured her that Timmy didn't have a pet snake, but he had been asking his dad about a puppy. As of yet, that was not going to be his favorite thing. I wondered what it would be.

As it turned out, Rick had a court case that morning and was not able to go with us. Timmy had decided his favorite thing for the moment was the new Spider-Man costume he had selected for Halloween, even though it was nearly a month away. Timmy has this thing for Spider-Man and superheroes. I tried to persuade him to pick something else, but in the end, Spider-Man Timmy won out.

Each of the children had a "Favorite Thing" box they had made with their original artwork to decorate it. Inside was the thing they were going to talk about. He wanted to wear the costume, but the instructions said they were to put their favorite thing in a bag, and they would then put it in their box. I looked at all the boxes along the stage in front of the children and chuckled nervously at the thought that one of them might contain a snake! Timmy kept looking at me and smiling. He wasn't nervous, just excited. I could see myself in him as I watched him fidget waiting for his turn. Maybe Timmy Martin had a streak of professional in him too.

The class members took their turns sharing alphabetically. Timmy was toward the end of the program. Each child stepped to the front by the microphone, stated his or her name, and said, "This is one of my favorite things. It is a . . ." They then opened their box, pulled out the item and explained what it was and why it was important to them. It seemed like a really good foundation for public speaking, even for five-year-olds.

The first five children's favorite things included a Smokey the Bear, a Mr. "Z" action figure, a baby doll, a Lego set, and a batch of chocolate chip cookies that the little girl and her mom baked. That was a real hit!

Just before it was Timmy's turn, another boy, Juan, stood up. I had met his mother once or twice before, but I really didn't know the family. They were Hispanic and seemed really nice.

When Juan opened his box and pulled out his favorite thing, I was unprepared for his explanation and my reaction.

"My name is Juan La Rosa. This is one of my very most favorite books. It is the book that tells all about my family."

He held up the book and turned through the pages one by one, explaining that the pictures and story were all about his mother, father, grandparents, brothers, and sister. He was beaming with pride and excitement. I was not the only parent straining to see the book. It appeared to be a small hardbound book about eight inches square with maybe twenty to thirty pages.

When he sat down, Timmy stood up and excitedly opened his box.

Mrs. Sorenson had to remind him to tell everyone who he was. He giggled and looked at me with a sheepish grin.

"Oh yeah. I'm Timmy. Timmy Martin."

He glanced back at Mrs. Sorenson and she nodded to him to continue.

"This is my most favorite thing. It's my Spider-Man suit. Spider-Man is my favorite hero, and I'm going to be like him on Halloween."

I am sure I blushed a little with a mother's pride, but my mind was still thinking about Juan's family book. There was something about a child calling a book about his family his favorite thing. That seemed incredible to me. I couldn't wait for the program to finish so I could get a closer look at that book!

As soon as Mrs. Sorenson finished the program and thanked the children for sharing with their friends, I made a beeline first to Timmy and then to Juan and his mother. After giving Timmy my congratulatory hug, I saw about four other moms headed toward Juan's mom. But I got to her first! She remembered me from our earlier meeting. She greeted me as I approached her.

"Hello, Mrs. Martin. Good to see you again."

"Thanks, and please forgive me, but I've forgotten your first name."

"It's Elena, and yours?"

"Oh, I'm Karen. You have to be proud of Juan. He did a very good job."

"Yes, I remember you. Thank you. I think he did good."

About that time, the other moms were standing around us. I continued. "The family storybook he showed us looked amazing. May I see it?"

She looked at Juan and he smiled and took the storybook out of his box. It was clearly evident the other moms wanted to see it too. They all crowded around as I looked over the cover. *The La Rosa Family— 2010* was the title over a beautiful picture of the their family in an outdoor setting.

"Is all about our family," Elena said with a little pride showing through as she motioned to the cover picture.

I turned the cover to the pages. Each page featured one or more pictures of their family members involved in some family activity.

"We have lots of tradition and parties and we put some in the book."

Her English was a little broken, but we all got the picture. I wanted to take more time reading the details, but I could see the other mothers were just as interested as I was. I was impressed. The quality of the book was all so . . . *professional.*

"Where did you get it?" asked one of the other moms.

"We worked together to make it on the computer, and they sent it to us," Elena said a little sheepishly.

"Who is 'they'?" two of us asked in unison.

"Is my sister. She does it. She helped us. Is her business." Elena smiled.

I had a lot of questions, as did the other moms, but we all had kids tugging at us to go over for the refreshments the room mothers had prepared. I thanked Juan and Mrs. La Rosa and asked before I was whisked away by Timmy to the cookies, "Elena, I would like to talk with you more about your book sometime. Can I call you about it?"

"Oh, sure. You call me. I can tell you more."

After the refreshments, I kissed Timmy, and told him I would be back to pick him up after school. I took his Spider-Man suit and walked out to the car. I hoped I could catch Elena in the parking lot, but she must have still been answering the other mom's questions.

As I drove home, I couldn't get that book out of my mind. I kept thinking about it. *The La Rosa Family Book*. I heard myself say almost out loud, "The Martin Family Book." I knew that my curiosity and interest would have me calling Elena before the end of the day. What I didn't know was where that phone call was going to lead me.

As soon as Rick walked through the door, our superhero-suited son was there to tell his dad all about the program. I showed him the pictures I had taken and doted on Timmy's presentation a bit. Rick suddenly transformed after dinner into an evil-eyed menacing villain that required Spider-Timmy to rescue me. They wrestled on the living room floor, and despite Rick's superior size, somehow Spider-Timmy seemed to end up on top as the winner. Fully vanquished and full of spaghetti, Timmy and Rick settled into their bedtime reading ritual.

That was my first opportunity to get back to Elena about the book. When I called, Juan answered the phone.

"La Rosa residence, Juan speaking."

I had noticed Juan's politeness on the other few occasions I had been around him. He was charming, and his warmth and respectfulness spoke well of his parents and family.

"Juan, it's Timmy Martin's mom. You sure did a great job today in the program!"

"Thank you, ma'am. I will get my mother." It took her a minute to get to the phone.

"Hello, Mrs. Martin. Sorry, I was getting Aleta to bed."

"Oh, that's okay. Should I call back a little later?" I offered.

"No, no, she down now. This is good time."

"It was good to see you again at the school. And I am so impressed with Juan. He is such a gentleman when answers the phone."

"Thank you. Sometime he remembers, but sometime he forget."

"Well, he sure remembered today! I have to work on that with Timmy. What's the secret to your success with Juan's manners?"

"Is easy. Is Captain Crunch," she said matter-of-factly.

"Captain Crunch?"

"Yes. When they remember their manners they get to choose the cereal. When they forget, I choose. They choose Captain Crunch, I choose bran flakes. Next week maybe they get Captain Crunch again."

I laughed but took note of her reward system.

"Uh-huh. So that's the secret! Well, please tell him I thought he did a great job with his part on the program today."

"Thank you. He was very nervous about standing up in front of everybody. But I think he did good."

There was more than a little motherly pride in her response and it was well deserved.

"Elena, I was really impressed with the family storybook Juan showed us. Can you tell me a little more about it? You said your sister makes them?"

"Yes, she helps me to makes the books. She has many storybooks for her family. She does it with her computer. This one we did just las' month. Was so easy! Maybe you like to see my sister's books?"

"Are they like yours?"

Yes, and many more. She is coming to my house, I think Wednesday. Maybe you come and meet her?"

"Does she make storybooks for other people?"

"Yes, but mostly she helps people to make their own storybooks. She be happy to show you and tell you. Is her business. She works mostly at her house. She does this maybe two years. She likes it very much. You like to come and meet Carmen.?"

I was now more intrigued that ever. "I think I would like to do that. I think I would like that. When should I come?"

"Wednesday, I think ten in the morning, while the boys are in school. Is okay?"

"Great, I'll plan on it."

I told Rick about the La Rosa's family book and of my interest to understand more about how they make them. I knew he was listening politely and that to him it was probably just another girl thing. I wished he had seen it. I knew he would be interested if he saw it. That night I kept thinking about it. I was curious and excited to find out about making the books.

I don't know what I was expecting that Wednesday when I met Carmen. Looking back now, I realize how valuable the information she gave me has become. We have become really good friends.

Carmen is a beautiful and talented young woman about my age. She had been working as a legal aide before her daughter was born. She had planned to go back to work after her maternity leave. Then, after she used a friend's gift to make a baby storybook, Carmen changed her mind. I'm not sure if she just didn't want to miss out on the baby time or if she just loved making the storybooks so much that she didn't want to go back to work at the office. At any rate, Carmen described what she did as a personal publishing consultant. She explained how she helped people to capture their precious moments and stories of their families and put them into what she called "storybooks." It was a simple and exciting process that was the perfect thing for me. I immediately became her next client. My goal was to have the *Martin Family Book* done before Rick's birthday in a little over a month. She assured me I could do it and that she would coach me through the process.

The little family storybook was absolutely amazing! Everything about the book was extremely professional. Rick opened it after his birthday dinner with Timmy and me. Timmy knew we were giving daddy a family book, but I hadn't dared show it to Timmy, lest he slip and reveal the secret to Rick. As Rick opened the book and saw the cover, he gave me a questioning look and then opened it. Within a minute, I saw tears welling up in this court-hardened attorney's eyes. He wiped them away as he read our family storybook for the first time. His silence said it all. Rick later told me that storybook was without question, the single best gift he had ever received. I don't think he will ever again think that my storybooking projects are just another "girl thing."

The family storybook quickly became Timmy's favorite bedtime story, and Rick and he get the message about my love for them and about how special our family is again and again. They love seeing the pictures of our family and themselves. I think that is a "guy thing." That was my first Martin family storybook.

Carmen and I became really good friends. The storybooks are just what I needed for being more effective in my quest for being more intentional about my parenting. Now I'm working on our next Martin family storybook. It will be another surprise for both Rick and Timmy. I think it will give Rick goose bumps to find out that this time it will feature *four* of us.

WORTH YOUR TIME AND TALENTS—PERSONAL AND PROFESSIONAL FULFILLMENT

"She openeth her mouth with wisdom; and in her tongue is the law of kindness. She looketh well to the ways of her household, and eateth not the bread of idleness. . . . Her children arise up, and call her blessed; her husband also, and he praiseth her." (Proverbs 31:26–28)

These days, being "just a housewife" or "just a stay-at-home mom" seems to mean that you don't have anything better or more important to do—that you aren't capable of doing something more significant or professional. How could anyone with family perspective and real love get that *so* wrong? Guarding and guiding the next generation of world's leaders, scientists, theologians, philosophers, doctors, lawyers, teachers, and parents has got to be the most important and worthy of all professions.

Proverbs tells us much about the importance and worth of virtuous women. It tells how her virtues lead her to speak wisdom and kindness and how she works hard to take care of the needs of her family. It also tells us that her children and husband praise her and call her blessed. These are indeed the rewards Karen found in making her storybooks.

The wisest investment a woman can make with her time, talents, and her experience will be in her intentional parenting. Other professional women may look at their title plate on the door, read their name in the corporate annual report, and may be toasted by colleagues and competitors. But it is intentional mothers who will be praised in the courts of heaven by family members and angels.

Intentional parenting is proactive character-building and heritage-making. Every mom who snaps a picture at a birthday party, at the zoo, at the school program, or of the spaghetti-covered toddler's face *is* a family heritage-maker. Every mom who collects drawings, report cards, and ribbons; makes scrapbooks; or seems driven to collect, retain, and preserve the evidence of her children's success, is being intentional about the most important things in her children's lives, and her own.

Every dad who plans and conducts a picnic outing, family vacations, or attends a child's baseball or soccer game *is* being intentional about his parenting. Every parent who helps to organize and conduct a family reunion, birthday parties, and remembers and makes anniversaries a priority, is an intentional family heritage-maker. Every parent who establishes family values, boundaries, rules, and standards is being intentional and is helping to build the children's character.

These intentional parents are not just picture-takers nor picture-keepers; intentional parents preserve and promote their family's heritage and life to protect and direct the success of their children and their family. Storybooks are all about strengthening the family unit to ensure their pride and commitment to family security and success.

Intentional parents connect all the pictures, pieces, and stories of family history and weave them with the memory threads of their ancestors' beliefs, standards, and values. They identify and celebrate their family heroes, past and present. Their children come to know who they are and what they stand for by the example of their parents and by the heritage of their progenitors.

Intentional parents find great satisfaction and personal fulfillment in preparing their children to stand up and to stand out.

Being intentional about parenting is something every parent can do. A great place to start, like Karen, is with your family story. It could look something like hers did:

Front Cover: Recent picture of your family in front of your home.

Title: *The Martin Family Book—How We Came to Be*

Page 1: How it all started—a scanned copy of your wedding announcement and a picture from your marriage or reception and a couple of paragraphs about how you met, dated, fell in love, and married.

Pages 2–3: Rick in the beginning—a short story, maybe three or four paragraphs, about Rick's early life and family pictures of him and his family before meeting Karen.

Pages 4–5: Karen in the beginning—pictures and a short story, maybe three or four paragraphs about Karen's early life and family before meeting Rick.

Pages 6–7: Courtship and Marriage—more of the pictures and story about meeting, dating, falling in love, and getting married.

Pages 8–9: Before the Kids—pictures and the story about school and work interests prior to their first child.

Pages 10–11: First to Arrive—the story of pregnancy, anticipation, birth and life to that point of the first child—pictures to match.

Pages 12–13: Second Child to Arrive—same thing for child number two.

Pages 14–15: Etc. to cover for the number of children you have.

Pages 16–17: Rick's Family—pictures and text about his parents, grandparents, and siblings on his side of the family.

Pages 18–19: Karen's Family—pictures and text about her parents, grandparents, and siblings on her side of the family.

Pages 20–21: What Our Family Likes to Do—pictures and explanation of family interests, sports, and activities.

Page 22: Things We Value Most—identify and describe your major values and beliefs, things you stand for, and your commitment to each other with representative pictures of the family.

It's a simple recipe for a short twenty-two-page family storybook that intentionally establishes your family heritage and character. You can bet that it will become an instant hit with its central characters and will be on the family's best bedtime story list. There are several ways to bind your book. Staples, three ring binders, and the like will quickly be destroyed. You will appreciate one of the several hardbound self-publishing options that are available like what Karen did.

LEGACY-SECURING INTENTIONAL PARENTING PROJECT SUGGESTIONS

The First Family Storybook—Plan and complete your first family storybook. And no, it doesn't have to be professional. You can be assured that it will touch some of your less-than-fulfilled interests as a mom and spouse. At the same time, it will be a great resource to your roles as intentional parents.

Gather Your Family Photos—Pictures are such an important part of family heritage-making and storybooking. Be sure your photo records are secure—both prints and digital pictures. Sort and have your prints scanned and uploaded to a secure storage system to protect them. Many, if not most, of them, are irreplaceable. There are too many horror stories of floods, tornadoes, fires, thefts, and moving losses to leave the images and memories of your family heritage at risk. When you have them scanned and uploaded, the task is easy and fun. It will take a little time, but it is a real trip down memory lane that will reconnect you to family stories you have almost forgotten.

Involve the Kids—Have your kids help you make a simple storybook for their dad for Father's Day or a birthday, or for no reason—just for a "We love you" gift. They can put a picture of them and their dad with a simple story of why they love him so much. Make sure you get a page or two in the book too. Be sure to have a clean handkerchief ready for him when he opens the book.

Capture an Activity—Take pictures of a birthday, outing, or other special event and combine them into a storybook. Practice writing the unusual, unique, funny, and touching aspects of the story. There is an important difference between a storybook and a photo journal book. Photo books focus on the pictures; storybooks focus on the family.

Kid Books—Have your kids make little storybooks with drawings and handwritten stories as practice and preparation to become full partners in the family heritage-making and storybooking process. Don't be surprised if a couple of these projects end up being good enough to publish. Think of the impact that can have on a child to know that he or she is a published author!

Family Storybook Album—You can begin collecting, writing, and publishing an annual family album. When you do digital storybooking, you can work a few minutes or hours or days on a project, close it, and start right up where you left off when you have more to add to the project. You can do a scrap, post, or binder book and add a page or two at a time as you complete them. Or you can complete the year of pages and finish the binding to make copies for family members for Christmas or New Year's gifts. Organize your digital pictures by placing them in a folder labeled by month (January 2013, February 2013, and so on). Your monthly pictures will jar your memory so you can journal the important family events well before they fade.

Help Someone—Find someone at a retirement care center or shelter or a shut-in and interview him or her about his or her life. Help him or her select pictures about important events and aspects of his or her life that the person does not want his or her posterity to forget. You will likely have to do the work of putting the storybook together because that person just doesn't have the technical experience on a computer, nor the confidence, eyesight, health, or mental stamina to do it solo. These projects of vicarious family heritage-making services will ensure that you save the meaning of lives that are soon to end. It is a treat and a reward you will not want to miss.

NOTES

1. David O. McKay, quoted from J. E. McCulloch, *Home: The Savior of Civilization* (1924); in Conference Report, April 1964, 5.

9

THE TRADITION MAKER

Things and Times to Remember

KIM HEAPS IS ARGUABLY THE FAVORITE ADULT AT the Crestview Elementary School. She represents the best part of the day—lunch. She has worked at Crestview since the school opened. Last year she had second-generation students greet her. These were the children of children she had known as sixth graders when the school was new.

Every year there are new students who are the brothers or sisters of students who have known and loved her. These siblings come with the expectation that Ms. Heaps makes the best food and the best friend. Somehow, Ms. Heaps always knows when it is their birthday. She always has a little something to make their birthdays a special treat when a birthday student passes by her in the lunch line. She is a living legend at Crestview.

Kim is no less a legend in her own family. She is the favorite aunt for all the girls and for most of the boys. If she were a little more of a fisherman too, it would have been a unanimous first place with the boys as well. While no one is taking a poll, all the nephews and nieces look forward to her visits, parties, reunions, and her gifts. To quote them, "They are *awesome*!"

But Kim is not just a great cook and party planner. She is always the first one chosen for family softball teams. She has hiked about every trail on the state mountaineering guidebook, and she knows more knots than the local Scoutmaster. She can fix the bikes, build bird houses, and is the family's best handyman. But her greatest title is that of the family tradition maker. Kim singularly assures that all of the important Heaps family traditions are carried through each year. Just like Tevye from *Fiddler on the Roof*, for her, family and traditions are inseparable.

Oddly, with all of that talent and love oozing from Kim, Cupid has thus far passed her by. Perhaps that's why she seems to have so much love and time for her nieces, nephews, and elementary school kids. Maybe it's that she is so involved with her extended family and the community that Cupid hasn't been able to catch up with her to make a match. That was not the only thing that had not found its way into Kim's life. Kim did not own a computer, nor did she want to learn to use one.

So far, Kim had been able to avoid the face-off with the technology monster. Although she knew that sooner or later she was going to have to succumb to the demand. Her nephew Chris had offered to show her how. He said it would be "so easy," but then he was a whiz kid in his sophomore year in computer technology at the college.

That offered gift, and a few visits with Chris, became the key that opened the door to an entirely new world for Kim. Who would have ever guessed that Kim would be the first in her family to have a computer in her kitchen!

KIM'S STORY

Okay, I admit it. I was wrong. But I had my reasons, or so I thought. I was what my nephew Chris called a computer illiterate. He said I was a world-class lunch lady, a world-class aunt, and that he had more fun with me growing up than most of his friends combined. But he said he was worried that we were growing apart because we no longer could speak the same language—computers!

I told Chris that sounded like some generational gap nonsense. He was hitting me up again about learning how to use a computer. I told him that I didn't need a computer and that I had nothing to compute.

I kept putting Chris off until one Saturday morning he just showed up at my front door with the computer in a box. He wouldn't take "no" for an answer and proceeded to set it up at the kitchen table. I wasn't going to risk offending him again. So I decided that I had better humor him. I sat down and watched as he gave me my first lesson—how to turn it on.

For some reason, I let down my guard as he continued to reveal how to go from typewriter to word processing on the computer. Maybe it was Chris's excitement about sharing his own passion with me, or maybe it was because I now knew how to turn the thing on, but something changed in me that day. The result was a deal maker! I would fix him dinner each night he returned to help get me up and going on "my" computer.

I had been racking my brain trying to figure out what I would give for my next family Christmas gift. I didn't think that I was ready to tackle a family history, but now with my computer in the kitchen, I might just try getting an updated family calendar together.

I'd thought that maybe they would be okay with a case of Auntie Kim's Apple Butter and some fresh rolls for the gift this year. The debate was which to do—cooking the apples in the kitchen or making a calendar from my Apple in the kitchen? The more I thought about it, the more excited I got about the calendar.

Chris came over to eat dinner with me and to get me ready for the Internet connection that was scheduled for the next day. All through dinner we talked about how I could set up a family calendar and what could go into it. All the dates, reminders, pictures, even a few memories of some of the family's best traditions could all be incorporated into a digital family calendar.

"Auntie," Chris said, "just think about it, you can have each month with pictures of the family members whose birthdays fall on that month. We could put a small picture on their birth dates. We could list all the important family events for each month. You could put your favorite recipes for the holiday treats and feasts of the month. Heck, we could even feature ancestors on their birth date months or anniversaries. You could feature all the great things about the Heaps family legacy. Best of all, we could print a calendar for you to give for Christmas presents. You could update the calendar each year and add or take away what you wanted. It would be really simple, and it would sure be fun for the rest of us. Really, it would be so easy!"

The things he talked about seemed too good to be true! That first calendar was a learning process. Now I am on the fourth edition, and every year it gets better and easier. Yet it seems to be the best Christmas present I can give. I certainly get more compliments and thanks for the annual gift than I ever got for the apple butter and rolls. We have discovered that one of the most important things to keep the traditions of family is the reminders and pictures of those events from last year that we incorporate into the new year's calendar. That is how the whole Auntie Kim Calendar Tradition got started. Now everyone in the family calls it "The Heaps Family Calendar," and I still keep the computer in the kitchen.

THE POWER OF TRADITIONS—A HERITAGE OF FEASTING AND FUN

"And thou shalt rejoice in thy feast, thou, and thy son, and thy daughter, and thy manservant, and thy maidservant, and the Levite, the stranger, and the fatherless and the widow, that are within thy gates." (Deuteronomy 16:14)

The cyclic events of nature and the significant events of history have always spawned celebrations of progress and remembrance. Most of those celebrations included a feast. Ancient Israel and modern Jews and Christians participate in religious celebrations and feasts. The feast of Tabernacles, the Passover, the Festival of Unleavened Bread, the Pentecost, and the Feast of Weeks had specific dates and ritual processes.

The most common tradition and celebration is the Sabbath day. While the specific day varies among various groups, the commitment to observe the event is common throughout the world among most religious sects. Remembering and participating in traditions is an important part of a religious life. Jews and Christians rest from their labors on Sunday. Muslims have their Friday call to communal prayers. In Western society, often the biggest family meal of the week is Sunday dinner. For so many, that is a time and a tradition to get together and to share in the joy of family and heritage.

The common, traditional celebrations listed on most Western calendars for reference and for coordination of scheduling priorities vary somewhat country-to-country. In the United States, the commonly observed holiday celebrations and feasts that have become traditions for most families include: New Year's Eve, New Year's Day, Martin Luther King, Jr. Day, Presidents Day, Valentine's Day, Easter, Memorial Day, Independence Day, Labor Day, Veterans Day, Thanksgiving Day, and Christmas.

Hundreds of other community and cultural group defined holidays can overload your calendar and make it hard to find room for family-specific events and traditions. Businesses and communities often seek to leverage those holidays as opportunities for increasing business and shopping activities.

The original and traditional significance and purpose for many of the holidays has faded for many modern observers. The original purposes for the celebrations and feasts have largely given way to the focus on "time off work and out of school" that avail time together with family and friends for trips and parties. The holy days have become holidays and days for marketers and business to promote their products and services.

This shift away from the tradition's original focus on remembering and celebrating a specific event, person, or achievement has weakened the traditions and heritage-enriching power of the events. It is remembering the purpose and understanding the meaning of the celebration that engenders thoughts and feelings of remembering, gratitude, and recommitment. These are the real powers of family traditions and their celebrations.

It is wonderful to gather with family and friends for any celebration. However, we would never think of participating in a birthday party without honoring and celebrating the person whose birthday it is. To do this would miss the real purpose and opportunity of the celebration. The intentional heritage-maker should consider how to use the heritage-enriching opportunities at their celebrations and feast for their "traditional" holidays as well. These are grand opportunities to revisit and recommit family members to family heroes, values, beliefs, and heritage.

FAMILY TRADITIONS

The best and potentially most powerful traditions are those associated with the people and the significant events and celebrations of your own family. There are three powerful aspects for leveraging the power of your family's traditions. They include anticipation, participation, and reflection.

Families look forward to their traditions. The longer the tradition is in place, the more it becomes a mile marker on the family annual calendar, and the more it will be anticipated as an important and heritage-enriching activity for the family. Participation starts with the planning of the tradition. Planning for the tradition celebration should involve as many members of the family as possible. Planning includes reminding all family members to clear their calendars for the event. Preparations can include purchasing a card or gift for the person being celebrated, helping to decorate for the event, or preparing food. Talking about the event and sharing anticipation excitement with those to be honored or celebrated also adds to the unifying significance of the event.

Participation in the tradition is a reminder of the importance and reason for the event or person being celebrated. Participation should be more than just being there. Participation is active and happy involvement. The term *party pooper* can refer to someone who does not attend. It can also be someone who does attend but does not really engage in the celebration. This person can be a wet blanket on the celebration that robs it of its warmth and unifying value. Teaching the family to really look forward to and to engage in the celebration strengthens family traditions.

The tradition's full cycle and highest value is achieved in revisiting its memory. It is in the reflection and savoring the event that gives the tradition its unifying influence. It is in the remembering that the greatest influence and heritage-building purpose is achieved.

Emblems of the celebration in the home (the gift, pictures, stories, albums, and books) extend and expand the celebration's influence, even for those who did not participate. Heritage-makers leverage the purpose, anticipation, participation, and memories of their family traditions.

LEGACY-SECURING INTENTIONAL PARENTING PROJECT SUGGESTIONS

List and Calendar—Start now to calendar all your current family holidays, vacations, reunions, and traditions. Find places on the calendar where you may have two or more weeks without some tradition and creatively add simple traditions to close the gap. They can be simple feasts, themed outings, picnics, or dates. The key is the constant reminder of things you do together as a family or as parents.

Define and Plan—Create a detailed overview of each of your major traditions. Define what you will traditionally do and what will make the tradition unique, fun, and memorable. Focus on the values, beliefs, and remembrances that will be included in the tradition. Assign various elements of the tradition event to responsible members of the family.

Family Counsel—Have a family gathering to discuss, plan, assign, and begin the implementation of your traditions. Discuss and implement the anticipation, preparation, participation, and reflection aspects of the traditions. Your explanation of what traditions are and how you plan to become a tradition-celebrating family will depend on the age and maturity of your children. Taking these first steps will begin to lay the foundations for strong commitments to the traditions and heritage it builds and the legacy it can carry forward.

Flyers—Use flyers to announce and invite people to events. You can make simple flyers and post them on the refrigerator and family bulletin boards or even mail them to children to add to the special nature and anticipation of the event. The flyers can be simple who, what, when, where, and why notices. You can also include preparation assignments or participant emails as reminders and can be effective ways to help them remember the upcoming event.

Talk It Up!—Excitement is often found in talking about the event. At meals and in conversations with family members, build the purpose, anticipation, significance, and excitement of the tradition. Ask the kids about their excitement for the activity. Let them invest in the event.

Dress It Up!—You can make things special and important by dressing up for it. While it doesn't need to be formal attire, it might be a great idea to do something formal once in a while. Set the table formally. Let your children help you. Remember, a little praise goes a long way. Best dress, especially for dads, can add a dimension of importance to the event. Teach the family good table manners and etiquette. Teach your young men to stand when a lady enters or leaves the room and to assist the ladies into their chairs. Teach them that these things are done not because they are girls and need the help, but because they are men and that is their privilege and duty. Teaching the kids to dress up and to clean up for important events is an important aspect of good grooming and culture. It will give them confidence and grace in public and in events where their peers will likely be looking to them for leadership and example.

Capture the Event—Assign someone to act as the family picture taker and someone to write the story of the activity for the family album, storybook, and newsletter. Moms and dads may need to help in the story and picture taking until the children can do it on their own. Letting your children carry those responsibilities is the core value of having the traditions. They are laboratory activities to provide confidence-developing experience in all the aspects of the tradition and its associated celebrations and feasts.

Tell the Story—We talk about the most important things in our lives. We talk with each other and with friends and associates. Sharing the experience and associated values and joy of our traditions will encourage your children to be intentional about their traditions and parenting, and will deepen your family's appreciation of these special activities they do together. One of the best ways to tell the story is to write the story of the event and add it to your family's annual storybook or scrapbook album. Ideally, you will do this while the memory is fresh and before you download and forget your pictures.

Savor the Tradition—Savoring is the process of enjoying the memory, without the stress and pressure of planning, preparing, and making it happen, after the stress and mess are gone. The review of the event in conversation and in seeing the pictures and reliving the story adds to the sweetness of the tradition, like opening and using a jar of jam you made together last fall. No mess, just sweetness. By the way, home canning is another great tradition to consider.

Thank You—Just as you would give a thank-you card to a host of a party or event you attended, give family members thank-you notes or cards for their work and contribution in making the activity a success. This honors their help and teaches them another important lesson about being gracious and appreciative.

10

NOT PERFECT BUT PERFECTING

Heritage-Making Borrowed and Built

F RIENDS OF KELLY REDD WILL TELL YOU THAT SHE IS
the most intentional person they know. They will tell you that she
is an overachiever to say the least. She is always the first in line for
any worthy cause or service. She's quick to consider, commit, compete,
and complete whatever she takes on. It is not just her name that is Redd.
Everything about Kelly is "red." Friends all agree that she has a "bright"-
red personality and character.

Kelly is a bright, energetic, enthusiastic, eternal optimist. She seems
to have a positive attitude about everything. Many who know her envy
her ability to get it all together. Some see Kelly's life as just about perfect.
She seems to have a perfect husband—who has a perfect job—perfect
kids, a perfectly tidy house, and the perfect yard. But looks can be deceiv-
ing, especially when the look that comes back from the mirror is not so
perfectly convinced.

Kelly's response to such allegations will likely be, "Perfect! Are you
kidding?" Like all perfect stories, all you have to do is turn the page to
find that Kelly's story is a long way from perfect. Her story is still being
written and some of the chapters are triumphs and some are tragedies.

Much of Kelly's situation and story are common to most women.

Trying to figure it out and get it together is no easy task for even the best multitaskers. What may not be so common was the absolutely amazing transformation from her difficult, sometimes tragic childhood. Her story is a testimony of how a few genuine, caring, and selfless people can change the head and hearts of a rebellious teenager. It is also a testimony of how one man could see into the perfect possibility of a woman whose will and determination had been forged in the fire of affliction and self-preservation.

KELLY'S STORY

I suppose that those who know my past would be amazed at just how far I have come. The fact that I even survived my childhood is a miracle. I was born to a mother who was little more than a child herself. I don't know who my father was. I endured the transitions and abuse of three stepfathers before I was fourteen. I have four siblings from those relationships. All of us developed a pretty negative view of family life from the effects of the constant upheaval. We were all victims of too little love and affection, too little acknowledgment, and too much loveless touching and hurting.

I guess I was naturally pretty. Because of the situation of my childhood, that was not an advantage. Being cute and living in the wrong area of town always seemed to draw the wrong kind of attention. I learned early that even relatives couldn't be trusted to be allowed to be left alone with me. It's no wonder why I developed such a powerful distrust of people, especially men. I came to shun many of the people I knew more than total strangers. That too was a dangerous attitude that deepened my distrust and anger.

Without some unseen help and some incredibly good people, that attitude could have made my early life story much more tragic than triumphant. I guess you could say that my family roots were pretty shallow. Thank goodness I was grafted into a different part of the family tree. It is still amazing to me, I guess to all of us, that graft took and my new roots have overcome the shallowness of my past.

Things had gotten so bad at home that at fifteen I left my house; It really wasn't much of a home. I went to live with my Uncle Bill and Aunt Vicki Morris. They were the only stable people I knew in my family up to that time. Before then, I don't think anything in my life felt safe or secure. The Morrises were really good people. They had three grown children,

Rick, Roni, and Rachel. Aunt Vicki said that *R* in their name was to remind them to choose the "**r**ight." Uncle Bill laughed and said it was to remind them to "**r**epent." Before coming to live with the Morris family, I didn't know what "repent" was, and I wasn't all that sure about what was right either. That all changed after I began drawing in the nourishment and felt the nurture of their home, family, and the effects of their intentional parenting.

The Morrises' three "Rs" were all older than me, and they all took a little sister interest in me. They are all much like their parents—really good people. They were and continue to be a shining example of what an intentional family that has got it together is like. I like to think that I was grafted onto the roots of their family tree because God knew that would save my life and give me a life worth living. I guess I'm still trying to thank him and prove that belief to be true.

Living with the Morrises became a window for me to see a different and wonderful world of family. However, my short-lived childhood and too-fast young adult life often put me in difficult situations and conversations with them. I never doubted that they were committed to me and to my happiness. I had never experienced that kind of commitment before the Morrises. Through it all, I came to know that significant personal transformation often takes that kind of interpersonal commitment.

By the time I graduated from high school, I had some of my rough edges rubbed off and some of their goodness rubbed in. The combination prepared me for an exciting albeit challenging adventure. That adventure was a new beginning that began with my perception of me. Mine was a journey of trying to figure out who I really was. My adoptive family helped me to see who I really could and wanted to be. Becoming that person is a work in progress.

The Morris family was active in their church, and I came to know them as very faithful people. Now I look back and see them as very faith-filled people. I didn't realize then just how much of that faith was being leveraged for me at the time. Eventually it was that faith and constancy that convinced me that *their* way to a happy-ever-after was what I wanted. To be sure, my journey has proven that "happy ever after" does not mean happy all along the way! It also has proven that learning to leave the past in the past and the effects of the past behind you is not easy, but it is possible and that it is worth the struggle.

I was smart enough to get by in school, even amid all the turmoil of my grade school and junior high school years. Like most kids, I was not smart enough to do as well as I could have and should have done. That started to change when I became a member of the Morris family. Average was not good enough for them, and they encouraged and pushed me to do better. Before long, average was not good enough for me either! I think that's what started my passion for personal perfection. The Morrises guided me to self-discovery and self-actualization through what I have come to know was their way of intentional parenting. They knew who I could be and who they wanted me to become long before I discovered and embraced that vision. I think of them and their parenting as the craftsmen of my character.

At first, my high school experience was bittersweet. It was bitter because of my lack of clear direction and the constant feeling of being different and not good enough. At the same time, it was sweet because with the Morrises I was safe and not afraid of the people who I lived with anymore. By the end of my sophomore year, the graft in my life was taking on some of the strength of their roots. I didn't have their blood, but I was being infused with their values and heritage. Although that heritage came from a different line of the family, they were able to help me discover and embrace it as my own. Now I am passing on that same heritage to my family.

Like too many kids growing into adults, I had to battle the effects of too much of the wrong kind of attention from people who were not who I thought they were. I was scarred from all types of abuse. I had been ignored and often sought self-esteem from others in self-defeating and destructive ways. The challenge of my childhood had led me to have low self-esteem and low expectations for myself. That was the reality of my early school years. The thought process of those patterns was difficult to change. Changing or transforming my mind was hard work, and it could not be accomplished alone. Changing how I thought about me came by association with people who thought differently about me. That has become one of the grand lessons of my life. Transformation is a shared journey and a shared way of living. Discovering who you can be, who you choose to be, and accepting the new you is the very process that makes you who you are. It is an intentional transformation that others can start and influence, but that you must discover, embrace, and complete.

I think that is what family is all about, our joint transformation. The parents are raising the kids, but in the process, the kids are raising and transforming the parents. Raising the children is how parents learn to be intentional about their priorities and their heritage and character developing efforts. It's a journey, and for me it has become a perfectly exciting, challenging adventure. It lets me take the lessons of my past and use them as stepping-stones, rather than stumbling blocks, on my journey to discovering and knowing me. This, my heritage, then has become the substance that I draw on for my own intentional parenting of the values, standards and character discussions I have with my own children.

Before the Morrises, I had few close friends. Looking back, I can see that good friends and family friends played a vital role in transforming my thinking and my choices. The new friends were also transplants from my new associations with their friends and members of their church. Some of those girls have become lifelong friends. They continue to fill a deep need I suspect every woman has for understanding and nonjudgmental companionship and communication. Really, they are the sisters I never had. They are the friends that know that neither me, nor my life is perfect, while others may see the pretty blonde who appears to be so with it. Still, the woman looking back from the mirror reminds me that I am definitely working on it, and so is my family.

By the time I graduated from high school, my birth mother had done some growing up too. She had a steady job and a steady husband that treated her and me much better. We both see our lives of the past as victims of circumstances that neither of us could change then. Even though I call her Mom, I look at her more as a friend now. "Mother" has a different meaning to me now. I think she really understands that and that was why she was supportive of the Morrises adoption of me after high school. Really, Aunt Vicki was the mother who rescued and raised me. Her influence and counsel continues to give me a healthy, hopeful, and healing perspective on the occasional reminders and pains that come from my less-than-Morris-like childhood. She did not give me life, but she definitely gave my life new meaning, perspective, and purpose. It was she who helped to birth my character. I will always call her Mother.

I guess all girls need continued mothering and mentoring. I've got a lot of learning ahead of me, but some of the toughest lessons are clearly behind me now. I have to take regular refresher lessons to help keep me clear on who I am and where I am going.

Now my priorities have transformed or shifted from a focus on me to a focus on intentional parenting of my own family. That priority change all started when Kyle Taylor decided and convinced me that he couldn't live without me. I think the truth is that he chased me until I caught him!

The story of our meeting, dating, fighting, making up, and getting engaged were worthy of a harlequin romance novel! I'm still amazed that he put up with my up-and-down, on-and-off roller coaster relationship! Kyle was and is the perfect change agent for me. He contends that I was the perfect catalyst to make him want to settle down! The truth is that we are really good for each other. I think he discovered who I really was or could be even before I did.

I still get goose bumps when I think about the continuing journey of our courtship! Like all fires, we have to take care to feed the flame. He really follows his father's example of treating his mom with respect. I guess you can tell I think he's a pretty perfect guy, most of the time.

It would take a whole book to tell you even a few of the mystery, adventure, and drama stories of our meeting and marriage. Just learning to talk to each other was like learning a new language for me! Learning to listen to each other was like an advanced psychology course. I'm not sure which was more difficult for Kyle—learning to dance with me or learning to share the TV remote! We're still working on both of those family-life skills and challenges. However, I think I am getting better at letting him lead in the dance of family living. And these days, he hardly ever picks up the TV controller. But then come to think of it, neither do I!

One of the hardest things for me to learn was to figure out and accept how to counsel with Kyle and then learning to take turns leading. In any relationship there needs to be communication, consideration, joint decision, and then action. The leadership of that action is usually coordinated or lead by one of the partners. It was tricky to explain to him what I wanted and then make him think it was his idea all along! No, actually, that was something we both had to learn, and we are still learning. Helping Kyle lead required me to fully trust and let go of my need to control. Now I find great satisfaction in being his counselor and partner. It's a different but most rewarding kind of partnership of shared control and trust. We still step on each other's toes occasionally, but we know when we do and we are getting faster at apologizing and getting back into step.

That understanding came doubly hard for me because I didn't have that example of a good husband or father in my early years. Also Aunt Vicki and Uncle Bill did their counseling with each other in private, so I didn't see exactly how they did it. Previously, I had no role model for me to see how a stable husband and wife processed decision-making. Oh, the stories I could tell about battles won and lost in the early years of our marriage! I finally figured out that I had all the influence I needed when I was committed to *what* was right, not *who* was right. We also discovered that discussing and making decisions should never be done when either or both of us were tired or rushed. That was a important discovery. We do our best communicating and decision-making when our knees are on the floor and when are heads are on the pillow. I highly recommend it!

We also discovered that we were different in our communication needs. I suspect we're not that much different from other men and women. At least my friends seem to echo our experience. I am a talker, and he is a doer. It's that simple. I need to talk about things. I need to tell the story. Kyle wants and needs to fix it, take care of, and to be done with it, so he can move on to the next thing to fix. He only wants to listen long enough to understand what he needs to do, to get it taken care of, and to get done with it, regardless of what it is. I on the other hand need to tell the whole story. It's the telling that's important to me. That drives Kyle nuts! I need to use a lot more words doing it than he thinks is necessary to give him the general picture so he can get the issue handled.

For a while, that made me think that he was a terrible listener and really didn't care about how I was feeling about "it." Finally, I got through to him. I explained that sometimes I didn't want him to fix it. I just wanted him to hear me out. I needed him to understand and acknowledge that "it" was a big deal to me whatever "it" is. On another communication front, we've found that generally Kyle doesn't like talking about his work. He comes through the door and unless there is some crisis, and often there is, I ask what happened at work. You probably know the answer. The conversation usually goes like this.

"Hi, honey! How was work?"

"Okay."

"What happened?"

"Oh nothing much."

Nothing much! How can he say that? He's been away nine or ten hours, and nothing happened? In my first hour I had to navigate through three crises at the same time. I was getting the wash in and the garbage gathered and out to the cans. Then I was handling six phone calls with friends and neighbors who needed my advice on their crises and our schedules. By the time Kyle got home, my list of what happened was so long it would take the rest of the night just to fill him in on what he missed while he was at work doing. Nothing much!?

Anyway, it used to drive me nuts that Kyle would say nothing happened at work. What I've discovered that is just another of those "man thing" differences. Men generally don't want to rehash or reprocess their battles. They want to leave their work at work. They need to retire to their castles.

Turning a hectic house with several little destroying angels into a castle is definitely a challenge for the best intentional parent. More often than not, it is a losing battle. It is a task that I'm far from perfect at. Our castle is rarely perfectly ready by the time I hear King Kyle drive up. What's helped me was to get Kyle in the habit of calling when he's leaving his work and heading for home. That way I can gauge and initiate our last-minute clean-up crusade before His Majesty's return. I think he's on to me, though. When Kyle gets home and I'm a little behind in my housework, he picks up a broom or puts on an apron to help. I can thank his dad for that bit of example and helpful heritage. And no, you can't borrow him.

We have also discovered that multitasking is not Kyle's forte. He agrees that he would make a terrible stay-at-home Dad or castle keeper. We have both come to accept that the perfect home is a transitory thing. Like our welcome mat says:

Welcome

Although you'll find our house a mess,

Come in, sit down, converse.

It doesn't always look like this.

Some days it's even worse!

We share one job and priority, which we discuss often—our commitment to intentional parenting priorities with our children. Our shared determination is to do everything we can to give them as perfect a family foundation as possible. We want to help them to develop the standards and character traits they will need to be successful in their lives and with their families. That doesn't mean that any of us are perfect people, or that we expect them to be perfect and to get everything right. What it means is that we are committed to have as perfect a home life as possible. We are building a foundation of shared family values and priorities—together.

We are making certain that our children feel loved and are aligned with our family standards and rules. Getting the kids to understand and embrace them is a work in progress too. I must admit that sometimes it feels like a battle in progress! I want them to have what I didn't have, and Kyle wants them to have all the advantages he did have. Sometimes they let us know that they want something else entirely. Our negotiations are learning experiences for all of us. We try to make our children active participants in the process of our parenting discussions.

Our family started with Michael. He was about as perfect a baby as a mother could hope for—especially a first baby. Redd number two, Melanie, was a different story. She definitely had a timetable and mind of her own. When I found out that another little one had finally agreed to join our family, I had a bit of a meltdown. Michael was entering third grade, and Melanie was in preschool. I began reflecting on some of my early school experiences and monsters. One Sunday afternoon, Kyle could tell I was struggling with the worries of what our kids might be facing. Thankfully, he was willing to listen and to counsel with me about what we could do to protect our children.

He reminded me how we'd had the important conversations with them about how they could protect themselves. Kyle helped me realize that the boogiemen of my childhood were not only hiding at the school and playgrounds. For the most part, they had been in my neighborhood and friends' homes! That was the big difference for our children. Our home was a place of security, and they had been prepared with family standards and values that I hadn't been raised with. They knew how to be safe and to choose the right.

I'm sure that Kyle thought that I was being a little overreactive. The likelihood that someone was going to offer Michael drugs or show him pornography at his first day of third grade may have been a bit much. But it wasn't all in my head either.

We had heard some pretty terrible things from other parents in the community. Kyle could have put my concerns off, but he didn't. He had his own experiences with the boys at his school and knew all too well what was ahead for Michael in the years to come.

The school experiences that were most damaging to me came in sixth and seventh grade. They were extensions of abuse and low self-esteem tied to my home life. Kyle and I were clearly ahead in the process of preparing our children to recognize and reject the kind of things we knew that they would be exposed to. We had intentional open conversations with Michael about what was not good and what he should do when he heard or saw or was approached with something that our family didn't do. We would have those conversations with the other kids at the appropriate time too.

We had been intentionally building the foundations for healthy open communications about what many would have considered "older issues." Michael responded well to our open and frank conversations. I think there is real power in opening that door before it must be broken down. It's all about being forewarned and feeling that they can talk with us about anything—and he does. We have had important and timely discussions with Michael about dirty pictures and dirty words. The door of communication is open to all topics with our kids.

Both Kyle and I were perfectly clear that the need for those kinds of intentional parenting discussions would need to come at a much younger age than it did for him or me. One Sunday afternoon, we decided that we would move those priorities to the top of our list for family heritage discussions. We discussed our heritage and searched our family history to find stories of family heroes who represent the values we want our children to have. I should say we drew from Kyle's family heritage and I borrowed a few stories from the Morrises. My family history and heritage stories take some real creative avoidance to make something good out of them.

Helping the kids see the character trait in their heroes, especially family heroes, encourages them to include those traits in their lives. Michael and Melanie are gaining a basic understanding that their choices show and define their character. I wonder how many of their friends' parents even mention the word *character* to their children, let alone are intentional about helping them understand and develop it. That's all the more reason why we must do it and do it well.

Our plan may not be perfect, but it's proving to help us clarify and strengthen our family values and expectations. I think it also empowers our children with the seeds of leadership and self-security that will help them compete and contribute in the future.

When a friend invited Michael to share some candy he had stolen from another student, Michael's negative response and report of the incident to us was a direct result of one of our family hero discussions. In fact, family heroes have become the kids' favorite part of our family heritage stories. The best part about our efforts is that I never worry about what Michael may have been exposed to. He tells us. And he's proud when I tell him honesty is making him one of our family's heroes too.

As I said, ours is not a perfect family or perfect story. It is a continuing story of trying to get it right, or at least the best we can. We do our best and often we mess up a bit and have to retrench and learn a little more patience with the kids and ourselves. That patience is not yet a trait any of us have mastered, even though it's on our list. I think I have realized that patience may be the ultimate perfecting influence on our own and our children's character. I hope that both stories, mine and ours, will give you hope, perspective, and ideas of how you can become more effective in your parenting. Just remember, it doesn't have to be perfect, it just has to be intentional.

HERITAGE-MAKING—IT DOESN'T HAVE TO BE PERFECT, AND NEITHER DO YOU

"But let patience have her perfect work, that ye may be perfect and entire, wanting nothing." (James 1:4)

"Be ye therefore perfect, even as your Father which is in heaven is perfect." (Matthew 5:48)

James counsels to us let patience have her perfect work. Certainly intentional parents, even those that are perfectly intended, will need patience. Perfection is an ongoing process. So also is the perfecting of a family's heritage and its influence upon the character of its members.

Kelly's husband adores her. Her children love and bless her with smiles and hugs. They are not a perfect family, but they are a perfect example of a family being led by parents with virtues that secure, sustain, and perfect them. Theirs is a family whose children will be secure in knowing who they are, what they stand for, and that they can talk with each other about anything. They are clear about their values and standards. That is the basis for their character and the fence of their security.

You too can determine to make the commitment and to spend the time to establish those values, standards, beliefs, and traditions to help secure your children. You can develop a clear definition and distinction about your family's standards. Do not leave the meaning of what kind of people your children are and what "family" and "life" mean to schools, friends, neighbors, or media. You can rest assured that their values, morals, priorities, and definition of what is important are likely to be at odds to those you would have your children embrace. Become an intentional and proactive parent, just like Kelly and Kyle, about the legacy of your family heritage and your children's character.

Neither you nor your efforts have to be perfect. You need not be a homeschooler, full-time homemaker, or perfect parent or grandparent. There are simple yet practical tools to help you build the internal family security you want for your children. Others have and are blazing a trail that you can follow with your family and parenting. They are perfectly able and willing to help you discover the intentional parenting process that can help you succeed.

Remember the lesson about Kelly, the perceived perfect woman who is not as perfect as she appeared to outsiders. So it is with families that may appear to have their values, standards, and heritage all perfectly wrapped up. Those families will be the first to tell you that their heritage and legacy is a work in progress. Some days it's forward progress, and then other days . . . They are headed the right direction, but they certainly have not arrived. It is a journey. They will also tell you that the work is worthy and the process, though sometimes slow, is worth the work. The important thing is to get started and stay in motion, regardless of where you are in the journey or how long it takes.

Kelly didn't start with an ideal situation. She certainly didn't have the advantage of a good example or a strong family legacy to start with. Sadly, precious few do. But even her poor upbringing set the stage for knowing what she did and did not want for her children and family. Kelly had the example of her adoptive parents, the Morrises. Similarly, we all can borrow from positive examples from family, friends, and other intentional parents.

Associating with like-minded, heritage-focused relatives and friends can be invaluable in discovering and implementing our own parenting priorities. If you don't have one, finding a church family who share your views on family, values, and standards is a great place to start.

The foundation for effective intentional parenting is establishing a common language with your children. They need to understand your words and have a clear vocabulary of words that relate to the family beliefs, values standards, and priorities. Let's call this family lingo. So let's get started with a list of words intentional parents can use to create their family lingo.

WORDS ARE POWER

Values and standards need names just like children do. To be identified and understood, the concept needs a "handle," a name to talk about it. For example, *morality* is a handle that brings to mind ideas, concepts, and attitudes about *sexuality,* which is another more specific word. Do sexuality and morality mean the same thing? That depends on the meaning you give them. How you, the parent, define the word and how you use it in your home and family will be how your children understand and use it. Your words and definitions will not be viewed as "dirty words" like they were learned in the hallways and locker rooms at school.

We recognize that the larger a child's vocabulary, the clearer we can be in our communication and the more effective they can be in relating and working with the concepts. We teach them math words, sentence structure words, and science words to help them build an understanding of their world and how to live in it and to communicate about it effectively with others. Similarly, we must teach them words that define values and relationships and behaviors to help them communicate and live safe and successfully.

Learning big or adult words can be a grand adventure for youngsters, if it is approached effectively. If not, it can be awkward and "icky" for both child and parent. Parents usually err on the side of too little, too late with regard to when and how to teach these adult words and the associated concepts, beliefs, meanings, and standards to their children.

Let's get one thing absolutely clear: concepts, words, and standards relating to family values are a responsibility parents should never delegate nor abrogate. This is clearly the parents' responsibility and the core of intentional parenting. Make sure you begin these conversations before you consider preschool, as soon as the child can learn to repeat the words. Parents need to discuss and agree on when to teach these words and which words to teach.

IMPORTANT WORDS AND MEANINGS

The following is a list of words that every child needs to be clear about before they enter preschool. The depth of definition can be added to over time, but they need to have a feeling for the meaning and an attitude about the word (the beginning of family standards) before they are exposed to the words and associated meaning, feelings, and attitudes by others away from direct parental supervision. You must determine your own definition for use of the words. Consider the list and definitions and adjust and add as you deem appropriate to support your family values.

PARTIAL INTENTIONAL PARENTING PRESCHOOL FAMILY LINGO LIST

Faith—How we think and feel about Heavenly Father and Jesus. Our family believes in Jesus, and we choose to follow him and do what he wants us to do.

Sacred—Some things are sacred. That means that they are so special that we don't talk about them or show them to anybody but our moms and dads and Heavenly Father.

Kindness—Treating other people like we want to be treated and not being mean or selfish to them. Our family chooses to be kind to everyone.

Selfishness—Being unkind and treating ourselves better than we treat someone else. Our family chooses to not be selfish. We share and take turns so everyone can be happy.

Respect—Listening and taking our turns when someone is talking, especially parents and teachers, and not being mean. Our family chooses to be kind and to respect other people.

Reverence—Being quiet, listening, and using a quiet voice. Our family members are reverent when we are in special and sacred places and need to be quiet, listen, and think about what is being said.

Truth—The real way things happened and the way they were and are. Our family only tells the truth. We are truthful about everything.

Honesty—Telling the truth, not lying, and not taking things that don't belong to us. Our family is honest in what we say and do. We don't lie, steal, or take things that are not ours.

Heritage—The way our family does things and the things we believe in and our family rules. Our family has a strong heritage to help us be good and safe and happy.

Standards—The things we believe are right and wrong and important for what we will do and the things we won't do. Our family has important standards in our heritage. They are like our family rules. We know what we should and should not do and that is how we live.

Private Parts—The private parts of our bodies that nobody but our mom and dad and the doctor can see or touch or talk about. Our family does not show our private parts, nor let anybody look at or touch them, and we don't look at or touch anyone else's private parts.

Modesty—Dressing and acting so that we don't show very much of our skin and not wearing tight-fitting clothes. Our family dresses to look clean and neat and to not show very much of our bodies, not our private parts for sure, and we don't look at anyone else's body to see their private parts, not even through their clothes. That is being modest. We are a modest family.

Pornography—Pictures, or drawings, or movies of bodies without clothes or that show private parts. Our family doesn't look at pornography or talk about private parts and things like that except with our mom and dad. Because our mom and dad love us, they will never look at or show us that icky stuff either.

Sex—What moms and dads do with their bodies and private parts to bring new children into the family after they are married. Our family does not talk about sex except with our mom and dad when we have questions or want to know more about it.

Drugs—Things that make our bodies and our brains change the way they work. Our family doesn't take drugs or smoke or drink beer and alcohol because it is not good for our bodies. Doing those things can hurt us and make us sick, weak, and cause us to want more. Only the doctors can tell our moms and dads what drugs we should take as medicine when we are sick.

Alcohol—Drinks that make our bodies act differently and make us lose control of how our body is supposed to work and how our brain is supposed to think. Our family does not drink beer and alcohol or other things that make us lose control and can make us want to drink it more.

Safety—Doing the things that will help us from getting hurt or into trouble. Not breaking family or school rules and knowing what to do when someone tries to take us or make us do bad things. Our family chooses to be safe. We know when to say "no!" and when to scream and kick and run for help.

Peacemaker—Not getting into fights or arguments and helping to stop arguments and fights. Our family chooses to be peacemakers by sharing and being kind.

Good people—People who help us to keep our family values and standards and to learn how to be good and do good things. Our family members always try to be good people.

Bad people—People who try to get us to do bad things and not to follow family and school rules. Our family chooses to stay away from bad people and to tell our teachers and parents about them when they come around.

Leader—Somebody who shows people how to do the right things. We are all leaders in our family. We show our friends how to be safe and happy.

You may decide to add many other concepts and words that to these. However, these are the keys to establishing a foundation for our children's safety as they leave the security and control of your home and your watchful eyes.

For greater understanding and safety, children will need more words and more detailed definitions and standards at about the third grade. Then they will need more words and detailed definitions at the fifth or sixth grade, depending on their schools and the environment you find them in.

By sixth grade they need about as much understanding about principles and standards of morality as their parents needed at college age—maybe more. By then, hopefully you will have developed a full set of family values and standards vocabulary. Using the value list mentioned in the previous chapters and appendix will help, but it does not include sufficient words regarding moral security. You can bring these words and concepts into your heritage and character discussions as you feel appropriate.

Certainly secure and open pre-puberty discussions with sons about nocturnal emissions and masturbation are as important as discussions with daughters about menses and feminine hygiene. Sadly, too often these important discussions are not completed soon enough or are left to someone other than the parents. These conversations should include discussions about family values relating to sexuality, intimacy, and reproduction.

LEGACY-SECURING INTENTIONAL PARENTING PROJECT SUGGESTIONS

Pre-Parent Values Planning Discussion—Before your children make their debut into your home, discuss and decide as a couple regarding what family beliefs, values, standards, and rules you will have. Consider the family heritage you each bring to the marriage and the values you want to perpetuate and add to your family. The goal is for parents to be together on their views, attitudes, and expectations about family values, beliefs, and traditions. Develop your list and implementation strategy timetable. Talk with other parents about what they did and wished they had done.

Family Honor Jewelry—Create a family honor pendant or ring or other item of emblematic jewelry that represents full adherence to the family values and proclamation. Give one to each child at age eight. Present it to the child in a semiformal ceremony with all family members present. Have the recipient recite or read the proclamation and give a promise to the family of their allegiance to the family values, standards, and rules. At age twelve the item can be upgraded in a ceremony to honor the family member who has kept their promise from age eight. Be sure to have an official way for family members to return to the family with full commitment when the member falters in their commitment to any of the precepts of the document and promise. Then again, at age sixteen and nineteen and at their marriage you can reconvene an honor ceremony and upgrade the emblem item where possible. Perhaps at their marriage, the child (now adult) can be given their own copy of the proclamation as a template for their own family.

Family Counsel Conversations—During your regular weekly family activities, lessons, and conversations, consider discussing the family values and challenges that any member of the family has had to deal with either personally or as a peacemaker for someone else. These conversations can help to deepen individual understanding and commitment to the values and standards. It is a great way and time to upgrade the definitions of your family value and standard words.

Standing by Our Values Storybook—Design a family storybook with a page dedicated to a picture of a family member demonstrating a family value or standard. Write the text, or story if an actual situation can be used, that describes the value and how family members can stand by the family value in focus. Creating and reading the storybook together is a powerful way to implement the principles, values, and standards. It is also a great way to introduce friends who come to play as to what is and is not okay in your home and with your family.

Values Card Game—Make a card game with a different value or standard word on one side and the explanation on the other. Then on other cards, put a description of a situation that would require a choice of how to respond based on the family values. To play, shuffle, and stack the cards with the situations on them facedown. A family crest or logo would be a great face to the cards. Then place all the value word cards face up on the table. Let each player take a card from the stack, read the situation, and explain what the right thing to do is, and then find the matching face-up word card. This game could also be played as a matching or concentration game with small children.

Write a Letter—Write and send a letter or card to each child expressing how proud you are of their efforts to live by specific family values, standards, and rules. You can also put a secret note to that effect in your children's lunch boxes, on the steering wheel of the car, on the bathroom mirror, or in a pocket of their pants or coats. Surprise notes and letters say you noticed and took the time to compliment the family member.

Honor Party—Organize a family values honor party. It can be a special dinner where Mom reads the nominations for family value heroes of the month or quarter and describes why that family member was nominated. Two or three can be nominated to give coverage of situations and behaviors that merit recognition. Then award and honor one person with a toast of sparkling cider or a soft drink. Make sure every family member wins one value award. You can give them a certificate or an envelope with a movie pass, for example.

11

HERITAGE

The Details of Dashes
between the Dates

THE MASSIVE ROOTS EXTENDED LIKE GROTESQUE fingers outward from the banyan tree that stood like a sentinel at the gates of the overgrown cemetery. The iron gates had long since given way to the rust from saltwater spray and air of the ocean. The headstones were weathered and the names eroded by the wind and sands of time. Few of the hand-carved inscriptions were legible. The oldest remaining dates were mid 1700s. But the one Marjean was looking for was not there.

Captain Bruce Jensen's headstone, if indeed it were at this site, would bear the birth date of April 11, 1747. The exact date of his death was not known, although the story of his drowning would have placed it between fall of 1796 and early 1798. He, and the clues to a Jensen family treasure, was lost on a stormy day near the island. The mystery had been the subject of countless family gatherings. The marker they were looking for would have both dates, but it was the dash in between the dates of his life story that was the treasure Marjean was searching for.

The treasure was not in lost gold, rubies, or emeralds. The jewel she sought was a single pearl of information that held great value to the Jensen family.

They just needed the name of the young lass he had married two years before his fateful sailing. The name of his widowed wife would be the clue that would allow the research on the family tree to go forward. Without that pearl of information, that family line, like the treasure hunt, would likely remain a dead end.

MARJEAN'S STORY

We made our way from one grave to another, looking for the clue the local vicar had suggested might be at this location. He would continue looking through the death and burial records of the three old cemetery sites for which the small church group tried to maintain records. The chances of finding something that old were slim at best. Still, the vicar thought he remembered the name Jensen on one of the markers he had cleared from overgrowth. He wasn't sure, but it was worth the visit to the Rocky Point Cemetery overlooking the old village bay. He thought it was on the back row nearest to the rock fence corner.

It was getting to be late afternoon when Verl and I got to the site. The heavy growth around the outside of the small seaman's cemetery was beginning to cast foreboding shadows over the few remaining rock head-stones. As we reached the proposed location and started examining the markers, we found that the four-foot-high rock wall had sheltered some of the headstones from the effects of the wind and weather. Some of the inscriptions were still legible.

I bent over and cleared away some undergrowth from a large stone cross. Malcolm L— the rest of the name and the death date were broken off the corner of the stone. The birth date, however, was clear—August 1, 1783. That find raised my hopes. I took a picture of the stone.

Then I found another smaller stone with a faint inscription. I took out a piece of plain copy paper and a large charcoal pencil and made a rubbing. It was faint, but the technique worked. I could make out most of the letters. S-A-L . . . Y. Sally, I surmised. The middle name was clear, Othea, and the last, M-A-S-T-E-R. The dates were unclear. That was the only woman's grave I could identify. All the other partially legible names on the headstones were men.

It was Verl who discovered the odd shaped 2'x3' weathered stone facing the wall. It was third from the last on the second row in.

"Well, I'll be a turkey buzzard!" he shouted. "This is going to be good for the family! I think this is it!"

I had been trying my luck on another rubbing but quickly got up and made my way over to Verl. Verl stood gazing at the inscription. The name had been carved under a slight overhanging edge of the headstone. The stone wall had protected it from the erosion. There it was, just as the vicar remembered! Weathered as it was, the large deeply cut letters of the name were clearly legible: J-E-N-S-E-N

On the second line, faint, but still recognizable as, C-A-P-T . . . N B . . . The rest of the name was obliterated, but the dates were clear. No birth date or month, only the years: 1747–1788.

That had to be it!

My heart was pounding as I stared at the stone and then stepped to the side of what I assumed was the grave.

"Oh my, my, my, my!" was all I could say.

I looked back to Verl, who stood erect with a smile like a child who had found the last Easter egg. I took a piece of paper out to get a rubbing of the inscription. The death year, 1788, was earlier than we had been led to believe, but there it was, and the year was all we needed to keep the research going. It would be the missing link to find the late Mrs. Bruce Jensen, and that would be the link to the family treasure.

We spent the better part of the next hour clearing, cleaning, and photographing the grave while the shadows crept across the plot. We felt a strange reverence and peace as we gazed at the gravesite of this long-lost relative. A thousand questions beyond the date flooded my mind. The big question now was, "Who did he leave behind?" I strained trying to pull the memories of this distant relative from the bones that lay just a couple of meters beneath my feet. Oh, if only the grave could speak! If only from the dust he could tell his story. But then, that was my job— getting the rest of the Captain Bruce Jensen family story. Now I felt sure that I could.

The vicar was waiting for us in his small office at the whitewashed stone chapel in town. He too had good news. He stood as we entered and we both started speaking simultaneously. Verl interrupted our shared exuberance.

"Just as you said, your memory was right. Vicar, you just don't know how exciting this is for us! This is fantastic, wonderful!"

I wanted to hug him but didn't know if that would be okay.

"Yes, yes, Mrs. Watson, and I have yet another surprise for you. See here . . ."

He pointed to a large old leather ledger. It was not an original record of the cemetery but a copy of a copy that had been updated in the early 1900s. Whoever had made the copy had been careful and complete. To the side of some of the interment records were notes that must have been included in the original entries. The Vicar pointed to a name midway down the page.

"That's it! That's him! Bruce R. Jensen, Captain, born 1747, died September 11, 1788, buried lot C 117!" It was truly like finding a treasure.

It was the note on the next line that was the real treasure, even the jewel we had been looking for. I stared in near unbelief and then laughed at the irony.

"Well, will you look at that! Verl! We have found our pearl of great price!"

The note read: Next of kin—Mrs. Pearl B. Jensen—Huntingdon, England. Verl and I had indeed found the jewel they were looking for and it was indeed a "Pearl of great price." Pearl B. Jensen was the nameless wife that had been referred to in the old journal that had started our journey of discovery. What happened to Pearl and the treasure of their posterity? Did they have a child? Posterity? Are there living relatives? Now I could find out.

I have been an avid genealogist for well over twenty years. Verl has been a more recent convert. He says we spend a lot of time and money finding out about whom we are related to and is worried that we'll have to spend a lot more to cover up some of what we find.

Some of our retired friends prefer to knock and chase a little white ball around the grass, and others prefer to drown worms or jog themselves into a sweat. We prefer finding the stories of long-lost family heroes and villains. Now don't get me wrong. We sometimes take our turn on the golf course, and Verl even drags me along on an occasional fishing trip, and we love to get the cards out and play a few hands of Five Crowns with friends. Those things are part of our lives too, but the most rewarding part of our retired life is getting tired searching for dead people, morbid as that may sound. But it is an exciting adventure that has taken us to some hunts.

When we got back from the Islands, we passed the information on about Captain Jensen to others in the family. It didn't take long at all until the connections were being made. Pearl and Bruce Jensen had two children—a daughter, Carrie, and a son, Alvin, whom the captain had never seen.

Carrie had married John Bentsen and moved to America shortly after the news of her father's death. Her mother followed two years later. Alvin stayed in England and worked as a carpenter's apprentice for several years. Then he signed on as a seaman to pay for his crossing to America. Alvin joined his mother and sister in Boston in the spring of 1803. He went back to his carpentry work and stayed with his mother until her death at age seventy-two in 1823. Several members of the family were doing research on the Emily Bentsen family, but I felt compelled to follow up on Alvin to see what treasures his life and story might contribute to our family heritage.

After his mother's death, and inspired by some itinerate preachers, Alvin decided to move west. He soon became one of the frontier settlers in western Ohio and Missouri. It was there that he met and married Ann Rogers. The discovery stories like theirs is what makes heritage hunting so exciting! Theirs is a story of unyielding commitment to each other and to the principles by which they lived. Their story and character are now being infused into the heritage and hero lore of my children and grand-children. Alvin's life treasures are becoming our inheritance. His life is affecting the lives of his great-great-grandchildren, my grandchildren.

Alvin and Lydia Rogers Jensen carved out a life and a legacy along the American frontier, from the Erie Canal to the Mississippi River. Over the years, their children, grandchildren, and great-grandchildren contin-ued their westward migration. They made their homes, lives, and mark along the frontier trails and communities from Nauvoo, Illinois, to San Diego, California. Their stories could fill countless volumes. Some of the stories are heartrending. Some about made me bust a gut laughing! Some touched and stirred me spiritually. Others raised my indignation when I learned of the persecution and intolerance they suffered!

For the most part, the stories are inspiring. They reveal how one fam-ily's commitment to each other and to the values and the principles they believed in were the welding links that kept them together, even when they were physically apart. These are the stories behind their lives. This is the inheritance that came from a sea captain who found a Pearl of great price.

Perhaps one of my most wonderful finds in searching the Alvin and Lydia Jensen family legacy were copies of several letters they exchanged with each other while they were apart. The letters reveal some additional facts about the family and the struggles of frontier life. More important, they reveal the story of the love and commitment they shared and the deep respect and gratitude they held for their shared values and family heritage.

I intentionally put the letters into a storybook about the Jensens because I knew that it would tell the story and teach the values of their lives. They are real love stories that the girls of our family read and reread. Their stories influence how our girls think about marriage and family.

Alvin apparently felt compelled to return to his native England to reconnect to his relatives there. While Lydia did not fully understand his yearning, she supported his decision. He left Missouri in August 1838 and went by way of Boston to see his sister Carrie. The letters come from that journey.

October 1, 1838

My dearest Lydia,

I am well enough. Arrived Boston Thursday. Last journey largely uneventful save longing for you. I trust that my prayers for you and the children have been effectual and that all be well with you. Had little difficulty locating Carrie and John. John in poor health has consumption. Carrie cheerful and glad to see me looks to be so much of mother. Her family now is five boys and four girls. Gave to me a few of mother's things for memory. I will claim them upon my return as the extra to Carrie a burden now.

Jon has work for me at the mill. The money will help. Expect to take passage to Liverpool 19 of October. Hope to be with Uncle Martin family Christmas. Trusting my letter to them has arrived and that I will be again welcomed. Want to look in on Marybeth and William before London.

Lydia, I feel badly in leaving you with the final of the harvest and affairs and would not have taken this journey save these feelings and urgency to return. I do so miss the warm of your embrace and comfort of your company. Ben and Bethany surely shall be to your aid and support. Please do tell them again my love and deep thanks for looking out for you and the children. The gift of their health and smiles cheers me always. Present them with my affection and reminder of their duty.

My prayers to God for your health and welfare until I return.

I remain your faithful companion.

Alvin

The letter gave us several other clues about their family. Bethany, the oldest daughter had married Ben. We are following through on those leads. Alvin's reference to Uncle Martin turned out to be his mother's brother with whom he boarded and worked as a carpenter's aid after his mother left for America. Confirming his sister's five boys and four girls will be valuable to those who are searching Carrie's family. Her letter in response refers to a second letter from Alvin, which we do not have, but her response reveals more of her nature and the standards of the family.

December 20, 1838

My Dearest Alvin,

Words cannot convey the happiness of receiving of your letters! Oh how my soul yearns for your embrace and the sweet comfort of your presence. The snows have come and we are by candlelight in the scripture with the children nightly. The mob has not returned and all is quiet tho there is some word of a move to Coleville. We are secure and under God's watchful eye. Tho I trouble thinking of your daily trials, I am persuaded that providence is sustaining as my prayers request.

Ben and Bethany are here daily to see to my needs. The children are proudly yours in duty and service. They bid their love and good thoughts. We are well save some slight croup and fever for the twins of recent. God is gracious and faithful and we are warm and with sufficient and to share. The cow is good-natured and will not dry until spring thus we are with plenty of milk and butter to trade.

The late fall a welcome blessing to get the last of the corn, hogs and wood in. The neighbors look out for us as well and we will get by together. Addie is a regular visitor as her Henry is yet to return from his business. I enjoy her company and fellowship.

I received word from mother that daddy is fast ill and that the doctor considers him nigh unto death. She is faithful that her prayers will be answered and that he will yet return to vigor. Perhaps you can visit them on your return in the spring. I dare not think to go but entreat God to their needs. Perhaps Marybeth will minister their needs, as she is yet to marry.

Your letter 30 arrived today. Again, my heart was lifted and I felt to sing for joy! I was sorry to learn of Martin's passing. We will hope that your aunt will be sustained and return to health. Surely she was grateful for your presence to assist with his affairs and business.

I will as you requested write to Carrie with the news. She can respond to Elizabeth's interest in visiting her. As I remember she is some younger than Carrie, tho your senior by a few years. It is gratifying that she accepted your message with such zeal.

As for the situation with the move, as I have said tis but a rumor as yet. We have not seen the Browns nor received your package of them. Perhaps they were some delayed with the last storms.

You can take pride in Carlos. Tho but 11 years he is acting in your stead as a man. Mr. Crossman called today to trade flour for a ham. Carlos did the business and knew that four bags was the fair price. When Mr.

Crossman proposed five bags Carlos replied no sir, four bags is a fair trade and tho we know your good intention for five bags, my father would stand on a fair trade. We will have only four bags for the ham." Mr. Crossman looked to me and I reminded him that today Carlos was the man of the house and would do our business. Mrs. Crossman sent him with a jar of honey for us so the trade was sweetened without the extra flour. They are good neighbors and Carlos is becoming like his father, a man of honor and fair dealing. The girls were not as understanding of the refusal of the extra flour. I'll be speaking with them about our good name and reputation at prayers tonight.

Again dearest, we ever pray for you and trust in your continued safety and good health. Know that we are in His good hands as well. Let us hear from you again in due season.

Your loving wife,
Lydia

In the simple interchange of letters there is so much insight into their lives and hearts. It is as if we are watching them from behind a one-way mirror. Although the facts and clues to more information about the family members and their history come in bits and pieces, we see the character of the family and their principles both in and between the lines of the letters. It is also amazing to see common character that seems to be part of the Jensen DNA.

February 27, 1839

My dearest Lydia,
Your letter arrived and filled my heart with the warmth of your good nature and righteous determination. So glad is my heart to know that all is well and that my prayers are answered for your health and protection. Yet your letter causes me to yearn the more to return to your bosom. I do so miss your embrace and the assuring confidence of your eyes. I am sorry to learn of your father's ill health. I will surely attend to her father and mother upon my return through New York. It shall likely be late April before I can book passage.

Please convey my love and affection to Carlos and the girls. He honors me with his commitment to be the man of the house in my absence. Please advise Ben that it is my attention to be back in time for a late planting. I have yet some business with other family and friends and need to deliver my message to them once I can take leave of the rest of Uncle Martin's affairs. It is clear to me that I have been a godsend to them in this hour of need.

His passing has brought me more in contact with many relations for whom I might not have seen on my journey. I have met with some acceptance and with some skepticism in my message tho none have openly rejected me while I am caring for auntie.

I will leave for London shortly and will meet up with the other family members. I have been paid a fair wage for my work at Martin's business although I would have gladly done the service for but a bed and bread. I am to help Aunt Elisa sell the business to a Mr. Hogan come the first of March. He seems a fair enough chap tho I fear he would not have paid as fair a price had Aunt Elisa had to reason with him alone. She would have much the rather had me take over the business. I assured her that I was honored in her thot as she had no sons to carry it on, I deemed it in her best interest to sell.

My darling, I must admit that I weighted the thought of returning the family to England into a fine home and his business with some envy. Yet shortly I returned to the truth and riches of our own home, family and the cause that moves us forward together. Tho I would have spoken with you of the offer, yet I knew without the regard of your answer and counsel. We are in God's good graces and nowhere else would we be. Elisa can't understand my reason, yet she honors my decision. I hope she will come to honor and believe my message.

I would give you more of the mission and my labors but I have been faithful with my journal and will let that bear the record back to you upon my return. Tomorrow is the Sabbath and I will meet and break bread with the Elders and friends at Sweeny. My prayers will be for you and the children. Rest safe and assured of my faithful love and devotion.

Always your companion,
Alvin

As you would assume, we are anxiously looking for Alvin's journal. As of yet, that is another mystery and treasure hunt.

It is a grand adventure to search out our heroes and to connect to the roots of the legacy of their name and values! Those roots become stronger with each generation who read and hear their story. These branches of the family tree will weather the winds that challenge their connections to the family name and values because of the roots behind the records of these people. Finding the stories, not just the people, is what makes me a heritage-maker, and not just a genealogist. It is truly the details of the dash between the dates that are the life treasures that enrich our family heritage.

HIDDEN TREASURES—GETTING AND PASSING ON THE REST OF THEIR STORIES

"Tell ye your children of it, and let your children tell their children, and their children another generation." (Joel 1:3)

Joel warns us of the conditions that are to occur prior to and at the Second Coming of the Lord. He tells the people to tell their children and grandchildren the things they will need to know to prepare for the days ahead. Similarly, we should tell our children and grandchildren and the generations to come about the truths, values, beliefs, and standards that they would need to prepare them to stand firm in the challenges that will come in their lives.

This is the purpose of finding and sharing our family heritage past—the roots of our legacy. Through finding our ancestors and the stories about their lives, tragedies, and triumphs, we can discover and share the values they lived by. That is the fiber of our family heritage and the basis for the character and legacy we want to pass on and secure. Their stories will be invaluable to our children—it's their greatest inheritance. The kinship is in their genetics and carried through their bloodline. But the treasures of their values are carried through their stories into the hearts of their descendants. This too is the turning of the hearts of the children to their fathers.

The genealogy and stories of our ancestors and their character and values should be the foundations for the heritage of standards and character for our children. The most effective and powerful method of teaching those standards to our children, in addition to our examples, is through the medium of their stories. We have all seen parents and families who have suffered sorely from the consequences of the poor and destructive choices of their children. They might have been spared much of those pains had they and their children understood more about them. The whole linkage of fathers to grandfathers, to great-grandfathers and mothers the family tree and family line is the beginning of understanding the family legacy. They each have contributed to the collective family heritage and their stories empower intentional parents to influence their children's values and choices.

FINDING AND WRITING THE STORIES THAT STRENGTHEN HERITAGE

Family historians and genealogists give us the facts of *when* and *where* our progenitors lived. They can also lead us to the stories that tell *how* they lived. These stories are most valuable when they come from incidents where these departed family members' values have been challenged. They are the stories of how they took a firm stand to live by their principles and commitments.

Before we can make character-defining stands, we must know what our standards are. For most family-centered people, many of their basic values are the same. They are the values and standards of integrity, fairness, commitment, kindness and so forth. Unfortunately, in this age of unintentional parents and unintentional children, far too many parents have not been intentional about getting their own standards clearly and firmly entrenched. They often face the challenge of trying to teach from the standard of "do what I say, not what I do." That rarely results in strong positive values.

Many unintentional parents also assume that their children understand the family's values and standards and therefore theirs without talking about them. Even great examples need the clarifying and internalizing discussions about the family legacy. Finding and becoming acquainted with the family forbearers is a wonderful way to get started. Parents and children who have not discovered, discussed, or embraced the legacy of values of their ancestors will be vulnerable to the pressures of peers and life that will challenge them.

These are the vital discussions Joel was directing us to "tell it to our children" so that they could tell it to their children and they to their children. We tell it by story and by discussions of what those values mean and how they should affect family choices and behavior.

As we tell and write the stories of our family members past, there are a couple of keys to finding and including the values they lived by. Typically the individuals won't "toot their own horn" with stories about their own noble virtues, but someone needs to discover (ask) and write (tell) about these values if they are to be passed on to "the children." That someone may need to be you.

As you seek for and find information about your people of the past, you can mine the data and stories for these values for their living relatives. Look for journals, records, and stories so you can reveal who these people really were. Ask others what they know about the family member and what stories they may have heard. You may need to extract and extrapolate the values from the information and stories you gather. You may find bits and pieces that you may need to write into the story. This is how you can tell your children and their children and their children of the life and values and testimony of their family heroes.

Some helpful facts and ideas you may include as you discover who your ancestors really were:

She/he was known as . . .

People saw him/her as . . .

Wherever he/she went . . .

He/she wanted to be known for . . .

She/he would always . . .

She/he would never . . .

He/she wanted their posterity to remember them for his/her . . .

Simple things like their interests (dancing, fishing, travel, art, music, reading, the scriptures, school, learning, tidiness, grooming, timeliness, cooking, sewing, quilting, spelling, drama, speech, sports, and so on) can all be leveraged for positive association and interests for your children. Intentional parents can create connections to the ancestor's interests and values.

For example:

Grandpa Jefferson loved fishing. Matt loves fishing too. There is a heritage-making transitivity that can be used with Matt. Grandpa Jefferson and Matt both like fishing. Matt is like Grandpa Jefferson. Grandpa Jefferson always tried to be on time and to keep his things tidy and neat. Therefore, because Matt and Grandpa Jefferson are alike, Matt also likes to be on time and to keep his room neat and tidy.

Grandpa Jefferson is one of our family heroes. He would never take something that didn't belong to him and neither would we. He was always the first in line to help someone in need and so are we. We are a lot like Grandpa Jefferson. We are becoming heroes like him.

The interests, values, and traditions of these departed relatives become stronger and more valuable for intentional parenting with each telling, reading, and reminding of their stories. Their beliefs, values, and standards become the "traditions of the fathers" to ensuing generations. These stories become the threads of the fabric of the heritage of their posterity—*your family.*

LEGACY-SECURING INTENTIONAL PARENTING PROJECT SUGGESTIONS

Define yourself—You are now a genealogist and a heritage-maker. As you tell others about your genealogy interests and activities, add and explain your new heritage-maker specialization. When you do this, you will be amazed at how the distinction "heritage-maker" will draw questions and interest. It will also open doors of conversation that may lead to additional story resources from people who know something about the person or family you are researching.

Add the character—For those for whom you have done genealogical research and found some information or story about their lives, and the character aspects of their lives, identify some strong positive character trait(s) and then write or rewrite the stories with those character traits. Then share these traits with family members and add the newly discovered values and standards stories for that family hero.

Brand the Heroes—Make a list of the important values, standards, and character traits down one side of a piece of paper. Then make a separate list of family heroes and ancestors across the top of the page. Determine who is the best example of the value you want to portray and why. Then write a short story or explanation about why and how that family hero has become known for that trait. Share this character heritage with the children so that they come to identify and value the hero and the defining traits.

Ask Them—When you are finished researching at least the recent ancestors, ask yourself, "Now who are you, Mr. John Doe? What were your strong positive character traits and how would you like to be remembered by your posterity?" Then don't be surprised to discover evidence about character traits and standards that were important to the person. They, or their records, can speak from the dust as it were, to help you get their value message as well as their dates and lineage right.

Tell Their Stories—As you find family members who had positive character traits, be sure to tell their stories! Leverage the information. Make it a habit to add key values to the vital facts. It would be great to add a character line to the birth and death lines of the record. Remember, we want to know who they were, not just when and where they were.

Four Generations of Heroes—For many, if not most, finding our ancestors beyond four generations may be difficult. However, for those within our four-generation pedigrees, we should be able to find and write their story. Take on the task of labeling each parent, grandparent, great-grandparent and great-great-grandparent with one or more life-defining character traits. List their names and identify one or more hero traits for each of them.

Your Own Story—Write your own story regarding the values you cherish and what it means to be a member of your family. Express in the story how you want to be remembered. You will find that writing your story will focus your thoughts and actions to present-day opportunities to be that way. This is evidence of how active hero-making can affect your own family members. When they define themselves with the family character traits you have incorporated into your family heritage, they are building their character.

Tell the Kids—Find an opportunity to gather your children and grandchildren and tell them the brief life sketches of their great- and great-great-grandparents. Focus on the values they contributed to the family heritage and name. Then discuss the family charter and values and ask the child what they can do to make those values important and powerful strengths in their lives. Remind them that people they know already are identifying them by the values and character traits they exhibit in their lives every day. Suggest that each child pick one or two of the family hero values that they too will become known for in their family.

Time Capsule—At a family reunion or gathering, have each family member write a letter about his or her life values and intentions. The letter can be a promissory contract with the family to embrace and live by the family charter, standards, and values. Small children can draw a picture about how they are going to behave, and you can print the values on the page. Put them into a sealable container that can be kept or buried to be opened at a designated family gathering in the future, about five years. You can put a moisture-absorbing packet in it. After five years, you open the capsule and review the letters and other contents you have included. Then add new letters, pictures, and information about the family to the capsule for the next period of time.

12

AN INTENTIONAL HERITAGE

Begin Where You Are

BARBARA'S PAGE WAS EMPTY. THE LONGER BAR-
bara stared at the blank lines, the more her heart felt empty and
her eyes felt full. These were not the kind of heartfelt feelings she
had enjoyed at former gatherings of the group. There had been so many
wonderful discussions and classes in the past. She always looked forward
to these Thursday night meetings. They always left her happy with a heart
full of joy and friendship. Her eyes had been full, often overflowing from
laughter and gratitude. But tonight was different.

Barbara felt the tears starting to well up. They were not the tears of
gratitude and happiness she was used to feeling there. They were the tears
of regret for having such an empty page that made her heart feel heavy.
The class leader had asked that they list some of their best memories of
family activities from their childhood. That was the problem. Tonight's
discussion was about family heritage and how to capture and pass on that
heritage to children and grandchildren.

Barbara Shelton was a young single parent. She was living on a tight
budget and had only recently moved into the area and joined the women's
group at a local church. She thoroughly loved these women. Without
question, they had become her closet friends, probably the closest friends

191

she had ever had. Several of the older ladies had practically adopted her and Callie, her six-year-old daughter, as their granddaughters. Their interest was genuine and their influence was welcomed.

There were three other single-parent mothers in the group. They were all friends, all struggling to make a life, a living, and a home. The gatherings were a mix between educational classes, crafting activities, socials, and religious discussions. The problem with tonight's discussion about family traditions was the lack of positive family memories Barbara had to draw from.

The instructor was excited and animated as she started the class discussion that evening. She started out by handing each of them a piece of paper. She explained that they were going to start by discussing important family memories. When the instructor asked the group to list some of their favorite childhood family activities, Barbara sat motionless. Then the instructor suggested memories of activities with their grandparents. Barbara looked at the floor.

The class leaders were always sensitive to the single women in the group, so they barely touched on the ideas from memories of their romance and marriage. Barbara recognized and appreciated the thoughtful sensitivity, but tonight's discussion just reminded her of what she had missed out on as a child.

Barbara's sweet memories of her childhood were not of family gatherings, vacations, and holidays like others of the group. Hers were quiet times at the little park she lived by as a child. They were memories of butterflies, sunsets, raindrops, and snowflakes. She had sweet memories of fun and laughter with her small group of friends. There were happy memories of Mr. Murphy, as she called the stray cat that often visited her back porch. She had spent a lot on time on the porch when she didn't feel safe or welcome in the house. Mr. Murphy always seemed to show up when she felt most alone.

Okay, shake it off! she thought. *Let's get the show on the road.*

She swallowed hard, pulled a tissue from the box that was always on the table for the many tearful moments that came in these meetings. She wiped her nose to camouflage the wiping of her tears and picked up the pen. Janice Green, adoptive Grandma #1, saw through the tissue charade.

Janice and she had talked about her life before. Janice knew that Barbara's childhood was rough. Very rough. Barbara was an only child of an only child, single-parent mother. She had met her father only a time or two when she was very young. His side of their family history was completely blank, just like the page in front of her. Her maternal grand-parents had passed away in an automobile accident when she was in grade school. In the ensuing years, she had made some mistakes. An early preg-nancy, a disappearing spouse, and a hard life were the memories she was working hard to leave behind. Time and memories associated with Callie were what really mattered.

Janice pushed a chair up to the end of the table next to Barbara. Her understanding look was sympathetic, but not patronizing.

"Well, kid, looks like you're digging deep on this one," she said.

Barbara forced a smile and offered, "Just like my luck." Janice wrin-kled her brow, not understanding. "You know, if it weren't for bad luck, I'd have *no* luck at all! If it weren't for bad memories—"

Janice burst into laughter. "Uh-huh! Just like my knees! At least I've got them! Even if they *are* bad!" Janice chuckled and sighed.

Janice encouraged Barbara with advice based on the sage of her age. "Well, my friend, just hang in there. They say age has a way of discarding the bitter and making some of the bad better. Frankly, I figure that we just stop remembering and start forgetting all that stuff. Besides, it seems to me that you and Miss Callie are piling up a host great memories these days. You two do everything together!"

It was hard trying to answer Callie's questions about why she didn't have a daddy and grandparents. Figuring out how to pass on important family traditions and memories was tricky. Barbara had a good job at the local hardware store. Her income covered the rent, food, and utilities, and if she was careful, she and Callie could get by on what was left. Barbara was pretty good at making the money and the month end together, but it was a struggle to do much more than that.

Janice and the other girls were always bringing something by to help. Sometimes it was groceries, or hand-me-downs that were always nearly brand new and were special things for Callie. The best thing they brought was their friendship, encouragement, and the reminder that Janice belonged with them.

Janice motioned Barbara away from the table to help get some refresh-ments ready. In the kitchen, their conversation continued. Janice asked, "So how's work?"

"It's okay. You know, everybody needs boards and nails and dog food," Barbara reported.

"Anyone needing anything else?" Janice asked with a glint in her eye.

Barbara knew what she meant. They were all looking out for her and hoping that Mr. Right just might come in looking for a piece of pipe or a bucket of paint and discover what he was really looking for was Barbara! But, so far, he must have been satisfied with the old paint. She had sold a few buckets to guys who weren't wearing a ring, but most of them needed a new paint job themselves.

"Nope, no one looking nor worth my looking this week." Barbara shrugged.

"Well not every eligible painter knows the best place to find what he really needs. Fact is, some of them flat don't know what they are looking for! I guess the Grandma Brigade is just going have to start telling a few more of them what they need and where to go. My Frank tells me I can tell his boys where to go anytime I feel like it. And sometimes I do just that!" Janice laughed.

"Well, I figure if I just keep my eyes and ears open, one of these days we're going to run into each other, with or without a bucket of paint!" she assured her friend.

Barbara crossed her fingers and smiled they headed back to the meeting area with plates of cookies.

The instructor was moving on with her discussion about family traditions. As Barbara sat back down at her seat, she heard the teacher say something that pulled her back into the discussion.

"Traditions can be started anytime. You are in charge of them, and they can be your own activities, not just those that you did growing up. Traditions are created is in the making of them."

The implication for Barbara was profound. She had been blaming the emptiness of her present on the emptiness of her past. It was the past that was robbing Callie and her of their heritage. Or was it?

"Heritage is what you make of it?" Was that what she said? Barbara thought almost out loud. The idea was an epiphany. She did not have to rely on her empty list of past family memories and traditions to have a heritage—she could *make* them. She could be the heritage-maker for Callie and for herself.

Janice saw the sudden light and change in Barbara's countenance. "What's up, Missy Barb? You look like you might have just seen a ghost!"

Barbara turned slowly and looked at Janice trying to keep her ear on the next statement the teacher was saying about creating "intentional traditions and family heritage."

"Maybe I did. Maybe I did," she muttered. Then Barbara turned back to the discussion. It was one of those pivotal moments in a person's life when things get really clear and really exciting. For Barbara, the tears of pain had turned to tears of joyful discovery.

After the class, Janice pulled Barbara aside again and they reengaged in the conversation about memories and family heritage. Barbara told Janice about what caught her attention and turned off the tears and turned on the possibilities.

The conversation that followed Barbara's family history and heritage-making jumped into high gear. She determined that she would not pass on an empty list to Callie. Her daughter was going to have a lot of wonderful family activity memories. Barbara was going to find her their heritage by making it. Barbara was going to build an intentional heritage for her and Callie, and when Mr. Right came around, they would even share it with him.

BARBARA'S STORY

I'm a pretty tough nut. It takes a lot to crack me. But Janice can really crack me up.

That day in the church kitchen was a perfect example of how she knew when and where to put the pressure to crack me without crushing me. Every woman should have a friend like that. The fact that I *did* have one proved that I was wrong about only having bad luck. Janice was proof of some luck. I have come to realize that there was really no luck about that. It was and is a wonderful blessing. She helped me discover how to build my heritage. It started when I prodded her about her list.

"Okay, Janice. How many memories do you have on your list?"

"Just one, Barbie, just one. LIFE!"

"No, really. How many?" I chided.

"Oh, I don't know. I didn't number them. When you get to my age you sort of have the right to make up your own rules. So I just listed a few things that I've been thinking about lately. You know, things that I don't want to forget and that I don't want Frank and the kids to forget either."

I knew her Frank well enough to know that he was anything but forgetful.

"Frank forget? Are you kidding? I thought you said he had a memory like an elephant!"

"Oh he does, he really does. Trouble is, he has a very 'selective' memory. Frank seems to be able to choose what he wants to forget. If it's something he wants *me* to do, his memory is like an elephant's. If it's something I want *him* to do, it's like that memory was written in disappearing ink!"

"Sounds to me like you need to switch pens with him," I suggested.

"Now that's an idea! The real problem is that we both tend to make stuff up on the fly. Sometimes the things we think we did are only reflections of things we thought we should or would do but didn't—yet. The memory seems real to one or both of us, but neither one of us can remember for sure. That's really a problem when it comes to where we think we put things.

"Like remembering where I left my keys or where he put his cell phone. I'd swear I remember putting them on the washer, but then we find them on the nightstand. Frank tells me it's creative memory-making to avoid having to do something or go somewhere I really didn't want to do or didn't want to go in the first place. And then I remind him that this creative memory-making thing doesn't work when it comes to him taking out the garbage. He can't creatively forget where he put the garbage can.

"Hey, maybe I could do that too! I could creatively forget some of my bad memories and creatively make up some good stuff! I think that could be called selective creative memory-making." Janice laughed, but we both knew the idea had merit.

That was right in line with the thought flash I'd had earlier about making memories! It was what I wanted to talk more with Janice and some of the other girls about. I wanted to find out what they had put on their list, so I could just borrow the ideas as I determined what I wanted to do to build our heritage.

Janice quickly reminded me not to hurry up the forgetting process.

"Now don't you be too anxious to start forgetting anything! You're gonna find that forgettin' is gonna find you sooner than you thought and a whole lot sooner than you want. It comes with age. But you just might find that intentional memory making can work to your advantage."

Janice laughed, and it was contagious.

I continued, "What I mean is, maybe I should think more about the memories I should be making than the ones I don't have or am trying to forget. I could get some good ideas from the group as to things that they remember and cherish."

Janice caught on quick. "Uh-huh, I've got a bunch of great memories you can just borrow from me! That is if I could just remember where I put them."

We laughed together and the list was forgotten for the moment while we got more cookies and punch ready for the girls.

Something about that conversation kept coming back to me over and over the next few days. There was something to the idea about determining what traditions and memories I wanted to make with Callie. Now I was really ready to make my list.

I was always keeping my eyes open for Mr. Right to show up so Callie wouldn't share my empty daddy memories list. But, until he finds us, I figured I'd better be building a heritage of happy memories for both of us.

That painful list-making exercise turned into an exciting planning adventure for me. I got a notebook out and started to make the list of things we could do together to build our heritage. They were simple things: trips to the zoo, the paddleboats at the park pond, tea parties, and picnics. Stuff like that, that Callie and I would do together.

Then I started thinking about those memories of my own childhood. I had to help Callie become a butterfly and sunset connoisseur. Maybe we would even get a cat and call him Mr. Murphy. There would definitely be more time sitting on the porch, but not alone and not because we were afraid to be inside. We would create a tradition of "porch talk." By the way, that has become one of my most precious traditions!

There were a lot of heritage-making things that I was already doing but just didn't realize at first. Callie's birthdays, holidays, and regular special events were already traditions. We had a few exciting one-of-a-kind experiences. We have come to call these our *heritage adventures*. We have gone to the circus and on an overnight camping trip. Once we did a big trip to the city with a lot of window shopping and dreaming about "someday" things we would like to have and do. That was a hoot! We even had a five-mile bike ride adventure. That was a big deal for a six-soon-to-be seven-year-old and for a mom who hadn't been on a bike in ten years!

Then there are those activities that are the simple little projects we like doing regularly because they make us feel so good. These were making things together. We do crafts, bake cookies, and do little service activities, like taking Grandma Janice a plate of goodies. Callie loves baking cakes, bread, or cookies and taking them to someone as a reason for our service project visits. At first, it was more about making the treats than the service. Now I can see more delight in the giving and the serving than in the baking. She is always looking for someone we should do a "to the rescue" project for, as we now call these visits.

These are the best because we first had to bake the goodies together! Before we could do that, we had to go to the store to get the things we needed, together. Before that, we had to plan what we were going to do, together. Although we do a lot of our service activities on the fly, these projects are special because we do it all together.

So our heritage-making formula has become: "traditions"—the things we do annually; "adventures"—unique that are one-of-a-kind outings like concerts and special day trips; and our "to the rescue" projects—creative service activities that are fun, usually spur of the moment things we do. These make up our memory and heritage, making it a work in progress, and it's true we find heritage in the making of it.

Perhaps the most important memory-making activities we have is simply being and talking together about *us*. *Us* and *we* have become important family words regardless of how many there are in the family. We share a wonderful and growing sense of belonging and security when we have our "we and us" conversations. It's a pretty simple idea, but it is a powerful family heritage foundation, one I didn't have growing up. It wasn't just Callie that feels the security of those words and talks. I have come to see heritage as the collection of traditions, memories, and conversations a family shares.

I make sure that at least once each week we have an intentional family heritage-making activity, preceded by an comfortable "we and us" conversation. I wonder how mothers with several children can manage their heritage-making conversations and activities? But then most of them have a partner with whom to share this precious responsibility and opportunity.

Tonight we are going to talk about family values and standards. That topic was spawned by this week's women's group discussion. The instructor was Jody Aims, a divorcee with four great kids. I don't know how she does it, but clearly she has some great experience and ideas about building character. While all of us take turns leading discussions and lessons, she is everyone's favorite discussion leader! She just makes things fun and insightful. Her opening question was "What are your family's values and standards?"

Ask an open-ended question like that to our group, and watch out! There is no shortage of ideas and opinions.

What followed was an enlightening conversation that focused on a list of words and what they mean to us and how we teach them to our children. Faith was the number one value. Then we added honesty, kindness, obedience, morality, service, grooming, health, education, excellence, and gratitude. There were a lot of other really good trait concepts and ideas, but this is the one I knew that I had to share with Callie. So tonight we will have our porch talk about these values and what standards we should have about them. It's a short list, but it's a start, and I'm excited to see how Callie responds. I am going to begin the discussion asking Callie the same question that I was asked at the women's group meeting: "What does it mean to be a Shelton?"

Little by little, we are building our family heritage. That itself is an adventure! I believe that this will become a tradition for her to carry on with her family later in life. Each of our "to the rescue" missions is a reminder to me of what we value and what produces lasting joy rather than fleeting pleasure. We are striving to make this the *essence* of our family heritage. Janice says we are "building our heritage from scratch," and she reminds me that the best things in life are made from scratch. That is certainly true about her chocolate cakes! I think it's going to be true about our heritage too. I rarely think about the heritage I didn't have anymore.

Some may think that I am at a disadvantage in trying to build a family heritage while I'm single. But I am not alone in that quest. I have this great group of heritage-making friends helping me. They are helping me to build a heritage for Callie and me!

HERITAGE MADE FROM SCRATCH—
SERVING IT UP FOR YOUR FAMILY

"That the generation to come might know them, even the children which should be born; who should arise and declare them to their children." (Psalm 78:6)

The Lord commanded the Israelites to teach his law to their children and to teach those children to teach their children. This is how traditions and heritage are turned into a legacy. When one generation passes the significant values, rules, and standards to the next generation, the legacy is strengthened, even magnified, for the coming generation. The roots of importance and influence of traditions and values go deeper into the priorities of each generation that embraces them.

Today, precious few new parents have a clear set of values, beliefs, and standards with which to start their family's heritage. Like Barbara, their buckets may be shallow or empty. That's the unfortunate news. The good news is that every parent, couple, or single parent can start a legacy of family heritage values, standards, and traditions for their children anew. Janice is absolutely right. It's okay to borrow values and traditions from others if you can't find them in your past. Those who enjoy a deep-flowing legacy well of family heritage are more than happy to share and to help you draw up all you need!

If you, like Barbara, are building a heritage largely from scratch, consider what beliefs, values, standards, life priorities, and heritage-based memories you want to give your children. How would you have them describe their heritage and their memories when they pass them on to their children?

Contemplate the following list of considerations for family beliefs, values, standards, and priorities. These are among the important questions that intentional parents and families should consider as fundamentals of their family heritage. What are your beliefs and values regarding these life's most important issues and questions? These will deeply influence how your children govern their lives and families in the next generation and what heritage and legacy they will pass on to their children.

An *intentional family legacy* should have clear answers to the questions that arise around these considerations. These are the foundations for building your legacy. They are particularly valuable for starting the discussions of family and legacy in homes where it is primarily a single parent who is building an intentional heritage.

1. **God**—What are your family's values relating to spirituality and religion? What is your family's belief in God, the scriptures, prayer, the Sabbath, church attendance, church service, commandments, fasting, tithing, and offerings?

2. **Education**—What is your family's position on academics, schooling, college, homework, studying, reading, grades, school activities, school sports, and parent-teacher involvement?

3. **Community**—What will be your involvement in community service, politics, organizations, and contributions?

4. **Patriotism**—How will you celebrate and engage in the political process of choosing, supporting, and holding your elected officials accountable for their service and

representing your interests? How will you celebrate national and state holidays?

5. **Laws of the Land**—How will you treat the laws of the land: taxation; driving regulations; and other community, state, and national regulations and laws?

6. **Humanity**—How do you view and treat other people: neighbors, friends, associates, and strangers? What is your family attitude about ethnic diversity and associations with members of other ethnic communities and cultures?

7. **Family Rules**—What are your family's absolutes and nevers? What are your rules regarding TV, computer, telephone, friends, curfews, bathroom time, bedrooms, house and yard chores, washing, food preparation and cleanup, refrigerator control, use of the family car, allowances, dress standards, grooming, music, house guests, calendar planning, permission, school, homework, dating, drugs, language, pets, and family time and activities?

8. **Family Values**—What are the character traits and standards that you adhere to as a family? What is your family's standards for dress, grooming, and language?

9. **Recreation**—What are the activities your family focuses on (sports, camping, fishing, hunting, cultural activities, movies, music, theater, concerts, dances, sports, and other family-focused activities)? How do you approach holidays and determine family vacations?

10. **Health**—What are the health-sustaining activities your family engages in? What will and what won't your family members eat, drink and take into their bodies? What do you do as a family to help keep physically fit and active?

11. **Division and Sharing of Labors**—Who has primary responsibility for managing the finances, paying the bills, doing the various household and yard duties? How can and should the non-responsible spouse and children support and help with those duties?

Parents are wise to discuss preemptively how they feel, or should feel and act, regarding any of these considerations. If they wait until an issue or misunderstanding of family standards arises, it is much more difficult to defend and hold the offending person accountable. Assumed standards are the weakest kind. Discussed and agreed-upon standards are the best fences and basis for corrective consequences when they are necessary.

If these standards are discussed early and reviewed often as positive aspects of the family's heritage, they will become accepted values. If not, they are more likely to be seen as controlling and unfair rules. Parents have the opportunity to establish values and standards when children are young. If they wait too long, the tide changes from pride in "this is who we are and how we live because we are the Jensens," to complaining arguments of "nobody else's family has this many rules!"

Older parents will concur that often the very rules that children are challenged with are those that they will most adamantly pass on to their own children. As children age and mature, their former frustrations often turn into appreciation for the defining, developing, and protective role of family standards and rules. This is yet another evidence of "training up a child in the way they should go, so that when they are old they will not depart from it" (Proverbs 22:6).

Family value communication activities and memories are vital to bringing alignment and unity to family standards. The inferred message should be "we are a special and unique family because of what we *do* together, as well as what *we don't do*." The following are recommendations for building solid family relationships, communications, and heritage-strengthening memories. Quality is vital, but it cannot replace consistency and frequency for validating family values, standards, heritage, and unity.

LEGACY-SECURING INTENTIONAL PARENTING PROJECT SUGGESTIONS

Pray Together Daily—The adage "the family that prays together stays together" is true. Parenting and family life management is tough in our time. Every couple, every parent, and all families need the power and influence of prayer and God. Pray in your homes, with your families, and at your own bedside. Intentional single parents will surely need to take more regular turns praying with and about their children. The example of your prayers about the legacy you are building in your home and with your children will be a powerful influence in establishing the priorities and focus of that legacy in the minds of your children.

Identify and protect a specific four-hour block of time each week that is family time. Ensure that the priority is not violated. When it must be for some emergency, make sure the one missing apologizes and explains the situation and asks for family support in advance. The meeting can be a meal or an activity—going bowling, to the movies, out for a treat, yo a ball game, and so on. Or it can be a family room discussion about what's going on with each family member. It can be a great time for parents to brag about the achievements and activities of the children. It is also a great time for parent(s) to trust the children with a little information about what is going on in their lives and work. This is not easy, but it is the very foundation of intentional parenting.

The gathering can also be a great time for refocusing on family values, standards and traditions. It can be a great time for planning and coordinating the week in advance. Remember, treats and surprises are important to children. They can be the ones surprised or they can create the surprise treat for mom and dad. These regular gatherings can be planning and anticipation time for major holidays, vacations, and other big family events.

Single parenting of family time is rare and precious. It is also most often by necessity the shortest and on the leanest budget. The key is consistency, even if it is a walk around the block, a backyard picnic, or trip to the library. When the parent makes that time with the children the highest priority and discusses family topics when they are in their activity, it "formalizes" the activity, which becomes part of the legacy.

Date Nights—Have a weekly Mommy and Daddy date night. It is vital that children see Mom and Dad dates continuing the priority of their romance and courtship. It has been said that one of the greatest gifts of heritage a man can give his sons and daughters is the sweet and tender love and courtesy he shows his wife.

Mothers and fathers should report how fun it was to take their sweetheart to dinner or movie or church activity. It doesn't have to be expensive to be valuable time investment with your spouse to strengthen your marital vows. It can be as simple as walking hand-in-hand around the block, sitting on the porch swing and talking, or just cozying up to the warmth of a fire while listening to music and dancing. The sweet giggles of the girls and laughter of the boys over the continuing romance of their parents is evidence of powerful teaching. That will help to set a pattern for them to feel to report their dates and activities to you as well.

It is so easy to get too busy. Holding each other accountable to the commitment and investment of weekly family and couple time is vital. The dividends of following through will prove to be the best investment you can make in the heritage and family success of your children. As they follow your lead and then lead their own children with that same example, that heritage will do much to secure the marriages and families of their posterity.

In cases of a single parent, if they are dating, bringing the children into a discussion of who, what, where, and how you enjoyed the date makes it a shared family thing. If the parent is not dating and can afford a sitter, it is a good thing for the children to see the adult involved in some personal development or personal interest activity. Here again, discussing the activity with the children when you return can make it a shared, family-connecting time.

Daddy-Daughter or Mommy-Daughter Dates—Hold monthly daddy-daughter or mommy-daughter activities for your girls. Let the girls in your family dress up when it is their turn for a special activity with the parent(s). It can be a special shopping trip, to a movie, skating, to a concert or play, a nature walk, or even just to get an ice cream cone and to talk one-on-one with that daughter. Parent(s) can make simple invitations for the daughters to make the event extra special (even if they have to enlist Mom's help).

Ask your daughter questions about what is going on in her life, what she has been thinking about, and if anything is troubling her. Tell her how proud you are of her and how glad you are that she is living by the family heritage standards. You might also ask her for some advice about something you are thinking about. Treat her like an adult and then really listen.

Do a Boys Night Out—Parent(s) can take one or all of the boys on an outing once a month. They can go out to a ball game, bowling, or for treats. Ask questions about their lives, school, friends, thinking, and challenges. Get their advice on some family or parenting issue or decision. Listen to them talk about life, school, their thoughts, and their concerns. Thank them for their thinking and sharing. Tell them how proud you are about the young men they are becoming and how they choose to live the heritage of the family.

Single moms can enroll extended family members and close male friends to provide male interest and interactions for these actives.

Mother's Time—Moms should seek special one-on-one time with each child throughout the month. Include them in homemaking and baking and shopping activities that can give you time to talk and listen. Set goals with them to qualify for special purchases of something they would really like to do or have. When necessary or appropriate, you might suggest, "Let's talk with Daddy about that and see what he thinks."

Similarly for those more rare cases where the single parent is a dad, he can enroll the women in his extended family or close female friends to provide the female-targeted activities and experiences. The parent then can participate vicariously by having the child tell him or her all about the activity.

Pillow Talk—At the end of each day, determine that you will reserve a few minutes to connect as partners and parents to discuss the day and keep each other appraised regarding the children, issues, priorities and decisions that need to be made. Practice TPK to keep your relationship and your family strong and timely in your heritage-making. TPK? Simple—TALK, PRAY, and KISS.

If you are an intentional single parent, make the Pillow Talk time with your children just before family prayer and before their bedtime to discuss the day and to remind each other of the values and heritage you are working on together. The pillow can be yours or theirs.

Calendar and Report—Put your family memory making and communication activities on the monthly and yearly calendar. Have the kids help keep track and report on completion of the activities and commitments. Making family time the top priority while they are young will help to secure their cooperation when they are teens and face the competition of friend time conflicts.

Whether you are a couple or single, the preparations and anticipation of planning and calendaring is a powerful tool. The important family and individual activities and appointments that affect family priorities and calendars is another way to enroll all members of the family in the notion of *us* and *we*—family.

Storybook—Write up each of your major family activities and events, combining pictures and the story in a scrapbook, expandable-post book, binder, or bound book to commemorate the activity. Include what each participant had to say about the activity.

Family Proclamation—Create and frame a family proclamation that outlines your family values, standards, beliefs, and traditions. Have every member of the family sign it, and leave space for additional family members. Grandparents may coordinate with married children to create an extended family proclamation with signatures and copies for all family members.

In single-parent homes, there is often an unspoken feeling of incompleteness that can make children feel that their family is not really a real family without the other parent. Single parents can use family language to help soften that feeling. For example using the term "Our Family Proclamation" may help to assure the children that their family is a family. Single parents are encouraged to use the phrase *our family* often.

13

INTENTIONAL DREAMING

*Determining Who You
and They Really Are*

MELANIE WAS ALWAYS A DREAMER. WHEN SHE was five, her teacher was Mrs. Carolstien, who made all the "little peeps," as she called them, feel special and important and smart. She told them that they were going to have a lot of fun learning things that big people needed to know, things like numbers and letters and how to write and read. It was all so exciting! Mrs. Carolstien told them that they could do anything and become anything they wanted to become. Melanie believed her. She just knew she could be a ballerina or a teacher or a scientist—that's what her friend Andy was going to be too.

Melanie loved talking about what she was going to become. She changed her mind about that sometimes, but that was okay. She felt smart and important and special, and so did all the other little peeps. Mrs. Carolstien asked all of them what they dreamed of becoming. She explained that dreaming was what people think about and get excited about and plan to do and be. She said dreaming was a way to plan so their minds would know what to do. They all loved talking about their dreams and what they wanted to do and become. Mrs. Carolstien said they were all little dream machines because they could dream so well. She said that they could do anything and be anything that they could dream about. Melanie loved to talk about her dreams! She and several of her new friends liked talking about becoming moms.

Mrs. Carolstien told them that everyone should have dreams. She said people should choose to do things that would help their dreams come true and even told them about her dream to become a grandma. She said to have her grandma dream come true she first had to still be a good Mom. Melanie was sure that she was going to be a good mom.

Then when Melanie was six, her new teacher didn't talk about dreams. She decided that Mrs. Richards didn't know about dreams. Once they drew pictures of what they wanted to become. That was like dreaming.

Then when Melanie was eight she dreamed about having a pony. She wanted to have one for her birthday, but her mom said she couldn't have a pony because they didn't have a place for it. Melanie was sad and didn't understand. She thought that she could have anything she could dream about. She talked to her mom about it. Her mom said that some dreams take more dreaming, more planning, and more time to come true. Before a pony dream could happen, there first had to be a dream about where to put the pony, and a dream about how to feed and take care of the pony. Those dreams had to come true too. Melanie understood, but it was hard to dream about a barn and a pasture. So she stopped dreaming about a pony and started dreaming about a new ten-speed bike. Sure enough, on her next birthday there was her bike just liked she dreamed it would be. Her dad had a man bring his pony so all she and all the kids at the birthday could have a ride. Her dad was helping her with her dream. She would save her pony dreams for later.

When Melanie was twelve, she dreamed about being the secretary for her seventh grade class. She made posters and asked her friends to vote for her. But another girl was dreaming about being the secretary too. Melanie knew that there couldn't be two class secretaries. She wondered if the girl with the biggest dream would win.

When the other girl won the election for class secretary, it was disappointing to Melanie. She didn't tell anybody, but she wondered if she wasn't dreaming hard or good enough, or maybe her dream machine wasn't working. She even stopped thinking about dreaming.

When she was sixteen, Melanie thought a lot about going to the homecoming dance with a cute young man named Parker. But he asked someone else to go with him, so Melanie didn't go. She took that pretty hard. While she didn't mean to, the older she got and the more disappointments she faced, the more Melanie stopped thinking about the power of her dreams.

She discovered that wishing is often what one does after the fact. That is, they wish something had been different. Whereas a dream was always something you were looking forward to and planning.

As Melanie grew older, she thought about Mrs. Carolstien and dreaming. She wished she understood better how it all worked. She still believed in dreams and dreaming, but she found herself only hoping and sometimes drifting down into doubting about the things that were really important to her.

One thing was clear: dreams felt good and doubts felt bad. Melanie decided that growing older somehow made her dreams and doubts get all mixed up, and it was hard sometimes to separate them. Like most adults, she didn't try to dream for fear that the doubts would come and take her dreams away and leave her feeling worse. She even wondered if her doubts were more powerful than her dreams.

When she went to college, Melanie decided she wanted to become a nurse. The classes were not easy, and she really had to study quite hard. Then a miracle happened; she met Stan. He was cute and smart and his dream was to become a doctor and to be a dad. They fell in love and got married. Melanie used her dreams and dreaming to plan the wedding. For the most part, it was all just as she dreamed it would be. She realized how much happier she was when she was using the power of her dreams to get the wedding just as she created and saw it in her mind.

After they married, Melanie continued attending school, but it became difficult to get her assignments completed, do well on the tests, maintain their home, and help Stan with his work. Paying the bills got hard—too hard. They decided that it would be best if Melanie stopped going to school and got a job to help pay the bills. So she put her dream of becoming a nurse away with her pony dream and got a job.

Melanie and Stan were happy, and being married was wonderful. Melanie still dreamed of being a mother, and sooner than she thought, she found out that a baby was on the way. They knew that Melanie would have to stop working, but Stan was nearly done with his schooling and it would be okay.

Baby Paul came the same day Stan got a letter from the Texas medical school he had dreamed would accept him. That was a day of dreams coming true! Melanie was a mother, and Stan was on his way to becoming a doctor.

Baby Paul was nearly three when Stan entered his residency at the hospital. Although they couldn't believe it, two months later, Melanie found out that another baby was on the way. When the sonogram indicated that their baby was a girl, Melanie was super excited and worried again. Dealing with two babies in the small apartment and having less space and less money, was a scary thought. She also discovered that worry and fear push dreams and dreaming away.

Stan was a good and loving husband and enjoyed playing with Paul and helping out as much as he could, but it was still hard. They both dreamed about the time when they could have a place of their own.

Melanie was feeling the wear and tear of the three previous years of work, then the pregnancy, learning to cope as a new mom, supporting Stan in his schooling and the stairs to the apartment. Baby Maryanne was more beautiful and perfect than Melanie could have imagined or dreamed. It was wonderful to have another child, but she couldn't remember ever being so tired.

What Melanie dreamed about most about during that stage of her life was for a few more hours of sleep, a few fewer messes to clean up, and for Stan to bring Chinese or pizza home for dinner. When Stan could give her a break to run to the store, that was also a dream come true.

Once when he could see that the load was wearing on her, Stan scraped together fifty dollars and gave it to her with a simple homemade card that read,

> Sweetheart, I'll be home on Thursday from 9:00 a.m. to 2:00 p.m. so you can pay a visit to StyleWise.
>
> Love you, Stan

The card made her cry, and although she objected to spending the money, she was excited about *her* time out at the salon! She started dreaming about it from that moment on. She had been struggling with the face in the mirror lately. She didn't have a problem with just her hair but the lifeless look she saw. It was not at all the excited, energized look of the dreamer she had been. She was feeling drained and a little lost within herself. She discovered that dreams and dreaming are energizing and actually affect how she looked.

The trip to the salon worked short-term wonders for Melanie. Her new 'do brightened the face in the mirror. She started dreaming more about the time when they would be done with the residency and they could get on with their dreams of a home and a medical practice of their own.

That dream came true eight months later when they accepted a position at a clinic back in Stan's hometown of St. Louis. That had been his big dream, the shared dream that had sustained and driven both of them.

They settled in, and the life stresses changed and the variety made it easier to manage the demands of the new house, the kids, and Stan's sometimes-erratic schedule.

It was her friend Nikki who first told her about the intentional dreaming and parenting seminar. Nikki was going to attend the seminar and wanted Melanie to consider attending with her. When Melanie saw the seminar flyer she became seriously interested. The flyer read:

"Who Are You—*Really*?"

The Dreams of an Intentional Parent

- Rediscover the dreams you left behind
- Discover the power of living intentionally
- Understand the priorities and power of intentional parenting
- Empower your children with a heritage of dreaming

It was to be a three-day seminar at a mountain lodge. There would be a small group of women from all over the country, coming together with the same interests. No phones, no TV, no Internet, no kids, no meal preparation, or clean-up! It was to be a retreat for women who, like Nikki and Melanie, were interested in becoming more intentional about directing the power of their dreams.

It had been a long time, *years*, since Melanie had taken more than a few hours for herself. The idea of a time out and a retreat for a few days was almost intoxicating. Melanie figured she could get her mom to come out to stay with the children. Melanie was sure Stan would be able to take a little time off to be with the kids too.

Nikki was already set to go. Her sister-in-law had attended the seminar and raved about the experience and the impact it was having on her life. The flyer had a contact name and phone for information. Melanie decided she would call that evening to get more information.

MELANIE'S STORY

In thinking about writing my story, I've been reflecting on how I saw myself as a child, what I dreamed about, and how I lost sight of my dreams and the very process of dreaming. I know that a lot of other women have come to a similar place in their lives. I'm not the only one who wonders about how smart, cute, important, and special I am. A lot of us start to wonder and worry about who we really are and if "I have lost me."

It's a struggle with our sense of identity and self-worth. Heaven knows there are ample reasons for that struggle! Wanting—no, *needing*—to know who you really are and if and how you are important to the grand scheme of things comes with the commitment and the challenge of being a wife and a mom. The wear and tear of being the spouse, mother, home-maker, teacher, church, and community servant, and everything else that comes at you in those roles can be daunting. It can cause busy moms to misplace more than her keys, glasses, cell phones, purse, and memory!

The multitasking of motherhood can find us having temporarily mis-placed our identity, if not our sanity. Sometimes it is misplaced for so long, or buried so deep, under the need to build and support the identity of our spouses and children, that our own identity seems to get com-pletely lost. That is when the mirror and our inner voice cries out, "Who am I—really?"

That's where I was. Don't misunderstand. I have a great spouse and super kids, but I still needed to feel like I was great and super too. The seminar with Nikki started a discovery of how I lost or misplaced me and helped me rediscover who I really am and how I can enhance the power of becoming by reconnecting to the process of dreaming.

It was an adventure full of laughter and tears and has developed a sig-nificant reawakening. As I begin my story, I want to assure readers who find my struggles and yearnings similar to their own that what you too may have misplaced in your past can easily be found—including yourself and your dreams. And it doesn't take a personal development retreat in the moun-tains to do it either. But if you get that opportunity, I highly recommend it!

I also want to assure you that there is a place for you to go to find what you have lost. More important than that, there are discoveries about who you can yet become that will help you to find and restart the dream machine in you. Your dreams of the past and the dreams you have not yet even begun to dream are waiting for you, and for your family, as you discover the power of intentional parenting, heritage-making, and the dream-maker within you.

The evening after Nikki invited me to attend the seminar, I decided to test the waters a bit with Stan to see how supportive he would be. I thought I knew how he would react, but I also knew how negative some of my friends' husbands would react. Knowing that made me want to send up a "weather balloon," so to speak. We have a equal partnership, and when I decide I want to do something, he is generally supportive.

I caught him after we had the kids in bed and he had finished his traditional review of the news headlines of the day. I have learned that conversation timing with a busy man, at least my man, is critical. He had just picked up one of his medical journals when I sat down on the sofa beside him and began the conversation:

"Honey, how would you feel about me attending a women's personal development seminar with Nikki?"

I watched his body language, eyes, and the word choices of his response. He looked up from the journal to me and lowered his glasses

"When?"

That was it? No hesitation? No scowl? No look of "What the heck for?" None of that? Just "when"? Times like that remind me why I love him so much. Stan and I had passed the first step in the process of planning. The second step would be tougher.

"I think Nikki said it is in about six weeks, maybe two months. It's in the mountains in Utah."

I watched again for any "in-between-the-lines" hints to his response.

"Too bad," he retorted, and then continued. "If it was a little later in the year, you could catch a little skiing too. I'd love to go back to Park City."

So far so good, but then Stan asked the next question that was on the test.

"What's it all about?"

I was proud of my response, but knew it could open the door to a conversation about how I was feeling that I really didn't want to start, at least not right then. So I padded it a bit.

"Oh, it's a group of women Nikki is associated with. It's a seminar about being intentional about your life and parenting. I'd be gone

Thursday through Saturday. I think my mom would be happy to come out to watch the kids. What do you think?"

This time Stan took his glasses off, a clear signal that I had his full attention. I didn't want to appear overanxious. In fact, I wasn't. I hadn't even called to check out the details and the openings yet. I didn't even know for sure if I wanted to or could attend. Stan's next comments caused me to realize just how interested I really was.

"Sounds like you're pretty serious about it. This isn't some women's midlife crisis course, is it? Is there something going on with you we need to talk about?"

"No, no. It's not anything like that—at least, I don't think it is. I need to call about it and get a little more information before I'm sure I even want to go. I just wondered how you'd feel about it if I decided that I really wanted to go. That's all."

"Hmm . . . okay. Well, I think we could manage with or without your mom. That's about the weekend Paul and I were talking about going out to the lake for a little camping and fishing. I think you should check it out, but we need to decide fairly soon so I can get one of the other docs to cover my shifts."

"Right. I'll follow up, and we can decide in the next day or two."

He nodded and went back to his journal. I stepped back into the kitchen and did a little victory dance! Stan had never been stingy or controlling, but somehow getting a general positive nod to doing something like this, something completely for me, felt like a win! It was certainly an open door. He didn't even ask about the cost of the trip.

I went into the bedroom to make my calls. I didn't know whom to call first, Nikki or the seminar contact. I decided that I really did need to get more details and answers before I could get back with Nikki.

The phone rang several times before a soft but enthusiastic voice answered.

"Hi! This is Patti."

"Hi, Patti. This is Melanie Crandall. We haven't met. I'm calling about the parenting seminar. I have a copy of the flyer, and a girlfriend suggested that I check it out."

"Oh great. And you're Melanie?"

"That's right, with an 'i-e.' Is this a good time to talk? I didn't know the time zone I was calling," I queried.

"Absolutely. It's a great time. Where are you calling from, Melanie?"

"Marion, Missouri."

"So you must be the friend of Nikki Marshall."

"That's me. But how did you know that?"

"I have to confess, Nikki called this afternoon to get some information, and she told me you might be calling. I'm glad you did. Should I give you the nickel tour and then let you ask questions?"

"Sounds good."

Patti was participant of a previous seminar and gave me a detailed explanation of the program. The more she told me, the more interested I was. There was an opening for me, and by the end of the call, I was ready to sign up.

My anticipation grew over the next six weeks. I was excited, nervous, apprehensive, and curious all mixed together. The week before the trip, Nikki and Paul came down with a bug and there were a couple of pretty anxious days and some pleading prayers to get them back in shape so we could go.

Like most of my worries, these too were in vain. That became one of my seminar *aha!* discoveries. Worry is so often the price we pay in advance for problems that usually never happen anyway. *Worry* is just another term for fear. I now understand that fear is the antithesis of faith and dreaming. It is equally as powerful as dreaming but in the *opposite* direction. Fear curtails possibilities while dreaming empowers them. Worry and fear are such a waste! I just don't do it anymore. That knowledge and understanding alone was worth the time and cost of the seminar! But I am getting a little ahead of myself.

Everything worked out just fine. The bug was only a twenty-four-hour slow down for Nikki and Paul. Mother's flight was canceled, but the airline was able to get her on another carrier, and she arrived without much delay. Stan was able to change his shifts, and he and Paul went on their camping and fishing trip. Grandma and Maryanne hung out and played with Barbies, had tea parties, and went to the park!

In spite of our worries, Nikki and I found ourselves turning off the cell phones and buckling up the seat belts on the plane. We breathed a sigh of relief that we were actually doing it. We were on our way! In just a few hours, we were meeting up with some of the other participants and driving and laughing all to the way to the mountain lodge where the seminar was being conducted.

The "retreat mode" experience, as they called it, was total silence for the first few hours of the seminar. That was interesting. Think about it. When in your life have you ever gone for even a short period without the noise or attention-demanding voices of the kids, TV, radio, the phone, the doorbell, the news—all that stuff. I told Stan when I returned that it was twenty women giving each other the silent treatment and loving every minute of it! You really do rediscover how wonderful the sound of silence can be. I rediscovered what it was like to just "be" again—it was wonderful! Even the word *being* has taken on a whole new meaning for me since attending the seminar.

The discussions and classes were truly as life changing as Patti told me they would be. And just as she couldn't tell me how that would occur through simple conversations and discussions, I can't tell you much more about the process either. I understand now how vital that group discovery experience was for igniting my intentional transformation process.

I could go on and on about the insights, thoughts, and mind shifts that occurred for me over the three days of the seminar. Many of those insights continue to manifest themselves even now, nearly two years later. It was really wonderful. I highly recommend it!

They started off the seminar with the question "Who are you really?" We each took our turn answering the question. Everyone started out the same with the answer "I am" and their name. Then we all followed similar patterns of where we were from, who we were married to, what he did for work, who our children were, what made them special, what we did at work, where we went to school, and what we were interested in.

The seminar leader's response turned out to be the basis of some insightful discussions and discoveries. He asked, "Is that really who you are? Is who you are what your name is? Is it where you come from? Are you who you are married to or what he does for a living? Is it who your children are or any of that stuff? Is that who you are?" Then he just let us really think about it.

After what seemed like an eternity, he asked again, "So, who are you—really?" We were much more hesitant to respond that time. I can't take you through the whole process, but I can tell you that that discussion and the discoveries that came from it were in themselves life changing for many, if not all, of us.

They had us think about how someone else would answer the question of who we are. How would they describe who we are beyond these superficial identifiers of our name, home, and family composition? They had us think of our name as a title on a file folder. The answers other people who know us would give to the question of who we really are is what goes into that folder to give meaning to our names. Who we are, through the eyes of others who know us best, is who we really are to them. Ultimately, we determined that who we really are has more to do with who we think they think we are. I know that sounds a bit strange, but it is a powerful discovery. We also learned that how we are with and treat other people is the real key to our identity.

I have used that conversation with my children, and I'm amazed at how powerful it is in guiding them to develop a clear sense of character traits and standards they want to be known for—by others and by themselves.

From that point on in the seminar, we used the terminology "I am . . ." to describe ourselves in the most important aspects of our lives. We learned that we all have stories about ourselves and that those stories may be true, only partially true, or completely false. They are rarely complete or up to date. In fact, most of our definitions of ourselves are based in the past and based on experiences, premises, and attitudes that are self-limiting and self-defeating of our possibilities and dreams.

The discussion on dreaming was incredible! Even Mrs. Carolstien could have learned some valuable insights. We learned that dreaming is an intentional process for programming the subconscious mind. We learned that part of the brain controls and directs the conscious mind to act in accordance to its perception of what is true and right. It is sort of mind-washing and programming at the same time. Learning how to harness that principle and power was another invaluable takeaway.

The most important thing I discovered was why dreaming is so important to children. It is their way of setting goals. Reconnecting to some of my own childhood dreams reminded me of how important and influential my dreams were to my thinking and behavior. We learned how that subconscious mind programs the conscious mind and how it directs our choices and supports active dreaming. I discovered that creating dreams is a vital intentional parenting tool. It is a tool I now use intentionally to help my family set and achieve worthy goals.

We explored the concept of how values, beliefs, standards, and traditions contribute to who we really are—our character. We considered how the stories of family heroes could be powerful resources for positive influence on family identity, heritage, and character.

We considered how "being and doing" were related but separate aspects of who we really are. Our first answers about ourselves were mostly about our doings. As we progressed through the seminar, we spent more time considering the *being* aspects of who we are. Then we explored how intentional parents can use the being and doing discussion in the home and with their children.

That was the last aspect to the question, the difference between who we were, had been, and who we really are and want to be. The realization about stepping out of the past, through the present and into the future was little mind-blowing. However, it gave us the clear realization that we were truly free to declare who we are and then back it up with consistent behavior. I hope you can get your head around that idea! At first, it was a little strange, but when it clicked, it was the most freeing and empowering concept of the seminar.

The discussion about heritage-making as a tool to help define and transfer family values was also amazing.

Perhaps the most important thing I discovered is that I was never really lost. I was always right there following my dream to be a mother. My kids have personality quirks and like me they are far perfect. But they are mine, and their happiness and success in life was and is the biggest and most important dream of my life. It is a lifelong dream. That dream is coming true more rapidly now that they and I understand the power of intentional dreaming as the process for setting and achieving goals.

I realized that I wasn't alone in losing sight of my dreams occasionally. The seminar helped all of us to see that and rekindled my sense of peace and joy about the progress I was making. The concepts of creating an intentional family and an intentional heritage are helping us to give our children a rich legacy of values, beliefs, traditions, self-esteem, confidence, and a clear vision of their character—who they really are.

I know exactly who I am. I am happy and fulfilled to be a woman, a wife, a dreamer, and the mother of a family who knows who they really are, where we are going, and how we are getting there. We are each important and special. I am surrounded by other important and special people.

You have read some of the stories of these other amazing special people in the previous chapters. They each came from different places and situations but with a common interest in finding out who they really were and what they could really do with their experience, talents, and love of family. I hope our stories, will encourage you to consider joining us in the adventure and the joy of being intentional about the parenting you employ to establish your family heritage and values.

And now, I must go feed my pony.

LEGACY-SECURING INTENTIONAL PARENTING PROJECT SUGGESTIONS—LIVING WITH VISION

"Where there is no vision, the people perish." (Proverbs 29:18)

The dreams, hopes, and influence of intentional parents hold the power to direct and change the world. Through intentional parenting, important values and priorities are instilled in minds and lives of children. The plans and preparations that intentional parents make and implement in their homes will have the greatest influence on the attitude and actions of their children. These parents and children are the men and women who can lead the world to better choices.

Intentional parents develop a clear vision and embrace a vital mission. They are committed to directing the development of their children's dreams and character traits. They instill time-honored family values and priorities in the hearts of their children. Your children's influence too can make a difference in the world they and their posterity will live in. This can be part of your family heritage. That can be one of your dreams and theirs.

As Melanie's story describes, part of being an intentional parent and one of the greatest elements of intentional parenting is understanding and employing the power of goal setting and planning. We refer to this process of goal setting and planning as intentional dreaming. Living intentionally is to live with a clear vision for your future and having a plan that gives you confidence and faith that you are in charge of your life, not just creatures of circumstance.

Our use of the term *dream* is more directly related to the biblical concept of *vision*. That is, seeing in one's mind's eye, or as in Proverbs 29:18 to have a vision or plan or understanding. Without that "vision," or purposeful understanding and direction, the people perish. So it is with individuals and families. Without a vision, a family or child's progress, purpose, and success is likely to perish or to be only partially fulfilled.

So how does an individual establish a vision to live by—a dream to believe in and to reach for? How do parents instill the attitude of positive possibilities and the power of active dreaming in their children? How can parents give their children a heritage of dreaming? We remember the words of the song "Happy Talk," from the musical *South Pacific*, that remind us, "You've got to have a dream. If you don't have a dream, how you going to have a dream come true?"

At the core of the message about dreaming is the belief in intentional, self-determined vision, improvement, and freedom. A dream is a vision of something you want to see come to pass—come true. Understanding the creative power of the human brain's frontal lobe to envision and create a pre-reality dream of how something could be is amazing.

This extraordinary, exclusively human, divine trait we call dreaming is the key to the power of achievement. It can truthfully be called "spiritual creation." It is the mental, creative basis for seeing a future not yet real in the world, yet real in the mind of the dreamer—the visionary. This is the process for successful goal setting. This is the planning, mapping, directive, and aligning power that brings the right words, actions, resources, and influence to bear to manifest the dreams of the mind into the physical world.

Consider the great dreamers of history, those who lived, led, and changed their world by dreams and a vision of what could be.

T. E. Lawrence put it this way:

All men dream: but not equally. Those who dream by night in the dusty recesses of their minds wake in the day to find that it was vanity: but the dreamers of the day are dangerous men, for they may act their dream with open eyes, to make it possible.[1]

Remember John Lennon's plea, his dream, and his imagination-at-work in the lyrics of "Imagine"?

You may say I'm a dreamer

But I'm not the only one

I hope someday you'll join us

And the world will be as one.[2]

"I have a dream today!" said Dr. Martin Luther King, Jr.[3] That dream and he, the dreamer, were met with seemingly impassable opposition, leading to the untimely death of the dreamer. Yet his dream outlived him, and we continue to live by and in a better world where that dream has come true.

The visions and dreams of great dreamers shape our world. Your dreams and visions can change your world and your family's world. Teaching your children to become dreamers and visionaries can shape their world. This is a heritage and a legacy of invaluable worth.

DREAM STEALERS

As with those who did not want to see the dreams of Martin Luther King Jr. come true, so do all dreamers face opposition from the "dream stealers" that surround them. Sadly, all too often some of those dream stealers are found within our own homes and among the friends and associates who should be encouraging our passion and success. Even well-meaning parents can be dream stealers. They can unintentionally inflict dream-shattering doubts, fears, and dream-killing rejection.

In an effort to protect their children from the disappointments of misguided or immature dreams, parents, siblings, friends, teachers, and even their heroes can snatch, crush, and kill their dreams. Usually dream stealers are themselves the victims of stolen or crushed dreams. They have had their dream machines turned off.

Learn to recognize and avoid the influence of dream stealers and their dream stealing comments. Above all, do not be a dream stealer yourself, especially of your own dreams. You will find great power for your own dreams as you believe in and encourage others to dream and to follow their dreams and then celebrate with them as their dreams come true. Belief is the life giving heartbeat of a dream.

THE ROLE OF BELIEF, DISBELIEF, UNBELIEF, AND FAITH IN DREAMING

As Mark indicates, "If thou canst believe, all things are possible to him that believeth" (Mark 9:23). We understand *belief* to be a positive attitude and accepting position on some proposition, some vision, some proposed fact, or possibility some dream. *Disbelief* on the other hand is the opposite. It is an active rejection of the proposition, or proposed fact as false, untrue, and unachievable. *Unbelief* is that attitude of neutrality, the lack of positive acceptance and belief, even without the presence of full disbelief. In other words, doubt. That is also a destroyer of dreams and the power of vision or seeing in the mind's eye.

It was their unbelief that kept the people of Nazareth from being able to "see" and witness the miracles of Jesus.[29] For people of faith, vision, and dreams are just that: a matter of faith. But faith is not merely belief; it is a strong and undoubting confidence that leads to action, which results in the miracle of creative power that accomplishes the vision or dream.

This creative power is available to every human being. It is seeing (vision), focusing desire and passion (dreaming), and positive expectation (faith). It produces and directs the necessary alignment of people, resources, actions, and conditions to "come true," to become reality. It is a priceless divine gift of empowerment. With that gift, the power of the human mind and can conceive and turn the loftiest of dreams into wonderful realities.

We should endeavor to teach our children and families to understand and use that divine gift intentionally. If we can succeed in doing so, even to the degree of a mustard seed, it can work miracles in their lives.

Knowing this we must also not allow dream stealers into our homes and we must teach our children to reject, even have pity on and pray for all would-be dream stealers. These are dream-making priorities of intentional parenting and dream-maker parents.

DREAM BIG

As children, our dreams are grandiose declarations of who we are and what we can do. A child's play is active dreaming, pretending, and preparing for the manifestation of their vision and dreams. It is only the cessation of the dreaming that curtails the dream's progress toward reality. As they change their minds, their play and their dreams, the former dreams fade away or melt into new dreams. Sometimes they resurface to be refined. For children, dreaming is an adventure of learning and refining the goal-setting, envisioning, and dream-making process. It prepares them for the time and the dreams that matter most and that will frame who they become.

The problem with most adults is that they shrink their dreams to fit their notion of today's or even yesterday's realities. By shrinking their dreams, thoughts, and vision of what is possible, they shrink and deny their true divine creative power. It leads them from unbelief to disbelief. That quickly dismisses and steals their own and anyone else's dreams of a better way and a better day.

The famous quote from Marianne Williamson's must-read book *A Return to Love: Reflections on the Principles of "A Course in Miracles"* is a great reminder of the attitude every dreamer should understand and live by:

Our deepest fear is not that we are inadequate. Our deepest fear is that we are powerful beyond measure. It is our light, not our darkness that most frightens us.

We ask ourselves, who am I to be brilliant, gorgeous, talented, fabulous?

Actually, who are you not to be? You are a child of God. You're playing small does not serve the world. There's nothing enlightened about shrinking so that other people won't feel insecure around you. We are all meant to shine, as children do.

We were born to make manifest the glory of God that is within us. It's not just in some of us; it's in everyone. And as we let our own light shine, we unconsciously give other people permission to do the same. As we're liberated from our own fear, our presence automatically liberates others.[4]

LEGACY-SECURING INTENTIONAL PARENTING PROJECT SUGGESTIONS

Believe in Dreaming—If you, like nearly all of us, turned off, turned down, or misplaced your dream machine, be clear that it can be found and turned on again. While the explanation of the process sounds simple, the incredible power of the human will and creativity of the brain's frontal lobes is enormous. Your dream machine (brain) creates powerful emotional and bioelectrical influences that will guide your choices and actions to achieve your goals. It is real. It is powerful.

You just have to understand how it works generally and how to turn it on. You turn it on by believing that it is real and begin to use and trust it. You can spend a great deal of time researching this incredible mental power. You can become convinced that it is what separates the most successful people from the "normal" less successful. You may even discover and become convinced that it is a natural power that children have and that it can be diminished and "turned off" by pessimistic and doubting persons of influence in their lives. But taking advantage of your discoveries will require you to exercise the dream machine with vision, belief, faith, and dreaming. You have to have a dream to have your dream-powered mechanism make your dream come true. So DREAM, dream big, get excited about, talk about, and believe in your dreams.

Use "I AM" Programming—You program your dream machine with positive, present-tense self-talk with above-normal volume and energy. This self-talk must be recognized as serious dream building rather than what the brain normally hears and ignores as simple daydreaming or wishful thinking. This high-energy self-talk may feel awkward at first. However, it awakens your subconscious mind. It cannot differentiate between what is present, past, and future, what is real and not real in the physical sense. The subconscious mind believes what it is told by you, your story, but you have to get its attention with powerful self-talk.

Your conscious, reasoning mind contrasts the "real" physical world against your subconscious vision, your dream world. You can override that contrast produced by doubt and fear with your strong, frequent, believing "I am" statements to the subconscious mind. You may even name your subconscious mind. Call him George, or her Jan, or whatever. Some use their own name. This is really you talking to you. This will help you to visualize to whom you are speaking to and to whom you are giving directions. Say, "I am . . ." and add any characteristic that you want to program into your nature. Declare, "I am . . ." and describe yourself living your dream. You will find a list of values in the appendices helpful for this exercise.

Detail Your Dreams—The more details you can provide to your subconscious mind, the more it can put the dream puzzle together into an actionable plan or program and expectations for evidence (behavior) that the dream is real. If it is a new car you are dreaming about, detail the car with make, model, color, features, and feelings. Yes, feelings. What does the leather seat feel like? What does it smell like? What does pushing the accelerator sound and feel like? Your subconscious mind can access your memories of those details and put them together for a "real" mental experience of the dream.

Window Shop—Go to the home show, car dealer, clothing store, baby store, or wherever you can recharge the sensory experience of what you want to dream about. Then mentally re-experience that as you tell "George" how things really are, your dream. Help your children dream by taking them to see the bicycle, new dress, college dorms, professional sports games, car dealers, or anything they want to dream about. Too many parents would shy away from these window-shopping trips because they don't want their children to get "their hopes up" or to be disappointed. Feed their dream machines. Help them keep them tuned up and revved frequently.

Have, Do, Be—Most adults dream about things they want to have. Children start out dreaming more about what they want to be—for the moment. Their dreams are often short term while adults extend their vision into long-term, lifestyle dreams. Both adults and children also dream about things to do and places to go. Balance your dreams with a wholeness of things to have, to do, and what to be. For most adults, the vision and dreams of what they are ("I am") are the most powerful for implementing intentional transformation influence by their subconscious minds. Try describing yourself as you would like someone to describe you to others when you are not present. How would they tell your story?

Associate with Dreamers—The world is full of naysayers and dream stealers. Sadly, they may be friends or even members of your family. If you are serious about harnessing the power of your dream mechanism and power of goal achievement, you will need to surround yourself with believers, dreamers, and optimists. People who understand the process and need for positive support and belief to the subconscious mind can help keep you focused on your dreams. Find, or establish, a group of like-minded dreamers who have similar values. This can be a church group, a business think tank, a dream team, or a civic service group. You may need to help them understand the concepts and the language of the dream machine principle and the brain's creative and directive power. You may have to become the dream team leader for your group.

Dreamers Act with Abundance—Dreamers think and live from a position of abundance. They know that God is the giver and the resource of all. Non-dreamers hold tight to what they have because they don't understand the principle of abundance.

Knowing and acknowledging that God is the source of all good will help to absolve the fear of temporal scarcity. Remember, fear kills dreams because it harbors doubts, and doubts kill belief and action. The twins of fear and doubt block the power of faith and confidence in the source and process. Live abundantly, especially with your children. However, do not reward non-dreaming, non-action behavior. Doing so will infect your child's dream machine with a deadly virus belief in something for nothing. Dreaming is not passive. Help them set goals and encourage them to achieve their "mini-dreams" so you can provide the resources for their rewards. Don't set goals that are too high or too low. Dreaming requires active stretching to grow the capacity and the capability of the dreamer.

Be Better—Dreamers are positive, happy, and energetic people. They live in the positive expectation that every day is better. Ask them how they are and their answer is "better!" Not that they were sick, or worse, but because every day dreamers are marching forward to the better life they envision for themselves, their family, and the world. Think about it. Given the choice of living with a smile and a hope versus a frown and fear, what will you choose? Now that you understand the power of intentional dreaming and transformation, when someone asks, "How are you?" answer with something that they aren't expecting, something that shakes their pessimism: **"Better!"**

Dream Your Heritage—An intentional family heritage is the goal for dream-making and heritage-making parents. In essence, it is the discovery of the successful heroes and character traits, values, and beliefs of the past and programming them into the expectations of your children. You help them program their subconscious minds with the picture (dream or vision) of who and what they are and how they do and don't behave.

In short, you create the vision for the subconscious mind and help the children to dream themselves into that reality. Heritage is both the picture of the past and the filtered and enhanced picture of the present expectations and that vision of the future for the family members and individual members of it. Here again, details are vital. The "dos" and "do nots," commandments, and the "shoulds" and "should nots," combine with the "always" and "nevers" to create a mental picture of who they really are.

Laugh—Dreamers laugh, a lot, especially at themselves. They understand that dreaming is a process and that there will be great days and not-so-great days, but they forgive, forget, and forge ahead—laughing rather than crying over the "spilled milk" and "whoops" that happen. They understand that life does happen. Dreaming is ever present, so you don't fail. You just start again, with greater determination to use the process more effectively and enjoy the journey while you are at it. Embrace the hallmark expression of one of the greatest dreamers and achievers of all time, Napoleon Hill, who said, "Whatever the mind can conceive and believe, it can achieve."

DISCOVERING, DETERMINING, DEVELOPING, TRANSFERRING, AND SECURING YOUR FAMILY LEGACY

The values, beliefs, standards, traditions, and character traits that are the elements of your heritage that you receive, select, or accept from your ancestors and those that you generate proactively or intentionally on your own become the elements of your heritage. That heritage successfully passed on to the next and succeeding generations becomes your family legacy.

The intentional discovery, clarification, development, and establishment of that heritage is the first process for securing your family legacy. Following on that process is perhaps the most important intentional parenting priority parents can have. It is an investment of time and purpose that can pay huge dividends in the quality and the security of family life and your children's self-esteem and character development.

Some parents will find significant resources available to them in terms of the heritage and family legacy that comes from their parents and ancestors. Others may have to plan and initiate the elements of their heritage and future legacy from scratch. For most of us, our heritage and associated family legacy will be a journey both of discovery and creativity. We will take the good that we want to carry on from the past legacy of our family progenitors and heroes and we'll want to add to, or customize, how we apply that heritage and those values in our own home. The most important aspect of the process is the clarification of you heritage and the concept that it becomes the meaning of your family name. That is, it is how your children and those who know them and you would describe the kind of people you really are to someone who did not know you.

The activity and project suggestions in the book can help you engage your spouse, children, and extended family in the legacy project. Talking about it with them will further help you to clarify what you want to have your family achieve through the process. Putting dates and specifics to various projects, discussions, searches, and traditions will give tangibility and priority to your work. You will be surprised as you talk with others about your intentional parenting family legacy project at just how interested and encouraging they will be. Don't be surprised if other family members and friends want to join and follow your leadership in similar pursuits.

Visit the author's website and blog to share and read the experiences of the process. As you connect with and even generate other intentional parenting friends and associates, you will find that the sustaining and encouraging support is reciprocal. This heritage-based approach to parenting can become a worthy cause that your experience can contribute to. Your experiences positive and challenging can be a vital resource

especially to those single parents and broken homes. Your greatest contribution, aside from securing your own family legacy, may be in helping
other families to develop and secure theirs.

Remember that even the most clearly defined and purposefully
implemented heritage and values will always be challenged. Sometimes
those challenges may end in lapses of consistency and dedication to your
heritage and their character. Remember that those lapses can become an
opportunity to strengthen what was weak enough to be bent or broken.
The intentional parents discussion in the aftermath of a breach in the
family standards is an exercise that can strengthen the offender, the parent,
and contribute to the loving acceptance and durability of the legacy.

Use your discussions about finding, building, and embracing your
family legacy as a kind and thoughtful way to turn your children's hearts
to their fathers (and mothers) and their fathers (and mothers) hearts.
Define yourself as an intentional parent. Incorporate the language and
vocabulary of heritage into your daily conversations. That in and of itself
will draw you and your family to the most central of all heritage values,
the value of family.

Please embrace the intentional parenting family heritage motto of
live, learn, love, laugh, and leave a legacy.

NOTES

1. T. E. Lawrence, "Seven Pillars of Wisdom," 1922, accessed April 2013,
    http://gutenberg.net.au/ebooks01/0100111h.html

2. John Lennon, "Imagine," *Imagine*, Capitol, 1971.

3. Martin Luther King Jr., "I Have a Dream," speech given at the Lincoln
    Memorial, Washington, DC, August 28, 1963.

4. Marianne Williamson, "A Return to Love: Reflections on the Principles
    of "A Course in Miracles" Harper Collins Publishers, 1992.

APPENDIX A

Values, Beliefs and Standards
Word Resource List

THE FOLLOWING LIST OF WORDS CAN HELP YOU TO discuss aspects of your family heritage. Discuss the words and their concepts and meaning as they relate to your family beliefs, values, standards, character, and heritage. Write your insights next to each word.

Abundant _____

Accountable _____

Active _____

Adventure _____

Ancestors _____

Belong _____

Brave _____

Character _____

Charity _____

Chastity _____

Clean _____

Cheerful _____

Committed _____

Compassion _____

Confident _____

Contribute _____

Courage _____

Courteous _____

Creative _____

Dependable _____

Devoted _____

Dignity _____

Disciple _____

Discipline _____

Dreams _____

Duty _____

Efficient _____

Elders _____

Empathy _____

Endure _____

Faith _____

Family _____

Fair _____

Fathers _____

Fit _____

Friend _____

Frugal _____

Generous _____

Gracious _____

Grandparents _____

Grateful _____

Happy _____

Harmony _____

Healthy _____

Heritage _____

Heroes _____

Holy _____

Honesty _____

Hopeful _____

Hospitality _____

Humility _____

Humor _____

Independent _____

Inspiration _____

Integrity _____

Intelligent _____

Intimacy _____

Joy _____

Justice _____

Kind _____

Knowledge _____

Leader _____

Liberty _____

Light _____

Love _____

Meek _____

Modest _____

Mother _____

Neat _____

Obedient _____

Optimistic _____

Orderly _____

Patient _____

Perfect _____

Persistent _____

Prepared _____

Pride _____

Promise _____

Punctual _____

Pure _____

Quiet _____

Reliable _____

Respect _____

Responsible _____

Reverent _____

Sacred _____

Sacrifice _____

Sincere _____

Spirit _____

Sympathy _____

Thankful _____

Thoughtful _____

Tidy _____

Timely _____

True _____

Trustworthy _____

Truthful _____

Understanding _____

Unique _____

Unity _____

Values _____

Virtue _____

Wise _____

Worthy _____

Yearn _____

Zeal _____

APPENDIX B

Heritage-Making Resource List: What You Have and Where to Find It

FROM THE LIST BELOW, IDENTIFY WHAT YOU already have and where you might find it. If you don't have it, note the stories that are associated with the item that make it significant to your family heritage.

I. FAMILY PEDIGREE AND ANCESTORS

A pedigree chart showing your genealogy

    Location _____   Description _____

    _____   _____

Family Records

    Location _____   Description _____

    _____   _____

I. FAMILY PICTURES, AUDIO AND VIDEO CLIPS, ETC.

Mother's mother (and family)

    Location _____   Description _____

    _____   _____

    _____   _____

Mother's father (and family)

    Location _____   Description _____

    _____   _____

    _____   _____

Father's mother (and family)

    Location _____   Description _____

    _____   _____

    _____   _____

Father's father (and family)

    Location _____   Description _____

    _____   _____

    _____   _____

Mother's grandmother (and family)

    Location _____   Description _____

    _____   _____

    _____   _____

Mother's grandfather (and family)

    Location _____   Description _____

    _____   _____

    _____   _____

Father's grandmother (and family)

    Location _____   Description _____

    _____   _____

    _____   _____

Father's grandfather (and family)

    Location _____   Description _____

    _____   _____

    _____   _____

Mother's great-grandmother (and family)

    Location _____   Description _____

    _____   _____

    _____   _____

Mother's great-grandfather (and family)

    Location _____   Description _____

    _____   _____

    _____   _____

Father's great-grandmother (and family)

    Location _____   Description _____

    _____   _____

    _____   _____

Father's great-grandfather (and family)

    Location _____   Description _____

    _____   _____

    _____   _____

Other progenitors beyond four generations

    Location _____   Description _____

    _____   _____

    _____   _____

III. YOUR IMMEDIATE FAMILY PICTURES AND MOVIES

YOU

You as a baby

    Location _____   Description _____

    _____   _____

    _____   _____

Preschool age

    Location _____   Description _____

    _____   _____

    _____   _____

Elementary school age

    Location _____   Description _____

    _____   _____

    _____   _____

Middle/junior high school age

    Location _____   Description _____

    _____   _____

    _____   _____

High school age

    Location _____   Description _____

    _____   _____

    _____   _____

High school graduation

    Location _____   Description _____

    _____   _____

    _____   _____

Major achievements and awards

    Location _____   Description _____

    _____   _____

    _____   _____

Talents, sports, church, and civic activities

    Location _____   Description _____

    _____   _____

    _____   _____

Dating age with spouse to be

    Location _____   Description _____

    _____   _____

    _____   _____

Your engagement

    Location _____   Description _____

    _____   _____

    _____   _____

Your wedding shower

    Location _____   Description _____

    _____   _____

    _____   _____

Wedding pictures

    Location _____   Description _____

    _____   _____

    _____   _____

YOUR SPOUSE

Spouse as a baby

    Location _____   Description _____

    _____   _____

    _____   _____

Preschool age

    Location _____   Description _____

    _____   _____

    _____   _____

Elementary school age

Location _____   Description _____

_____   _____

_____   _____

Middle/junior high school age

Location _____   Description _____

_____   _____

_____   _____

High school age

Location _____   Description _____

_____   _____

_____   _____

High school graduation

Location _____   Description _____

_____   _____

_____   _____

Major achievements and awards

Location _____   Description _____

_____   _____

_____   _____

Talents, sports, church, and civic activities

Location _____   Description _____

_____   _____

_____   _____

Dating age with spouse to be

    Location _____   Description _____

    _____   _____

    _____   _____

Engagement

    Location _____   Description _____

    _____   _____

    _____   _____

Wedding shower/party

    Location _____   Description _____

    _____   _____

    _____   _____

Wedding pictures

    Location _____   Description _____

    _____   _____

    _____   _____

III. FAMILY TRADITIONS, EVENTS PICTURES

Major holidays

    Location _____   Description _____

    _____   _____

    _____   _____

Major family events, vacations, and trips

    Location _____   Description _____

    _____   _____

    _____   _____

Family reunions

    Location _____   Description _____

    _____   _____

    _____   _____

Homes you have lived in

    Location _____   Description _____

    _____   _____

    _____   _____

Cars you have had

    Location _____   Description _____

    _____   _____

    _____   _____

Close friends

    Location _____   Description _____

    _____   _____

    _____   _____

Relatives not in the direct line above

    Location _____   Description _____

    _____   _____

    _____   _____

Family pets

    Location _____   Description _____

    _____   _____

    _____   _____

IV. JOURNALS OR FAMILY HISTORIES REGARDING ANY OF THESE

    Location _____   Description _____

    _____   _____

    _____   _____

    _____   _____

V. AUDIO RECORDINGS FROM ANY OF YOUR ANCESTORS

    Location _____   Description _____

    _____   _____

    _____   _____

    _____   _____

VI. FAMILY KEEPSAKES

Handicrafts

    Location _____   Description _____

    _____   _____

    _____   _____

Sporting goods, tools, or fishing gear

Location _____   Description _____

_____   _____

_____   _____

Jewelry, china, or cooking items

Location _____   Description _____

_____   _____

_____   _____

Old cards and letters

Location _____   Description _____

_____   _____

_____   _____

Clothing

Location _____   Description _____

_____   _____

_____   _____

Books

Location _____   Description _____

_____   _____

_____   _____

Awards, trophies, medals, and certificates

Location _____   Description _____

_____   _____

_____   _____

Toys, baby items, and musical instruments

Location _____ Description _____

_____ _____

_____ _____

Furniture or home décor items

Location _____ Description _____

_____ _____

_____ _____

APPENDIX C

Heritage Information Assessment

ANSWER THESE QUESTIONS TO REINFORCE YOUR knowledge of your family history and heritage. Invite your spouse to do the same. The survey and discussion will help you to discover more about heritage and what you may need to further define it.

For each question you answer, give yourself a point. If the question requires a yes or no answer, give yourself a point for "yes" and zero points for "no." If the question does not apply, then do not give yourself a point. Then tally the points to determine your score and to see how clear and how strong your family heritage is. If you find areas that need work, discuss with your family how to improve.

A) MOTHER'S INFORMATION

1. Where was your mother born? _____

2. When is her birthday? _____

3. What is your mother's maiden name? _____

4. What did your mother love to do most as a child? _____
_____
_____

5. What was her favorite subject in school? _____

6. What did she dream about doing or being? _____

    _____

7. What was her childhood nickname? _____

    _____

8. What character trait was she was known for? _____

    _____

9. Where did she go to school? _____

    _____

10. When is her and your father's wedding anniversary? _____

    _____

11. What is her favorite food, music, and movie? _____

    _____

    _____

                                              Score _____

B) FATHER'S INFORMATION

1. Where was your father born? _____

    _____

2. When is his birthday? _____

3. What is your father's mother's maiden name? _____

    _____

4. What did your father love to do most as a child? _____

    _____

    _____

5. What was his favorite subject was in school? _____

6. What did he dream about doing or being? _____
   _____

7. What was his childhood nickname? _____
   _____

8. What character trait was he was known for? _____
   _____

9. Where did he go to school? _____
   _____

10. When is his and your mother's wedding anniversary? _____
    _____

11. What is his favorite food, music, and movie? _____
    _____
    _____

                                            Score _____

C) ANCESTORS

1. Where was your paternal grandfather raised? _____
   _____
   _____

2. Where was your paternal grandmother raised? _____
   _____
   _____

3. Where was your maternal grandfather raised? _____
   _____
   _____

4. Where was your maternal grandmother raised? _____

_____

_____

5. Where did your paternal grandfather work? _____

_____

_____

6. Where did your maternal grandmother work? _____

_____

_____

5. What church did your paternal grandparents attend? _____

_____

_____

6. What church did your maternal grandparents attend? _____

_____

7. Where did your paternal great grandparents come from? _____

_____

8. Where did your maternal great grandparents come from? _____

_____

9. Where did your great-great paternal grandparents come from? ___

_____

_____

10. Where did great-great maternal grandparents come from? _____

_____

Score _____

D) FAMILY PEDIGREE

1. Do you have printed four-generation family pedigree chart or list?
   _____

2. What is the meaning (if any) of your family surname? _____
   _____
   _____

3. Do you have pictures of your parents? _____
   _____

4. Do you have pictures of both sets of your grandparents? _____
   _____

5. Do you have pictures of both sets of your great grandparents? ___
   _____

6. Do you have pictures of both sets of your great-great grandparents?
   _____

7. Do you have a copy of your family coat of arms or crest? _____
   _____

8. Do you have a copy of a family history book about your ancestors?
   _____

9. Do you have a copy of a journal written by one of your ancestors?
   Where is it located in your house? _____
   _____

10. Do you have a collection of important family stories? Where is
    it located? _____
    _____

    Score _____

E) FAITH-BASED VALUES, BELIEFS AND STANDARDS

1. What religion is your family affiliated with? _____
   _____

2. How often does your family attend church together? _____
   _____

3. How often does your family participate in regular family prayer?
   _____

4. How often does your family read and discuss the scriptures? ____
   _____

5. What is your family's understanding regarding salvation? ____
   _____
   _____

6. What are your family's Sabbath observance standards? _____
   _____
   _____

7. Does each member of your family have his or her own set of
   scriptures? _____

8. How often does your family have regular religious conversations?
   _____

9. Do you have religious icons and pictures in your home? Which is
   your favorite? _____
   _____

10. How often does your family offer a blessing on their food before
    they eat? _____

    Score _____

F) MEDIA, AND MORALITY STANDARDS

1. What is your family's age requirement for dating? _____

2. What are your family's standards for physical contact? _____
   _____

3. What are your family's standards for cell-phone use? _____
   _____

4. How often does your family talk openly about sexuality and morality? _____

5. What are your family's standards for movie ratings? _____
   _____

6. What are your family's standards for Internet use? _____
   _____

7. What are your family's standards about alcohol, tobacco and drugs? _____
   _____

8. What are your family's rules regarding electronic game use? _____
   _____

9. What are the rules on curfews in your family? _____
   _____

10. What are your family's standards about music choices in the home? _____
    _____

Score _____

G) CITIZENSHIP AND COMMUNITY SERVICE

1. How often does your family participate in the political process and vote? _____

   _____

2. What community service groups does your family participate in?

   _____

   _____

3. How often does your family use the public library and other community resources? _____

   _____

4. How often does your family participate in parades and other patriotic events? _____

   _____

5. How many family members are involved in community service?

   _____

   _____

6. How many family members are familiar with and discuss current events? _____

   _____

7. How many family members know their local, state and national representatives? _____

8. What is your family's standards toward a green and clean community? _____

   _____

9. Does your family have a national flag and display it appropriately?

   _____

10. How often does your family discuss the celebration purpose of national holidays? _____

_____

Score _____

H) FAMILY TRADITIONS

1. How often does your family have regular family night activities? What are the activities? _____

_____

_____

2. Does your family have and maintain an activity and event calendar? _____

_____

3. How does your family celebrate birthdays? _____

_____

_____

4. Does your family have an annual family vacation event? Describe it. _____

_____

_____

_____

5. How often does your family participate in family reunions? ___

_____

6. What does your family do to celebrate major holidays? _____

_____

_____

_____

7. What family traditions are unique to your family? _____

    _____

    _____

8. What sports or other activities does your family participate in?

    _____

    _____

    _____

9. Does your family give full priority to family tradition events? ___

    _____

10. What are some of your family's major annual traditions? ____

    _____

    _____

    _____

    _____

Score _____

I) FAMILY TREASURES AND ICONS

1. Where does your family display recent (within two years) family portraits in the home? _____

    _____

2. Does your family compile an annual family journal, scrapbook, or storybook? Who's responsible for it? _____

    _____

3. Is your home decorated with pictures of family members? If so, where are the pictures located? _____

    _____

    _____

4. Does your family prominently display trophies and awards? Where are they displayed? _____

_____

5. Does your family have a copy of a family history book? Who updates it? _____

_____

6. How often does your family create craft and building projects? Where are these projects displayed? _____

_____

_____

7. Who in your family takes, organizes, and labels photos of family events? _____

_____

8. What are your favorite family keepsakes and heirlooms? _____

_____

_____

_____

9. Does your family have audio recordings of grandparents stories? Who is responsible for them? _____

_____

_____

10. Does your family have a cookbook of favorite recipes? What are some of your favorite dishes? _____

_____

_____

_____

Score _____

J) FAMILY ORGANIZATION

1. How do you organize extended family? _____

    _____

    _____

    _____

2. How often do you have parent interviews with the children? ___

    _____

    _____

3. Who in your family is involved in planning activities? Is the whole family involved? _____

    _____

    _____

4. What are your family's rules regarding homework completion?

    _____

    _____

    _____

5. What are your family's standards and expectations regarding grades? _____

    _____

    _____

6. What is your family's chore system? Is it clearly defined and enforced? _____

    _____

    _____

    _____

    _____

    _____

7. What is your family's work ethic? Is it strong and healthy? ___

_____

_____

_____

_____

8. Does your family take a proactive role in healthy diet and exercise? How do you do this? _____

_____

_____

_____

9. Do you discipline in private with appropriate consequences? If not, what do you do? _____

_____

_____

_____

10. Can each member of the family explain your family's heritage and why it is important? Why is it important? _____

_____

_____

_____

Score _____

K) FAMILY SECURITY

1. What is your family's emergency contact plan? _____

_____

_____

_____

_____

2. What is your family's emergency evacuation plan? _____

_____

_____

_____

_____

_____

3. What is your family's family succession plan? _____

_____

_____

_____

4. Does your family have a minimum ninety-day food and thirty-day water supply? If not, how can you acquire it? _____

_____

_____

_____

5. Does your family have and live within a budget? What is the most important element of the budget? _____

_____

_____

_____

6. Does your family have a savings plan of 10 percent of net income?

_____

7. Does your family avoid debt except for a home, vehicle, and education? _____

8. Do family members each receive allowances or have other income? How much do they receive? _____

_____

9. Does your family discuss financial matters together? _____

_____

10. What is your family's anti-abduction plan (scream, kick and run)? _____

_____

_____

_____

Score _____

L) FAMILY COMMUNICATION

1. Has your family been taught to really listen to each other? _____

_____

2. Does your family hug each other and say "I love you" daily? If not, how do you express love to each other? _____

_____

_____

_____

3. Does your family have a rule of no yelling in the home, except for fire or emergencies? What is another rule you have to keep the peace in your home? _____

_____

_____

_____

4. Does your family all make loving eye contact and smile at each other daily? _____

_____

5. Does your family have and use a family bulletin board? What do you put on the board? _____

_____

_____

_____

6. How often do family members call living grandparents and close family relatives? _____

7. Does your family have a regular family newsletter or email system? What other ways does your family use to keep in contact? ____

_____

_____

_____

_____

8. Does your family write personal love or thank-you notes to give to each other? _____

9. How do you minimize electronic and maximize personal talk in your family? _____

_____

_____

10. Does your family eat at least one meal together daily? How often?

_____

_____

Score _____

M) FAMILY DREAMING

1. Does your family understand the power of *intentional dreaming*? What does it mean to you?_____

_____

_____

2. Are family members encouraged to have and share their dreams?

_____

3. Does your family use family events as dream exercises? What activities are used as dream exercises? _____

_____

_____

_____

4. Does your family write down dreams and discuss them often? How often? _____

_____

_____

5. Does your family encourage abundance and reject scarcity mentality? How? _____

_____

_____

6. Do your family members encourage each other to go for their dreams? How often? _____

_____

_____

7. Does your family have regular dreaming discussions and dates? How often? _____

_____

8. How does your family celebrate significant steps in dreams coming true? _____

_____

_____

9. How does your family encourage each other to develop and celebrate their talents? _____

_____

_____

10. How does your family express gratitude for the dreaming support of each other? _____

_____

_____

Score _____

COMBINED FAMILY HERITAGE FOUNDATION SCORE SUM OF A–L: _____

WHAT DOES MY SCORE INDICATE?

This scorecard is intended to help readers understand what the foundational heritage elements are and to encourage them to inventory those elements that they have in place and determine those areas where you can strengthen your family heritage. You can and should take pride in those items you were able to answer. However, the real opportunity of the assessment tool is to help you to become more *intentional* about your heritage-making activities and to fill the holes in your family heritage fence.

You can list the weakest categories and individual aspects of those categories and prioritize them for your heritage-making scheduling. For comparison purposes you could consider your score results like this.

RELATIVE STRENGTH OF FAMILY HERITAGE FOUNDATION RESOURCES

>100+   Very Strong Heritage foundation

80–100   Strong Heritage foundation

60–80   Average Heritage foundation

40–60   Fair Heritage foundation

< 40   Weak Heritage foundation

APPENDIX D

A Guide to Family Tradition Holiday Planning

LET'S LOOK AT THE LIST OF HOLIDAYS AND CELEBRA-
tions that we can leverage throughout the year and which we must
work our own family traditions around.

JANUARY

January follows arguably the most challenging of tradition and celebration months. We are usually ready for a pause in celebrating after a
month of the heavy schedule of Christmas activities. We will be ready for
a tradition of recovery and rest from the labors of our celebrating. So not
adding any optional family celebrations may be wise.

New Year's Day, however, is a great time to focus on the family. It
fosters a wonderful tradition of looking back and reflecting on the events
of last year. New Year's is most importantly associated with New Year's
resolutions. This can be a wonderful tradition for families to review the
year past and determine and declare how the new year is going to be much
better, and how they are going to be much better in the new year. It is also
the perfect time to start looking forward to the coming year's schedule.

If you live in the United States, *Martin Luther King, Jr. Day* is a wonderful opportunity for the family to remember and discuss the importance of our universal freedom and ethnic diversity. Celebrating the
liberating freedom of African Americans and the history and culture of
people of color is important for every family. Celebrating the life, dreams,
and accomplishments of Martin Luther King, Jr., can act as a reminder to

family members that commitments to principles and dreams can and do change the world for the better.

FEBRUARY

Valentine's Day is the celebration of love for families and friendship for children. Heritage-minded couples should ensure that the priority of a daddy-mommy date on Valentine's Day is the highest priority (behind family birthdays and anniversaries). Older children may have special non-family events to attend, and younger children may have a school Valentine's Day tradition with a party and cards.

Mothers can involve their children in preparing for the daddy-mommy date. Involving the children to help select the outfit, the restaurant, flowers, cleaning the car, making an invitation, and other shared preparations make this a *family tradition* rather than just a parents' date. Upon returning, parents can share their excitement and the joy of the date with the children. This expression of their love and joy in being together will do much to help children feel secure in the love and commitment of their parents to each other and their family. It will give children a positive pattern for their own adult Valentine celebrations.

President's Day is a patriotic tradition for many families. It is held the third Monday in February. For many people in the United States, it has become a three-day weekend outing opportunity for families and a marketing opportunity for merchants. Unfortunately, many, if not most, families miss the chance to celebrate the reason for the tradition—that of honoring Presidents George Washington and Abraham Lincoln and building on family values of civic service and national pride.

MARCH

St. Patrick's Day is a fun holiday that families can enjoy with its traditional green colors, shamrock, and blarney. A feast of corned beef, boiled red potatoes, and cabbage with various green desserts makes the tradition and celebration fun.

Occasionally *Easter* will also be celebrated in March rather than April.

APRIL

The child in everyone loves to play *April Fool's Day* tricks on family members. This too is a tradition worthy of just plain fun. The more Mom and Dad can get into the fun of the tradition, the more laughter, joy and family heritage-making memory value it will have. Breakfasts made with strange-colored or strange-flavored foods (purple milk, red pancakes, yokeless fried eggs, and so on) can be fun.

Wearing odd or mismatched clothing, making and sending funny cards, and playing practical jokes (safe and non-belittling) on each other can make the anticipated April Fool's Day fun and memorable. Mom may have to twist Dad's arm to join in the fun (or vice versa). She may have to remind him that the purpose behind the tradition is creating fun, laughter, and joy in family time together. The value is worth his bother. Dads need to have the little kid reawakened in them from time to time. They need to be reminded that neither they nor their boys will *always be boys.*

Easter, for Christians, should be one of the most important traditions and celebrations of the year. More so than Christmas, which celebrates Jesus's birth, Easter celebrates his redeeming Atonement and Resurrection. The challenge is managing the message through the onslaught of the Easter bunnies, colored eggs, and candy. So how does a deeply committed Christian family cope with and even embrace the purpose of the tradition? At least with Santa Claus, you can tie Santa and the gifts to the magi, the tree to the cross and the lights to the star. It is more difficult to find a tangent connection to bunnies, eggs, candy and new clothes.

Still, the fun and joy of Easter baskets, egg coloring and hunts, and picnics can be a wonderful family tradition, even for deeply committed Christians. We can have our family tradition by separating *Easter Saturday* with its bunny, eggs and candy from *Easter Sunday.*

Participate and enjoy the spring celebration with the Easter Bunny with all its eggs, gifts and fun on Saturday. Make it the celebration of spring that happens on the Saturday before the celebration and feast of Easter where we remember and speak of the gifts of the risen Lord.

MAY

Celebrated on May 5, *Cinco de Mayo* is observed in the United States to celebrate Mexican heritage and culture. This celebration has become a growing tradition in Mexico and especially along bordering communities in the United States. It is a wonderful opportunity to engage in the cultural contributions of the Mexican heritage with its food, music, parades and festivities. Families can help children learn to appreciate and embrace Mexican culture and heritage with a family tradition of a Mexican meal and maybe a piñata on Cinco de Mayo.

May Day, on May 1, is yet another celebration that can be woven into the calendar, though this is less common. Particularly for persons and families who worked in trades and factories, the roots of May Day have significant meaning. The holiday was birthed from the efforts to reduce the working hours of the day in the late 1800s from twelve to sixteen hours down to eight hours to allow workers to have more time with their families. Today it can be the celebration of the coming of spring, flowers and the summer to follow, but its history and influence on the heritage of many families makes May Day a holiday to consider.

Mother's Day is a day for dads to take a much bigger role in family heritage-making for this important cornerstone celebration. Schools and churches help children prepare cards, small handmade gifts and celebration programs for Mother's Day. Fathers can take charge of a special family gift for Mom and for preparing and cleaning up dinner on that special Sunday.

It takes a commitment from Dad to the overall notion of family heritage-making and traditional observance to really maximize the potential of this celebration to fully honor and show family love for the mother of his children and the homemaker of his house. Sometimes the older children will need to prod Dad to help him get the right gift, card, flowers, and meal. That too can be part of the tradition's *anticipation* and *participation*, as Dad involves the children in preparing the meals and sporting an apron as he spends his time with the kids in preparing meals on Mom's special day.

Dads should also remember that Mother's Day is the day they can express their deep appreciation for their wife's sacrifices in bearing and rearing the children. A special card and conversation from the father is another of the father's family-making privileges.

Parents should not forget their own mothers and grandmothers and include them in their feasts and celebrations whenever possible.

Memorial Day is an important family heritage-making day. It is often a three-day weekend, and many Americans hit the road for the first major outing after the winter snows recede. Its purpose, however, is remembering family members and heroes who have passed on. Traditionally it has been a day to visit cemeteries and clean and decorate the gravesites. The tradition can be a way to help family members connect to ancestors and to the roots of their name and the values, standards, and heroes of their family heritage.

JUNE

In June, we have *Flag Day*, a great opportunity to celebrate country and freedom. Families can fly the flag of their country, state, and family to celebrate and remind each other of their allegiance to each. Attending a local flag-raising ceremony and breakfast can be a wonderful Flag Day family tradition.

Father's Day is the big tradition and celebration for June. Even for single-parent moms, Father's Day can become *Grandfather's Day* so that the children are not robbed of the opportunity to celebrate the male figure in their lives. Grandfathers can help cover for missing fathers in the homes with many of the family traditions. Grandparents generally can be powerful family heritage supports with visits, phone calls, and celebrations.

JULY

July's tradition is focused on patriotism in the United States with the July 4 *Independence Day* celebrations. Here again, the holiday is often a three-day weekend event with major consumer programs and marketing to navigate through. It can be challenging for heritage and freedom celebrating parents to retain the purpose of the celebration.

Focusing on the national flag, the Pledge of Allegiance, the Constitution, the Bill of Rights, the Armed Services, and the history and heroes of our Founding Fathers and nation are a *must* for this priority heritage-making holiday. The busyness of the travel, picnics, feasts, fireworks, and visiting friends can have the flavors and conversations of national heritage woven through them, but it takes *parental intentionality* to do so.

Children get some of the patriotic focus in history lessons during the school year. Even that, however, is dwindling in many schools. The Independence Day celebration should become the family's way of remembering, connecting to, and celebrating their *national heritage*. The message for children should be that our family members are patriots too!

AUGUST

A casual glance at the August calendar might make you think that there are no traditions to deal with for this month. Not so. Every mom knows how important the tradition of back-to-school shopping is for her children. Whether it is clothing or school supplies, the time with Mom (and for some dads), back-to-school shopping is a precious one-on-one opportunity to celebrate the new school year with their children.

Parents can make these often hectic and frustrating events treasured family times with their children, but it takes a little preparation, anticipation, and planning to avoid the traps of marketing pressure. The key is the budget, the list, and the plan for lunch or treats. Being as clear as possible the night before about what you are going to shop for and purchase the night before is the goal of your pre-shopping planning session.

Empowering children, once old enough, to earn and save some of their own money to put toward the cost of their new clothing and supplies is another important intentional parenting tool. This really helps them learn to choose wisely, since they will have worked hard toward their contribution. "Name brand" items become less important when those items are at the expense of their own hard work instead of their parents'. This can be a wonderful tradition between children and parents each summer. They will be excited to have a traditional *family fashion show* on the evening of their school-shopping trip. Dads may be less enthusiastic, but should always be a good sport about this "show." It is also a great time to have the camera out to capture the growth, style and fun of it all.

The back-to-school events with children and teachers can also be just an added to *do to* on your list of too many *to do's*. Unless you see the activity as a tradition and opportunity for celebration of the child's continuing education and commitment to do well in the new school year. Determine now to turn this *have to do* into an exciting *want* to do for you and the children.

SEPTEMBER

Labor Day is the last three-day weekend and opportunity for a mini vacation, camping trip, or a visit to the amusement park or other semi-major family outing of the summer. It is also a great opportunity to clean the yard, participate in a harvest activity, and teach the family the value of *laboring together*.

It can be a time to honor those who do work for your family—the mailman, teachers, yard workers, mechanics, store clerks, hairdressers, babysitters, and any others who perform service and labors for your family's benefit. A note, call or visit of appreciation to some of these service people who have touched your lives would brighten their day. It can be a valuable reminder to children that there are people who are serving their family in so many ways. Labor Day is an opportunity to help your children develop the love of work and appreciation for service. You can also add the twist of appreciation for a healthy body to work and serve with and add a family health hike, bike ride, or other sports and healthy foods focus.

OCTOBER

Halloween, or All Hallows or All Saints Eve, as it was originally called, is a traditional event celebrated around the world on October 31. Although the origins are largely pagan and its observance is a secular holiday, it too can be the basis for fun family traditions. Families can avoid the scare, gore, and even the sugary sweets if they so choose. At the same time they can make the trick or treating vigil fun for the children, both outside and inside the house.

Once again, having your own family traditions around this holiday is the most important aspect of it for heritage-making. Parent involvement, particularly for small children can be a treat for both adult and child. Costume making, buying, modeling, and wearing together with meal and treats prepared around the theme of the holiday make it memorable and fun for the family.

NOVEMBER

November holds three important events. Everyone recognizes Thanksgiving as one of these two traditions. Unfortunately, few parents recognize the citizenship and national heritage developing importance associated with the tradition of voting in state and national elections on *Election Day*. We would be wise to make this a tradition *a priority* for our children as well.

Veterans Day, on November 11, is another important though little celebrated holiday. Veterans Day is a wonderful time to remind our families about the sacrifices and contributions that are made by members of our armed services to secure the freedoms our families enjoy.

Thanksgiving traditions and history are taught in schools but need validation from parents of their importance To secure real appreciation for the life and religious freedoms the pilgrims helped to secure for them, children need to know that their parents know and understand the real meaning of Thanksgiving beyond turkey dinner and pumpkin pie. A simple discussion before the Thanksgiving feast about its meaning, involving the children and adults, is often all that is needed to remind the family of the purpose behind the celebration. The importance of the religious freedom that was sought by the pilgrims and enjoyed by our families is conversation that should not be missed.

Special recipes, food preparation, the great feast and even the cleanup traditions make Thanksgiving one of the real anchors in family holidays and traditions for the year. Remembering the anticipation, planning, and full family participation in the preparations for the celebration is core to its family heritage-making effectiveness. Gathering together and inviting every family member to express his or her gratitude for what they have been given in their life is a vital tradition for every intentional parenting–based Thanksgiving celebration.

DECEMBER

December's *Christmas* traditions follow closely on Thanksgiving's heels. Indeed some family traditions for Thanksgiving include putting up Christmas decorations. Christmas with all its family, business, church, and friend get-togethers, parties, music, and visits can take up all of December and a good part of late November.

Families will likely have to pick and choose between more invitations and parties than their December calendars have available time slots. For the sake of family heritage-making, responses to these invitations will require thoughtful consideration to protect family heritage priorities. It will require some deliberation and negotiation to not let events of lesser importance rob the priority of events of higher heritage-making and sustaining importance for your family.

Parents can weave the real meaning of the holy day and Christmas story into the holiday traditions of gifts, trees, decorations, feasts, and parties throughout the month. Christmas music played throughout the month and singing Christmas carols are all part of the tradition of Christmas that intentional parents ensure are observed and savored. Dad or Grandpa can read the story of the Christ child's birth from Luke in the New Testament. The children can enact the nativity scene in costumes of bathrobes and dishtowel-wrapped heads. They can perform the ritual before an audience of family, with stuffed animals, and a baby doll in a makeshift manager. It will go far to keep the spirit and meaning of Christmas as a significant part of the family heritage.

It is easy to be swept along in the rush and commercialism of the season as the secular meaning and motives have overcome the traditions and meaning of celebrations throughout the year and especially at Christmas. However, the *intentional family* can retain these pure purposes, meaning, and defining message on the Savior and the family by implementing and retaining their own family heritage traditions.

New Year's Eve is December 31 and is the conclusion of the holiday season's celebrations. It is typically spent in watching sports activities and the turn of the year festivities at midnight. The intentional parent sees the opportunity to take a look back on the events, memories, and family traditions created or celebrated in the past year. It is a great time to look at pictures and work on your family annual storybook.

MANAGING THE CELEBRATIONS AND THE CALENDAR

Can you ever have too many traditions to celebrate? Sadly, the answer must be yes, based on the busyness of life and the crowdedness of the calendar. The key to powerful, effective, family heritage-enriching traditions is their purpose and the consistent priority we give them year after year. The issue is *quality*, not *quantity*. If you can find room for one other purely family-focused tradition in the month, in addition to the demands of the holiday calendar, you will be doing well. So, after the holidays, what needs to go on your family traditions calendar? Is it possible to manage and cope with all the demands and possibilities?

Families can manage the flow of traditions with their calendars, individually and with extended family members. To do so takes a lot of calendar coordination and individual priority negotiation. When we talk about priorities we must assume that the regular holidays are fixed to the calendar. We must also remember that birthdays, anniversaries, graduations, and individual family member important events trump other calendar priorities. Family must come first before work, community, church, and ESPN. Advance discussion, planning and calendaring of these events is vital for their success and their family heritage-sustaining value.

Okay, so you have talked, involved the family, decided on priorities and calendared the commitments. Now what is the next tradition to add? Oh yes, we cannot forget the family vacation and family reunions. Family vacations are the vehicle to have the family all together and all focused on the same things for an extended period of time.

VACATIONS

Whether the vacation is a trip to Yellowstone, Washington, DC, Disneyland or your favorite camping spot, vacations are the pinnacle of the family traditions year. Deciding on, planning for, saving for, thinking about, preparing for and finding yourself on your way requires a heap of family cooperation! Getting ready for and then later cleaning up from the vacation may make you wonder if it was all worth it. Reviewing the pictures, stories, laughter, discoveries, emergencies and miracles of the trip will prove the answer is a resounding "Yes! It was worth it!"

Vacations are usually seen as an end in and of themselves, but to a family heritage maker, they are clearly a deposit in the building of a *family legacy*.

FAMILY REUNIONS

Like vacations, family reunions can be challenging to calendar and manage. Sometimes vacations and reunions must be combined. Everyone wants to get together, but when? Then something always comes up for several of the committed participants. A good plan is to schedule family reunions every other year for each side of the family. That way you only have to deal with one family reunion each year.

For most families, selecting a location and facility is a challenge with families spread literally all across the world and with varying budget and time constraints. A simple Saturday rendezvous at a park in a community in a centrally located community may be the best option for many families.

A potluck lunch, some family history and heritage sharing, a family talent show or a little friendly family softball, volleyball, or Frisbee golf can involve all but the most senior members. *They* can be the referees. The great value of family reunions is that the children get to see and get to know their cousins and extended family. They come to recognize that they are a part of a bigger group with similar values and heritage.

Many families have formal family organizations that coordinate family gatherings, newsletters and even family funds to support family needs. In a society of such growing separation of families, individually and as family groups, it is a worthy consideration to establish and retain extended family association and unity. A family blog and occasional conference calls are great tools to stay connected to each other and your heritage.

CREATIVE TRADITIONS

We have identified the calendar priorities. Now we can add some totally unique and *family-specific* traditions. These can give family members a special sense of individual family significance and pride. Consider some of these possibilities.

Seasonal Traditions: The Spring Fling, the Summer Social, the Fall Fling, Harvest Days, October Fest, and Winter Fest.

Family Member Traditions: The grandparents party, parents party, Discovery Days, Fishing Fest, father-son outings, daddy-daughter dates, mother-daughter adventures, and The Great Treasure Hunt.

Special Traditional Non-Traditions: One-time calendared events like births, blessings, baptisms, bar mitzvahs, graduations, and other one-time events and parties.

FEASTS

Some of what makes a tradition memorable is the specific foods and feasting activity associated with the event. When you think of Thanksgiving, you think of? Right, roast turkey and pumpkin pie are on your mind and the menu. Some may think, roast goose when they think of Christmas dinner. Others want roast beef and Yorkshire pudding or ham and plum pudding. Birthdays invoke cake and ice cream; ball games must have hot dogs; and movies, popcorn. Winter caroling may require hot chocolate or cider.

Expanding the list with family-specific foods and recipes add more importance to the feast. Adding the family member's favorite foods to their birthday adds more feeling of *special* to the event. Indeed, having certain foods associated with certain activities, or even on certain days of the week, creates a *family tradition* in and of itself.

It is a tradition for families to feast together whenever they meet together. There is just something special about breaking bread together that unites and deepens relationships. That said, in our day, there is a significant reduction in the number of predictable, scheduled, home-cooked meals families participate in. The value of food preparation, eating together around the table, cleaning up and the conversation that is associated with these day-to-day feasts is invaluable.

More and more meals are eaten out and become *fast-food gobbles* rather than family planned and prepared meals. Eating out or getting takeout can also be a family tradition when it is tied to a special event. These eating out events can certainly be a welcome break for a busy mom to have someone else make the meal.

Too many restaurant and fast-food meals can minimize family interaction and communication that normally occurs around meal preparation and the dining room table. Traditional family mealtime gatherings and conversation is fast becoming a lost tradition. What is lost with family meals together includes the teaching opportunities mealtime gives intentional parents. There is loss of family discussions about life, challenges, and interests. The loss of family meal traditions weakens the bonds of family relations.

Eating out together periodically can also be a great tradition, especially when it is associated with some other celebration. Eating out often for convenience may be easier and may even have a cost-effective debate, but the *loss* in *family heritage* will come at a *high price*.

ABOUT
the AUTHOR

M ELVYN DOUGLAS CLOWARD IS THE PRODUCT OF his heritage. The values, standards, and traditions of his family, friends, and community continue to direct his sense of purpose, priority and the practices of his parenting, grandparenting, and professional services. He has been steeped in a rich experience base of personal and professional youth leadership. As one of Brigham Young University's youngest full-time faculty members, he developed and led the popular Wilderness and Pioneer Trek Youth Conference programs. He has taught and led generations of youth leaders in the art and science of experience-based character development. Now, as an author and speaker, his work focuses on helping parents to become more intentional and effective in establishing the heritage-enriched character of their children.

Learn more at www.douglascloward.com.

Mokena Community
Public Library District